Walking New York

Walking New York

GEORGE SPELVIN &
EVE DEVEREUX

TWENTY ORIGINAL WALKS
IN NEW YORK CITY

PASSPORT BOOKS
NTC/Contemporary Publishing Group

This edition first published in 2001
by Passport Books, a division of
NTC/Contemporary Publishing Group, Inc.
4255 West Touhy Avenue
Lincolnwood (Chicago), Illinois 60712-1975
U.S.A.

ISBN 0-658-01383-1

Library of Congress Catalog Card Number: on file
Published in conjunction with New Holland Publishers (U.K.) Ltd

Publishing Manager: Jo Hemmings
Series Editor: Michaella Standen
Design and editing: D & N Publishing, Hungerford, Berkshire
Cartography: Carte Blanche, Paignton, Devon
Production: Joan Woodroffe

Reproduction by Pica Colour Separation Overseas (Pte) Ltd, Singapore
Printed and bound in Singapore by Kyodo Printing Co (Singapore) Pte Ltd

Photographic Acknowledgements
All photographs, except the front cover, are by Chris Fairclough

Front cover: St. Moritz, New York City, photographed by The Stock Market
Back cover: Flatiron Building, photographed by Chris Fairclough

Contents

Introduction

This city is the center of the universe.
Mayor Robert F. Wagner

New York is a sort of anthology of urban civilization. The song that any city sings, she sings.
R.L. Duffus

New York is arguably the most exciting city in the world for walkers.

Many of New York's enthusiasts would claim it is the most exciting city in the world period, and there is much to favor this argument. Geography has constrained a city whose population is approximately 1.4 million within an island of area a mere 65 km² (26 square miles), so that, whereas others of the world's great cities may conceivably have as much to offer, none of them has it in such concentrated form: within a single block in Manhattan one may see as much, experience as much, do as much as one might discover in the whole of a small town. And it's not purely a matter of concentration: the manifold aspects of New York, crammed together as they're forced to be, interact synergistically to create something—something usually described as vigor or vitality or any of a number of other expressions affirming the city's *life*—that no other city on earth can hope to match. New York is well known as the city that never sleeps, but the description applies to more than just the fact that its streets are never empty: you can feel in your bones while in New York that, whether you like it or not, this city is always awake, always vibrating with its own life.

Another consequence of the concentration is that New York is a tremendous place to walk in. Indeed, New Yorkers tend to walk far more than do the people of other cities precisely because, for many journeys within New York, walking is quite simply the easiest, quickest, and most efficient means of transportation. We were once standing at a corner waiting for the lights to change when we heard two people talking about how they would get where they wanted to go. One said: "Shall we take a taxi?" The other responded: "I don't think we've got the time. Let's walk." For any journey less than about 15 north–south blocks, there really is no good reason (inclemencies of the weather aside) to consider any other mode of travel. For longer journeys the subway, much and justifiably maligned in the past but these days clean, cheap, and as safe as any other metropolitan subway, offers the most attractive option: taxis are not especially expensive by the standards of a major metropolis, but most times outside late night and the weekends they're agonizingly slow as they get caught in jam after jam; and the bus system, besides suffering from the traffic alongside the taxis, is so infernally complicated that many long-time New York residents still haven't worked it out. On balance, then, whether you design to do so or not, you're likely to find yourself doing a lot of walking during your time in the city.

And there's a lot to see. Someone once remarked—about a century ago, when the early skyscrapers were going up—that the difference between New York and other cities was that New York tipped its streets up on end. Those skyscrapers themselves are part of what New York offers the visitor, for this is architecturally probably the richest city in the world: while it cannot boast a Versailles or a Hampton Court, for obvious historical reasons, it can and does boast their more recent equivalents. At the same time, it has many of the world's finest specimens of strictly modern architectures, like the Chrysler Building, or the Flatiron Building, or the Rockefeller Center or, of course, the Empire State Building.

Aside from the architecture, you'll find in New York some of the world's finest museums, from the Metropolitan Museum of Art to the New-York Historical Society to the Solomon R. Guggenheim Museum to the smaller and more specialist establishments, such as the Museum for African Art or the Dahesh Museum. Scattered everywhere are striking examples of public art, both historical and modern. New York's ongoing program of public art is exceptionally vital. There are concert orchestras that are second to none, operatic and rock-music scenes that are almost unparalleled, thriving animation and broadcasting industries, street fairs, open spaces, flea markets, free concerts, Broadway theaters, bookstores, department stores, ferries, restaurants catering for virtually every regional palate under the sun—small wonder that some people have come to regard New York as being the whole world in microcosm.

And to discover all this you need nothing but some maps, perhaps a handful of subway tokens ... and your own two feet!

Key to Route Maps

Each of the walks in this book is accompanied by a detailed map on which the route of the walk is shown in blue. Places of interest along the walks, such as historic buildings, museums, and churches, are clearly identified.

The following is a key to the symbols used on the maps.

►▪▪▪▪▪►	route of walk	▪	park
▪	major building	●	subway or point of interest
†	church	▭	body of water
👥	public toilets		

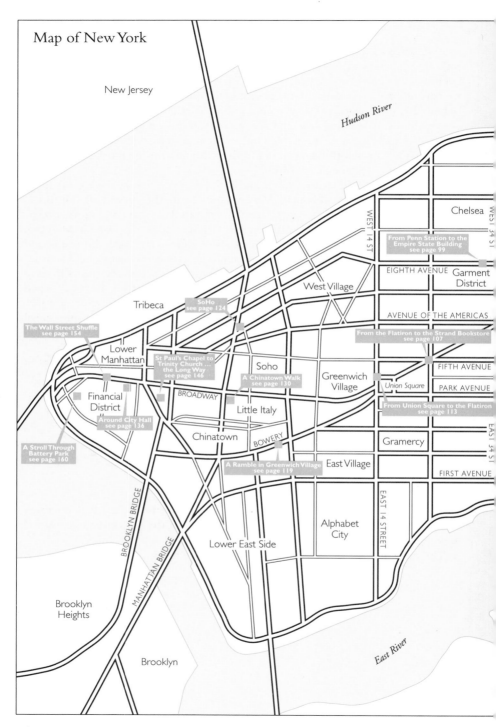

Map of New York

New Jersey

Hudson River

New Jersey

Chelsea

WEST 14 ST

WEST 34 ST

From Penn Station to the
Empire State Building
see page 99

EIGHTH AVENUE

Garment
District

West Village

AVENUE OF THE AMERICAS

Tribeca

SoHo
see page 124

From the Flatiron to the Strand Bookstore
see page 107

The Wall Street Shuffle
see page 154

Lower
Manhattan

FIFTH AVENUE

St Paul's Chapel to
Trinity Church ...
the Long Way
see page 146

Soho

Greenwich
Village

Union Square

PARK AVENUE

A Chinatown Walk
see page 130

Financial
District

BROADWAY

Little Italy

From Union Square to the Flatiron
see page 113

Around City Hall
see page 136

Chinatown

BOWERY

East Village

Gramercy

EAST 34 ST

A Stroll Through
Battery Park
see page 160

A Ramble in Greenwich Village
see page 119

FIRST AVENUE

Alphabet
City

EAST 14 STREET

BROOKLYN BRIDGE

Lower East Side

Brooklyn
Heights

MANHATTAN BRIDGE

East River

Brooklyn

8

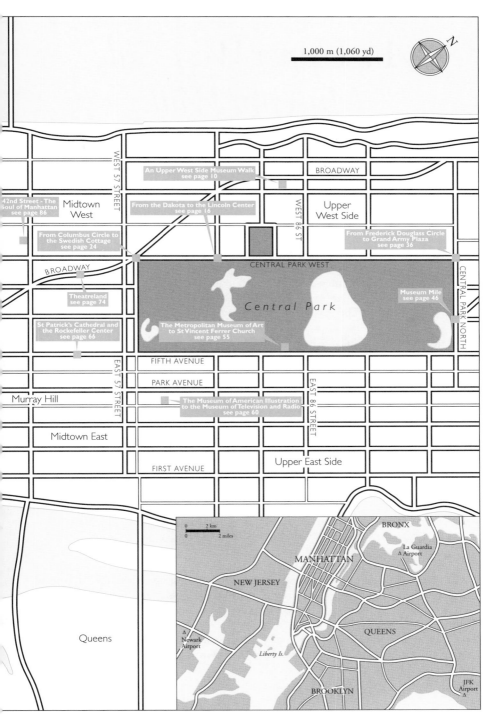

1,000 m (1,060 yd)

N

WEST 57 STREET

BROADWAY

WEST 86 ST

An Upper West Side Museum Walk
see page 10

42nd Street - The
Soul of Manhattan
see page 86

Midtown
West

Upper
West Side

From the Dakota to the Lincoln Center
see page 16

From Columbus Circle to
the Swedish Cottage
see page 24

From Frederick Douglass Circle
to Grand Army Plaza
see page 36

BROADWAY

CENTRAL PARK WEST

CENTRAL PARK NORTH

Theatreland
see page 74

Central Park

Museum Mile
see page 46

St Patrick's Cathedral and
the Rockefeller Center
see page 66

The Metropolitan Museum of Art
to St Vincent Ferrer Church
see page 55

EAST 57 STREET

FIFTH AVENUE

PARK AVENUE

EAST 86 STREET

Murray Hill

The Museum of American Illustration
to the Museum of Television and Radio
see page 60

Midtown East

FIRST AVENUE

Upper East Side

Queens

0   2 km
0   2 miles

BRONX

MANHATTAN

La Guardia
Δ Airport

NEW JERSEY

QUEENS

Δ
Newark
Airport

Liberty Is.

JFK
Airport Δ

BROOKLYN

An Upper West Side Museum Walk

UPPER WEST SIDE WALK 1

Summary: The greatest concentration of Manhattan's major museums is on the Upper East Side, but the Upper West Side boasts such internationally renowned attractions as the American Museum of Natural History and the New-York Historical Society, not to mention what is probably the most interesting (and certainly the least formal!) of them all: the Children's Museum of Manhattan. At the end of the walk are some monumental apartment buildings, including the famous Dakota.

Start:	The Children's Museum of Manhattan on 83rd between Broadway and Amsterdam.
Transportation:	Subway lines 1 and 9 to 86th Street.
Finish:	The Dakota, on 72nd Street and Central Park West.
Transportation:	Subway lines B and C from 72nd Street.
Length:	About 2.5 km (1½ miles).
Time:	About 1 hour plus visiting time.
Refreshments:	There are eateries on Broadway at the start of the walk, but not much thereafter.
Which day:	Not Monday or Tuesday for the Children's Museum. Not Monday for the New-York Historical Society.
Highlights:	Children's Museum of Manhattan
	Café Lalo
	Hayden Planetarium/Frederick Phineas and Sandra Priest Rose Center for Earth and Space
	American Museum of Natural History
	New-York Historical Society

Even before you leave 86th Street Station there's something to see. Take a look at the painted ceramic plaques along the platform walls. These were installed in 1989, and were done by students from Grosvenor House under the direction of Nitza Tufino.

Come out of the subway station at the exit marked for the southeast corner of 86th and Broadway and turn left down Broadway. Cross 85th and then 84th, which is locally called Edgar Allan Poe Street.

The Children's Museum of Manhattan

Cross 83rd and turn left. About halfway down the block you find the Children's Museum of Manhattan, its entrance raised from the sidewalk level and accessible by stairs or a ramp. The underlying principle of the museum is that children can learn by doing. It also houses the Helena Rubinstein Literacy Center, a sort of interactive, fantasy-oriented reading room. Bookish kids will also get a lot out of the permanent interactive exhibition called Seuss!, which, as well as displaying pictures from the tales, re-creates the landscapes of the stories and features such play and literacy items as a rhyme-making device. Elsewhere drawings by John Lennon (1940–1980) for his son Sean are on show.

Across the street from the museum is the Café Lalo, which is quite good for tea/coffee, light meals, and especially for European-style desserts. If it seems vaguely familiar to you this is probably because it featured in the movie *You've Got Mail* (1998), starring Tom Hanks as the ruthless heir to a bookstore chain and Meg Ryan as the owner of a little bookstore that faces closure; other locations around here are also in the movie, including the branch of Barnes & Noble that you probably noticed on the other side of Broadway as you turned into 83rd. The Café Lalo's international brunches are a mite curious in their conception: A "British Breakfast," for example, comprises coddled eggs with herbs plus the components of that afternoon specialty, a Devon cream tea!

Frederick Phineas and Sandra Priest Rose Center for Earth and Space

Having finished at either museum or café, keep going along 83rd, crossing Amsterdam Avenue to reach Columbus Avenue. Cross Columbus and turn right to cross 81st (a two-way street, so take care), where turn right to walk along the side of Theodore Roosevelt Park. Formerly Manhattan Square, this was renamed some decades ago

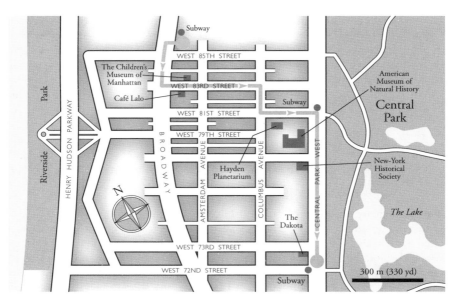

and was under renovation in 1999–2000; it is of interest mainly for its Dutch elms and as a means of access to what used to be officially and is now still popularly called the Hayden Planetarium, but should more formally be referred to as the Frederick Phineas and Sandra Priest Rose Center for Earth and Space, or just the Rose Center. This is part of the American Museum of Natural History, with one "suggested donation" covering admission to both.

From 81st you can see the impressive frontage of the Rose Center as you walk along. There are several ways to reach it, but we'll assume you choose to do so from Central Park West; continue to the end of the street and turn right, and the access is on your right. Named for Charles Hayden (1870–1937), the banker whose generosity permitted its construction and who only just lived to see the fruits of his benefaction, the planetarium was opened in 1935 and used a Zeiss projector. During World War II it was employed by the US Navy for training purposes; afterwards it kept pace with modern technology to present ever more dramatic displays. In the late 1990s it was closed down for complete rebuilding, at a cost of $210 million, as the Rose Center; it reopened in February 2000, although the David S. and Ruth L. Gottesman Hall of Planet Earth, concentrating on geology and the other Earth sciences, opened some months earlier, in June 1999. The architects were Polshek & Partners. The new planetarium *per se* is still the Center's main focus, using a Zeiss Mark 9 projector in a globe that is a full 26.5 m (87 ft) in diameter and appears to float unsupported within a 29 m (95 ft) glass cube; the technologies used within this globe fully justify the claim that this is a virtual-reality display, drawing on data from the Hubble Space Telescope and JPL.

The Rose Center: the Big Bang Theater

Below the planetarium, in the bottom half of the globe, is the Big Bang Theater: You can look down through a glass floor to witness a multisensory display of the universe's explosive birth, then follow the gently sloping Robert Heilbrunn Cosmic Pathway up through displays chronicling the 13 billion years or so that have elapsed since then. Below this area is the Lewis B. and Dorothy Cullman Hall of the Universe, which, while state of the art, is a somewhat more conventional museum facility focusing on astrophysics and cosmology—with, too, an important section on SETI. In a minitheater appended to the Cullman Hall you can take a virtual journey to the interior of a black hole.

All in all, this is an exciting place to be, and you may decide to curtail your walk here to spend some hours in the Center, and carry on with the rest another day. If so, you'll find a subway station (B and C lines, 81st Street/Museum of Natural History) right outside the Center.

The American Museum of Natural History

Otherwise, come out onto Central Park West and head toward downtown. Almost at once you're walking along the frontage of the American Museum of Natural History, which claims to be the largest museum in the world. Whether or not this claim is justified, it is certainly the largest of its kind. The museum was the brainchild of the scientist Albert Smith Bickmore (1839–1914) in the 1860s, and opened at the New

York Arsenal in Central Park in 1869–70. It was immediately realized that larger premises were required, and in 1874, funds having been raised by private subscription and from the city, new ground was broken at the current site, with President Ulysses S. Grant (1822–1885) leading by example and laying the cornerstone. It was not initially a success, however, being unfashionably far north and possessing an academic disregard for popular appeal in its exhibits; under the presidency of Morris K. Jesup (1830–1908) in the 1880s, however, all this changed. He also had the bright idea of opening the museum on Sundays, when working men and women could actually get to it.

The architects for this first stage of the complex were Calvert Vaux (1824–1895) and Jacob Wrey Mould (1825–1886), who were also responsible for the Metropolitan Museum of Art (see page 53); Vaux was, of course, also largely responsible for Central Park (see page 24). Later additions, during 1888–1908, were by the firm Cady, Berg & See; they include the Romanesque-style frontages on 77th Street and Columbus Avenue. The Central Park West and 81st Street frontages were constructed during a yet further wave of expansion during 1912–34 by Trowbridge & Livingston in a Beaux-Arts style.

Theodore Roosevelt Memorial

But the part you will be most aware of as you approach the main entrance on Central Park West is the Theodore Roosevelt Memorial, which forms the middle portion of this frontage and through whose colossal arch you ascend to enter the museum. Again in Beaux-Arts style and using the same pinkish New Brunswick granite as Cady, Berg & See had used, it was designed by John Russell Pope (1874–1937) and dedicated in 1936; the cornerstone was laid in 1931 by Franklin Delano Roosevelt (1882–1945). The bronze statue of Theodore Roosevelt (1858–1919) in the center is by James Earle Fraser (1876-1953) and was dedicated in 1940; the other statues, also by Fraser, are of John James Audubon (1785–1851), Daniel Boone (1735–1820), William Clark (1770–1838) and Meriwether Lewis (1774–1809). Although there can be little doubting the excellence of the architecture and statuary, there is something rather distasteful about the fulsomeness of the various inscriptions on the monument, which hardly fall short of beatifying Theodore Roosevelt.

Go up the stairs and into the Theodore Roosevelt Memorial Hall, often referred to as the Rotunda: This is one of Manhattan's most magnificent interior spaces. It measures 36.6 m (120 ft) by 20.5 m (67 ft) and is a whopping 29 m (95 ft) high. The height of the eight Roman Corinthian capitals is 14.6 m (48 ft). The centerpiece of the hall is a scene depicting an allosaur attacking a barosaur and her youngster. Three Roosevelt-oriented murals by William Andrew McKay decorate the walls: They represent the building of the Panama Canal in 1904–14, the Treaty of Portsmouth (1905), and Roosevelt's explorations in Africa in 1910, but the symbolism is reasonably obscure. You can get a leaflet at the desk that explains the interpretation.

This is another place where you could easily spend the rest of the day. As acknowledged by the display in the Memorial Hall, the biggest single attraction at the museum is offered by the dinosaur fossils and reconstructions. The special exhibitions tend to be pretty spectacular; they have pretty spectacular admission fees too, but these also cover your "suggested donation" for the rest of the museum.

The New-York Historical Society

Leaving the museum, turn right to continue downtown along Central Park West. Cross 77th. The big white building on the corner is the New-York Historical Society, whose entrance is a little way down 77th on the left. The Society was formed in 1804 with the aim of preserving primarily documentary material concerning the history of New York State in particular and the USA in general. It was somewhat peripatetic for its first few decades, acquiring a permanent home (at Second and 11th) only in 1957. The following year it was given the holdings of the New-York Gallery of the Fine Arts, which had opened in 1844 based on the personal collection of the merchant Luman Reed (1785–1836) and can be regarded as the USA's first attempt at a national gallery; among the artists represented were Thomas Cole (1801–1848), Asher Brown Durand (1796–1886), George W. Flagg (1816–1897) and William Sidney Mount (1807–1868). Until 1872 and the founding of the Met (see page 53), the New-York Historical Society was the city's only art museum, adding to Reed's core such items as the Thomas J. Bryan (1802–1870) collection and almost all of Audubon's 435 watercolors for *Birds of America* (1827–38). Also in the Society's collection are the world's biggest collection of stained-glass shades and lamps by Louis Comfort Tiffany (1848–1933) and the files of the architectural firm McKim, Mead & White, mentioned often in this book as responsible for some of Manhattan's finest buildings. The present building was erected in 1908, with architects York & Sawyer; the north and south wings were added in 1938 by Walker & Gillette thanks to bequests from Elizabeth Gardiner Thompson, Charles Griswold Thompson, and Mary Gardiner Thompson, to whom these wings are dedicated.

The Society's name conjures up a dry-as-dust image, but in fact there's something rather joyous about this museum, especially if you visit it immediately after having experienced the ponderous majesty of the Museum of Natural History. It is actually rather hard to appreciate just how much stuff there is here. For example, the library contains a staggering *two million* manuscripts, including the correspondence of George Washington (1732–1799) relating to the War of Independence and the subsequent implementation of the federal government; Washington's inaugural chair is also here. The Landauer Collection of Business and Advertising Ephemera (viewable by appointment only) contains Victoriana. The photographic collection numbers half a million items from the 19th and early 20th centuries. The recently (2000) opened Henry Luce III Center for the Study of American Culture ties the entirety of this vast collection together by allowing computer access to its treasures.

A Pretty Church Interior

Coming out of the New-York Historical Society, turn right and right again to continue down Central Park West. Cross 76th and you're outside the Church of the Fourth Universalist Society. This neo-Gothic building was erected in 1898 with William A. Potter (1842–1909) as architect; its tower is modeled on that of Magdalen College, Oxford. Through a plate-glass window you can get a glimpse of the church's interior; Manhattan seems to specialize in pretty church interiors, and this is another such.

Stately Apartment Buildings

As you proceed down Central Park West you next encounter an area of well-known apartment blocks—well known, that is, as the homes of the rich and high profile. On the northern corner of 75th is the Kenilworth, built in 1908 by architects Townsend, Steinle & Haskell in French Second Empire style. Between 75th and 74th is the San Remo, built in 1930 with Emery Roth (1871–1948) as architect; Rita Hayworth (1918–1987) died here of Alzheimer's disease. And between 74th and 73rd you find the Langham, built in neo-Renaissance style in 1905, the architects being Clinton & Russell. Most famous of all is the big fawnish apartment block between 73rd and 72nd, with its entrance around on 72nd: This is the Dakota, opened in 1884 as the height of exciting modernity. Nowadays it comes across as a grim, depressing building, and it's hard to imagine why the glitterati should flock to take apartments here. Henry J. Hardenbergh (1847–1918) was the architect, working at the behest of Edward S. Clark (1811–1882), then President of the Singer Manufacturing Company, who also built the astonishing Kingfisher Tower Castle up on Otsega Lake, and whose heir, another Edward, put up the money for the National Baseball Museum in Cooperstown. The movie *Rosemary's Baby* (1968), based on the 1967 novel by Ira Levin (b. 1929), was set here, so maybe the earlier comment about the interior was optimistic. Famous residents have included Leonard Bernstein (1918–1990), Judy Garland (1922–1969) and Boris Karloff (1887–1969), and of course John Lennon, who was gunned down on the sidewalk outside; the memorial garden Strawberry Fields (see page 33), inspired by Lennon's widow, Yoko Ono (b. 1933), is just over the other side of Central Park West.

This is the end of the walk, although if you're still game you can carry right on to the next one. Otherwise, the subway station is nearby.

From the Dakota to the Lincoln Center

UPPER WEST SIDE WALK 2

Summary: Many of the walks in this book are filled with museums, but museums and art galleries are not the only form of important cultural centers: theaters, and opera houses are of equal significance. This walk starts with a brief stroll down Central Park West and then diverts westward to look at a few of New York's palaces of performance culture. Along the way you encounter one of the city's most individualistic churches, and at the walk's end are the splendors of the Lincoln Center—or, more formally, the Lincoln Center for the Performing Arts.

Start:	The Dakota, on 72nd Street and Central Park West.
Transportation:	Subway lines B and C to 72nd Street.
Finish:	The Lincoln Center for the Performing Arts.
Transportation:	Subway lines 1 and 9 from 66th Street/Lincoln Center or subway lines A, C, B, D, 1, and 9 from Columbus Circle/59th Street.
Length:	About 2.5 km (1½ miles).
Time:	About 2 hours.
Refreshments:	There are eateries in and around Broadway and also on Columbus Avenue where the route crosses it.
Which day:	Any day.
Highlights:	Congregation Shearith Israel
	Christ and St. Stephen's Church
	Sony IMAX Theatre
	Dorothy and Lewis B. Cullman Center (New York Public Library for the Performing Arts)
	Museum of American Folk Art (but see text)
	New York State Theater
	Avery Fisher Hall
	Cork Gallery
	Vivian Beaumont Theater
	Juilliard School
	Alice Tully Hall
	Walter Reade Theater
	Stanley H. Kaplan Penthouse
	Daniel and Joanna S. Rose Rehearsal Studio

Come out of the subway station and turn to start walking in a downtown direction along the right-hand side of Central Park West. If you've done the previous walk you'll know which building is the Dakota; if not, skip back to page 15 to find out about it. As you continue downtown you pass further chichi and rather grim-looking apartment blocks, and you get the impression that you might catch a glimpse of the ghost of some trendy figure of the 1970s, now lost and adrift and *old* in an urban landscape that is slowly veering from the grand toward the decrepit.

A Synagogue

At the corner of 70th is a brightly white building, the Congregation Shearith Israel, the Spanish and Portuguese synagogue. The synagogue (the first in North America) was founded in 1654 by the first Jewish settlers in this country on Mill Street, on the site of what is now 22–24 South William Street; before that the community had had to make do with their homes or rented rooms for their places of worship. The building you're standing in front of was consecrated in 1897 and, according to the plaque, "this building is a striking example of the monumental Neo-American Classical style popular for public and ecclesiastical architecture at the turn of the [19th/20th] century." This, the fifth synagogue erected by the congregation since the first, in 1730, was designed by Brunner & Tryon. The building's frontage is very stately, with three elegant yet sturdy arches embraced by four fluted quasi-pillars. If the doors are open and you're allowed in (there seem to be no fixed hours when this might be the case), you'll be able to see a reproduction, in part of the space, of the original 1730 structure, complete with some of its furnishings.

Churches

When you reach 69th, turn right to go toward Broadway. Cross Columbus Avenue. Just before you reach Broadway you find on your left the Christ and St. Stephen's Church. This Episcopal church, only a single story high, is a very quirky little building—quite enchanting. Its red bricks and tiles and the various curves used in its construction make it seem like something out of an oriental print. The original St. Stephen's Church was founded on St. Stephen's Day 1805 on the corner of what are now Broom and Chrystie streets; the building was hurriedly constructed and shortage of money meant that inferior materials were used. Indeed, shortage of money has been something of a keynote in the church's history: The original mason had to sue to get his payment. Over the next half century the situation became untenable as all the wealthier congregants moved to more desirable locations further uptown, and in 1866 the original building was sold. For six long years the congregation had to make do with rented halls and the like as it looked for a new home. In 1873 St. Stephen's merged with the Church of the Advent on West 46th, but that premises too was soon decreed unsuitable, and the search for a home was on yet again. Salvation came in the form of a chapel that the Church of the Transfiguration was willing to sell; in 1897 St. Stephen's moved in, and has been here ever since. The purchase left the church with a vast debt, and financial matters were not eased when, in 1905, Christ Church, which had moved to nearby West 71st in 1890, sued St. Stephen's for infringing upon its parish boundaries; the bishop rejected the suit, but other pressures were put upon the church to try to get it to move once more. It was not until 1953 that the church was finally, for the first time in its history, able to clear itself of debt; on May 7 of that year a public burning of the now paid-off mortgage was observed. The 1960s, however, saw more hard times, not least through the construction of the nearby Lincoln Center, which forced many of the congregation to move out of the area. The rector of the time, Joseph Zorawick, pushed through a merger with Christ Church, in the mid-1970s, while at the same time instituting a dynamic range of social policies and projects for the church: feeding the poor, providing care and eventually low-cost housing for the elderly, aiding addicts, and reclaiming the homeless from the streets and rehabilitating them into society through the provision of food, training, and housing. In the 1980s the sale of the church's air rights to a local developer brought in $1 million to help these and other projects. Today the church is as active and involved in its community as its charming little building—which seats at most 250 before the folding chairs have to be brought out—seems to suggest.

Around the Lincoln Center: 66th Street

Turn left when you reach Broadway. Just after you cross 68th you find on your left the grandiose Sony movie complex. Do drop in to have a look around the lobby, which is a temple to lavish bad taste. The highlight is the IMAX Theatre on the fourth floor, which you can approach up some stairs that achieve an odd sort of grandeur amid the eye-wrenching pseudo-opulence of the rest.

Exiting the movie complex, turn left and walk down to 66th; cross Broadway and then cross 66th. Walk along the south side of 66th and the edge of the Lincoln Center for the Performing Arts, into which you'll shortly be venturing. About two-thirds of the way down the block you pass the Good Shepherd–Faith Presbyterian Church, which proclaims a bewildering array of affiliations on its front.

Around the Lincoln Center: Amsterdam Avenue

When you get to Amsterdam Avenue, at the end of the block, turn left. On your left, about halfway down the block, is the New York Public Library Riverside Branch. On the corner diagonally opposite you as you reach 65th is the Fiorello La Guardia High School of Music and Art and Performing Arts, opened in 1936 as the High School of Music and Art by the great New York City mayor for whom it was renamed in 1989, Fiorello H. La Guardia (1882–1947); it moved to the premises here in 1984. Also within is the La Guardia Theater, where the students present performances. The premises on 46th Street of the High School of Performing Arts, which the High School of Music and Art absorbed in 1961, is the setting for the TV series and 1980 movie *Fame*.

Cross 65th and keep going. Halfway down the block on your left is another branch of the New York Public Library, a more significant one than the last. This is one entrance to the Dorothy and Lewis B. Cullman Center, formerly known as the New York Public Library for the Performing Arts, which opened here in 1965 as the Library and Museum of the Performing Arts and was renovated with this latest change of name in 1999–2000. The library has various research divisions, the two most important being the Billy Rose Theater Collection and the Rodgers & Hammerstein Archives of Recorded Sound. Billy Rose (1899–1966) was a songwriter, nightclub owner, and,

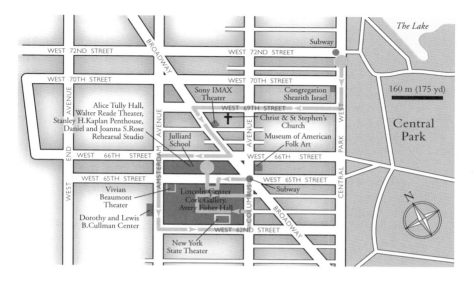

most notably, stage producer; he was married to the famous comedienne Fanny Brice (1891–1951). Rose left his entire fortune of $54 million to the Billy Rose Foundation, whose major endowment was the collection in his name at this library.

Around the Lincoln Center: 62nd Street

The rest of Amsterdam Avenue until you reach 62nd is a rather drab little stretch, and best traversed with the minimum of fuss. Just before 62nd, on your left, is the Guggenheim Bandstand (also known as the Bandshell), where various open-air attractions are presented. Turn left onto 62nd. On your right as you walk along it you can see, just beyond an apartment block, some of the buildings of Fordham University. This Roman Catholic university was opened in 1841 as St. John's College at Fordham Manor in the northwestern Bronx. Initially a theological college, in 1903 it added medical and legal faculties, and in 1907 it became Fordham University. Various other disciplines have been added to the array on offer, although it still seems strange that it should be called a university. It was as late as 1964 that Fordham became coeducational; this was a little after the law school and several other divisions had moved here.

Damrosch Park

To your left along much of this block of 62nd is an open area called Damrosch Park. The famous Damrosch family of New York musicians stemmed from the conductor, violinist, and composer Leopold Damrosch (1832–1885), who spent most of his life in his native Germany, where he was friend to composers such as Richard Wagner (1813–1883) and Franz Liszt (1811–1886), before immigrating to New York with his family in 1871 and becoming an important figure in the Metropolitan Opera and other institutions. Among his many achievements was to give Wagner's *Der Ring*

19

des Nibelungen and *Tristan und Isolde* their US premieres, which he did during the season of 1884–85. His elder son, Frank (1859–1937), another conductor, was choirmaster of the Metropolitan Opera in 1885–91, and in 1905 founded the Institute of Musical Art, which would eventually become a branch of the Juilliard School of Music. Walter Damrosch (1862–1950), yet another conductor, was a co-director of the Metropolitan Opera for half a dozen years after his father's death, produced the first US orchestral tour of Europe (by the New York Symphony Society in 1920), and conducted the first orchestral broadcast on national radio (1925). For 14 years from 1928 he hosted a weekly radio program with the NBC Symphony. Bearing in mind the importance of the Metropolitan Opera to the Lincoln Center from the very start, this little area is very aptly named. It is not, however, exactly scenic, unless you're lucky enough to be here when one of the frequent open-air fairs is being held; these typically offer the kind of expensive, determinedly hand-wrought artsy-crafty objects it would be madness to buy, but they can be fun to look around and certainly bring color to an otherwise somewhat monotone piece of Manhattan.

Around the Lincoln Center: The American Museum of Folk Art

As you approach Columbus Avenue you go along a monumental white stone wall on your left; this is the rear wall of the New York State Theater. The entrance to the City Center of Music and Drama is on your left as you go up Columbus, and the entrance to the theater proper is just around the corner, on the Lincoln Center's plaza.

However, just before you go in there, there's a museum it's worth making a quick detour for. The American Museum of Folk Art has since 1999 been constructing for itself a new building at 45 West 53rd Street, and plans to move there in the late spring of 2001. Nevertheless, squint across the busy intersection of Broadway, Columbus, and 65th to check 2 Lincoln Square; the museum's frontage is easy to pick out. Make the crossing, using whichever route seems best in light of the traffic flow, and have a look at this fascinating place. The museum concentrates on rotating exhibitions produced largely by self-taught or tradition-taught artists from all over the Americas although primarily the USA. The permanent collection is huge and of international importance; pieces from it are on display in the Daniel Cowin Permanent Collection Gallery and elsewhere in the museum. The museum is also home to the recently created Contemporary Center, which concerns itself with collecting, exhibiting, publishing and doing scholarly research into the work of 20th-century US artists.

This little stretch of Broadway also hosts a sort of informal book fair. Especially during the summer months, you're likely to find dealing tables up and down the sidewalks where usually friendly entrepreneurs sell secondhand and other books, as well as craft- and artworks

The Lincoln Center

Returning across the various thoroughfares, enter the plaza of the Lincoln Center up the stairs from the Columbus Avenue side. This plaza is officially called the Josie Robertson Plaza—as a birthday present in 1998 to his wife Josephine by the investor Julian H. Robertson Jr., who donated $25 million to the Center. Part of it was to establish the Josie Robertson Fund to support various artistic programs.

The largest performing arts center in the USA, covering about 6.5 ha (16 acres), the Lincoln Center for the Performing Arts was born from the desire of the Metropolitan Opera to move from the old Metropolitan Opera House at Broadway and 39th, a building famously stigmatized by the opera impresario James Henry Mapleson (1830–1901) as a "yellow brick brewery" and now demolished. The Opera had wanted to make a move much earlier, in the 1930s, to what is now the Rockefeller Center, but those plans fell through for shortage of money. In the 1960s the Opera's finances were in better shape, and the New York Philharmonic and the Juilliard School were likewise looking for larger and less antiquated premises. Robert Moses (1888–1981), who did much to shape modern Manhattan during his long tenure in a bewildering array of the city's public offices, selected the site, and money was obtained from various philanthropists including John D. Rockefeller Jr. (1874–1960) and especially John D. Rockefeller III (1906–1978). Construction began in 1959, and the various institutions moved in during the 1960s: the New York Philharmonic in 1962, the New York City Ballet in 1964, the Library and Museum of the Performing Arts (see page 18) in 1965, the New York City Opera and the Metropolitan Opera in 1966, and the Juilliard School in 1969. Today there are twelve performing-arts companies and educational institutions at the Center; the non-profit-making Lincoln Center for the Performing Arts Inc. manages the buildings. Guided tours of the complex go four times daily from the foyer of the Metropolitan Opera House.

The Lincoln Center: The Plaza

The plaza, with its famous central fountain, was designed by Philip Johnson (b. 1906) and is considered a superb piece of work even by those who harshly criticize the rest of the Center's architecture, most of which was done by Wallace K. Harrison (1895–1981) in the Formalist style, with unifying travertine marble frontages. The plaza is modeled on the Campidoglio by Michelangelo (1475–1564) in Rome. As you stand here in its mouth, on your left is the New York State Theater, home of the New York City Opera and the New York City Ballet; straight ahead is the Metropolitan Opera House; and to your right is the Avery Fisher Hall, home of the New York Philharmonic.

The New York State Theater was designed by Johnson, and its interior has a somewhat utilitarian feel; the auditorium, though, which seats over 2,700, is a wash of purple and bronze. The building was opened in 1964 in conjunction with the 1964–65 New York World's Fair. The New York City Opera was founded in 1943 at the City Center of Music and Drama at 131 West 55th Street by La Guardia and others as the City Center Opera Company, with the aim of bringing high-quality productions to opera lovers who couldn't afford to patronize the Met and to provide a proving ground for younger singers and musicians. Among its "alumni" has been the soprano Beverly Sills (b. 1929), who, after retiring from the stage, managed the company for a decade, until 1989. The New York City Ballet was founded in 1946, likewise at the City Center, by choreographer George Balanchine (1904–1983) and writer and arts patron Lincoln Kirstein (1907–1996) as the New York Ballet Society, changing its name two years later, in 1948; it came here in 1964, two years before the City Opera. You can go into the building and have a look around the foyer; do bear in mind that it gets unpleasantly crowded when audiences are milling around before or after a performance.

The Lincoln Center: New Metropolitan Opera House

Continuing around the plaza in a clockwise direction, you come to the Metropolitan Opera House or the New Met, as it is persistently called even three and a half decades after its opening. This is certainly the most majestic of the buildings at the Center, as even the briefest of forays into the foyer will reveal: The Grand Staircase, done in crimson and white, would be splendor enough even without the two enormous paintings (three storys tall!) by Marc Chagall (1889–1985) that mount almost vertiginously above it. It is from the foyer that the guided tours of the Center (see page 168) depart. Designed by Harrison, the New Met opened on September 16, 1966 with the world premiere of the specially commissioned *Antony and Cleopatra* by Samuel Barber (1910–1981). It seats only a little short of 3,800 people, each of whom (including those in the standing-room area) has their own "Met Titles" screen which displays the libretto, in English, simultaneously with the action on stage. On a downstairs level there's a bar, and there's a gift shop at ground level on the right of the ticket counters; some of the staff have been there since the New Met's opening, and if business is slack will talk absorbingly of the great events of the opera company's past. There's also a small museum on the lobby level where you can see paintings and busts of great composers, musicians, and opera singers; these were brought from the 39th Street premises when the company moved here.

The Lincoln Center: Avery Fisher Hall

Exiting the New Met, cut slightly left to the building on the third side of the central plaza. Originally the Philharmonic Hall, this is now the Avery Fisher Hall, renamed in 1973 after the inventor, magnate and philanthropist Avery Fisher (1906–1994), founder of Philharmonic Radio and Fisher Radios, who donated $10.5 million to the Center and also instigated and funded the Avery Fisher Prize, which annually grants $25,000 to a US musician. The acoustics in the 2,700-seater auditorium, however, hardly match those of Fisher's own audio equipment, despite great efforts to improve them over the past decade or so, and the auditorium also lacks a pipe organ, a bizarre omission that there are plans to rectify as soon as funds become available. Neither inadequacy is evident from the huge foyer, of course, which is the bit you can explore without buying a ticket for a performance. Everywhere around the walls and occasionally away from them there are exhibits of interest, from photographs of people important in the Philharmonic's history to artworks to artifacts like the baton used by Bruno Walter (1876–1962). A major treat is the small Cork Gallery, which is down an escalator on your left as you come in from the plaza. This gallery is devoted to the works of community arts organizations, which are allowed to hold exhibitions here for free assuming the work or the cause is adjudged worthy. Most of the time the underground gallery has a vitality that can often be missing from more pretentious art displays.

The Lincoln Center: Statuary and Theaters

Emerging from the Avery Fisher Hall, turn left and then left again to walk parallel with Columbus Avenue to West 65th, locally called Leonard Bernstein Place. A little way along 65th a viaduct crosses above the road. This is part of Paul Milstein Plaza, opened in 1997, up to which you ascend via stairs on your left. Here you find a row of the modern metalwork statuary you probably peeked curiously at as you crossed from the New Met to Avery Fisher Hall; all seven pieces look as if someone had gone berserk in a repairs garage. The cumbrous *Reclining Figure* by Henry Moore (1898–1986) in the middle of the plaza's pool stimulates the aesthetic passions barely more; dotted around elsewhere are what you might assume to be those mysterious objects the workmen leave behind on building sites but which are in fact further modern sculptures.

To the rear of the pool are, on the left, another entrance to the Dorothy and Lewis B. Cullman Center (New York Public Library for the Performing Arts), and, directly across the pool from you, the home of the Lincoln Center Theater. In fact, these are two theaters behind a single facade, the Vivian Beaumont and the Mitzi E. Newhouse, of which the larger and more important is the Beaumont, designed as a Broadway-style theater staging Broadway-style shows. The original designs for this building (probably the Center's best piece of architecture) were by the famous Finnish-born US public architect and furniture designer Eero Saarinen (1910–1961), who unfortunately died before it could be completed, in 1965.

The Lincoln Center: The Julliard School

Exiting the theater, turn left and then right to walk along the wall, where there's further modern sculpture, until you reach the stairs up to the upper part of the plaza. On your left is the Julliard School. The school was founded in 1904 by Frank Damrosch as the Institute of Musical Art using a donation from James Loeb (1867–1933), and was originally housed in the Lenox Mansion on Fifth Avenue at 12th Street. In 1920 it moved to Claremont Avenue, and then in 1969 it came here. In 1929 it had merged with the Julliard Graduate School—founded in 1919 as the Julliard Musical Foundation using a bequest of $20 million from the textile magnate Augustus D. Julliard (1836–1932)—to form the Julliard School of Music, whose name became the Julliard School in 1968. It is almost certainly the premier music school in the country, and takes students from all over the USA and indeed the world. The standard of music produced by the students is astonishingly high and you might want to take in a concert of theirs during your stay in New York. Premier among the school's various halls is the Alice Tully Hall, which has its main entrance on the north side of 65th, under the overpass on which you're standing; the hall seats just over 930, and its fine acoustics can be improved yet further for specific events because of the movable ceiling. Named for the important musical philanthropist Alice Tully (1902–1993)—among other awards she received France's Legion of Honor medal for her music-related philanthropy—the hall is home to, among others, Jazz at Lincoln Center and the Chamber Music Society of Lincoln Center.

On the left of the Julliard School are the Walter Reade Theater (the home of the Film Society of Lincoln Center) and, immediately beside the school, the Samuel B. and David Rose Building; at the top of the latter are the intimate Stanley H. Kaplan Penthouse and the Daniel and Joanna S. Rose Studio.

The walk is over, though you may want to look around the Lincoln Center for a while longer. When you've finished, the 66th Street/Lincoln Center Station has entrances on Columbus Avenue.

From Columbus Circle to the Swedish Cottage

CENTRAL PARK WALK 1

Summary: The story of Central Park began in 1856 when the city commandeered 315 ha (778 acres) with the intention of creating a designed open space for public recreational use. A landscape-architectural contest was held, and in 1858 the winning design was declared to be that put forward by Frederick Law Olmsted (1822–1903) and Calvert Vaux (1824–1895); Vaux had in fact been a principal instigator of the competition in the first place. The whole area, because of its rocky outcrops and swamps, was undesirable for real-estate purposes, but those very same attributes made it extremely attractive as a place that could be landscaped to bring a touch of the wild to a city that was already becoming far too universally urbanized for its own good.

It is hard to imagine the scale of the endeavor that was involved. Various shanty towns had to be flattened and their occupants expelled; the same fate was meted out, more significantly, to the residents of a black settlement that was sufficiently established to have a school and three churches, and, more genteelly, to the sisters and pupils of Mount St. Vincent, at the area's northern end (see page 39). Twenty thousand laborers took over two years of hard toil to complete the original task sufficiently for the public to be allowed in, and improvements continued to be made for some while after that. In 1863 a further acreage was purchased, bringing the northern border of the park up to its current position at 110th Street. Over 40 bridges were required, some to overpass the four main vehicular transverse roads that were dug below ground level through the nascent landscape, and some merely to ensure that pedestrians, riders, and carriages were not confronted by too many or too steep gradients. Parts of the park were constructed as wilderness, parts as cultivated countryside, and parts as formal lawns, arenas, or gardens. Some effort was made to preserve historical sites that lay within the demarcated area, and new structures were erected for curiosity value or for recreational and educational uses. Swamps were excavated and/or built over to make lakes. A maze of surfaced paths was laid through what was largely, to all intents and purposes, open countryside.

The end product was Central Park, one of the wonders of the 19th-century world, and in its way the greatest engineering achievement witnessed by a city that has seen many. Further modifications were made to the park during the decades-long reign as Parks Commissioner of Robert Moses (1888–1981), who added such items as the children's playgrounds, the skating rinks, and the sports fields. There was and still is much criticism of these additions, but, significantly, they're still there and obviously fill a need; to the casual stroller they serve as often pleasing landmarks that give structure to one's walk.

This is the shorter of the two Central Park walks in this book, and visits most of the popular attractions clustered toward the park's southern end. There is a further foray into the northwest of the park at the start of the first of the East Side museum walks (see page 46).

The park used to have an appalling—and completely justified—reputation as an extremely dangerous place to be: muggings and rapes were a real hazard. There is no longer any significant danger during daylight hours—indeed, it's safer than many other parts of the city—but it's foolish to wander around here after dusk. If you start either of these walks in the afternoon and it takes you longer than anticipated, so that twilight is coming in, give it up for the day. Chances are you'd be safe if you continued, but you'd be crazy to take the risk.

Start:	Columbus Circle.
Transportation:	Subway lines A, C, B, D, 1, and 9 to Columbus Circle (59th Street).
Finish:	The Swedish Cottage Marionette Theatre, Central Park.
Transportation:	Subway lines B and C from 81st Street (Museum of Natural History).
Length:	About 5 km (3 miles).
Time:	About 3 hours.
Refreshments:	There are occasional snack counters in the park, plus the moderately expensive Loeb Boathouse Café (off the route) and the very expensive Tavern on the Green.
Which day:	Any day, although weekends are best.
Highlights:	Trump International Hotel and Tower
	Merchants' Gate
	The *Maine* Memorial
	The Carousel
	The Chess & Checkers House
	The Dairy
	Sheep Meadow
	The Tavern on the Green
	Naumburg Bandshell
	The Mall/Literary Walk
	Bethesda Terrace
	Angel of the Waters/Bethesda Fountain
	Strawberry Fields
	The Ladies' Pavilion
	The Ramble
	Belvedere Castle/Henry Luce Nature Observatory
	Shakespeare Garden
	Swedish Cottage Marionette Theater

The subway station has a plethora of widely scattered exits, so when you emerge to the surface your best plan is to look around for, as landmark, the fairly unmistakable Trump International Hotel and Tower. This tall black glass-and-steel skyscraper, of which 15 floors are a hotel and the rest condos, was opened in January 1997, the architect being Philip Johnson (b. 1906). This was, before the remodeling, the Gulf & Western Building, and in the long ago there used to be an equestrian school here. Make your way toward it (one of the subway exits comes up almost beneath it), and have a look at the brightly polished silvery skeletal globe, made by Brandell of Miami, that stands in front of it.

At Explorer's Gate

The island across the way is called Explorer's Gate; cross to it with great care. In its center is a memorial to Christopher Columbus (1451–1506), consisting of a marble pillar 24 m (80 ft) tall and erected in 1892, with atop it, added in 1894, a statue of the navigator by Gaetano Russo. On the other side of the street, downtown, is 2 Columbus Circle, now the headquarters of the New York City Department of Cultural Affairs but originally built in 1965 as Huntington Hartford's Gallery of Modern Art. Hartford, heir to a supermarket fortune, loathed the type of modern art on display at MoMA (see page 64), and determined to set up his own rival museum. He commissioned Edward Durell Stone (1902–1978) to design a building that would match his aesthetics, seemingly not realizing that Stone had been, decades earlier, one of the architects of the detested MoMA. The best that can be said of the building is that Stone did indeed capture Hartford's aesthetics.

Through Merchants' Gate

From here you need to cross the busy, complicated intersection to the bottom corner of the park. The best plan is to retrace your steps to the globe outside the Trump, and then cross Central Park West.

Here you arrive at the plaza in front of Merchants' Gate, the most obvious feature of which is the massive memorial, designed in 1913 in Beaux-Arts style, to those who lost their lives when the USS *Maine* sank in 1898, an event that (whether accident or enemy action) triggered the Spanish–American War. The monument was erected in 1913 by architect Harold Van Buren Magonigle (1867–1935). The equally imposing gilded bronze statue on top of it is the immensely patriotic *Columbia Triumphant*, symbolizing America's sovereignty over the waves; it is by Attilio Piccirilli (b. 1866), as were the other sculptures associated with the memorial.

Beside the statue is Merchants' Gate itself. There are two ingresses to the park here, one a path and the other a roadway. The park is closed to motor vehicles 10.00–15.00 and after 19.00 on weekdays and all weekend from 19.00 Friday to 06.00 Monday—a good reason why this walk is best at the weekend! Most times, therefore, you have a choice as to which course to follow. The route given in this book assumes that traffic is a consideration, so use the pedestrian entrance (on the left) here.

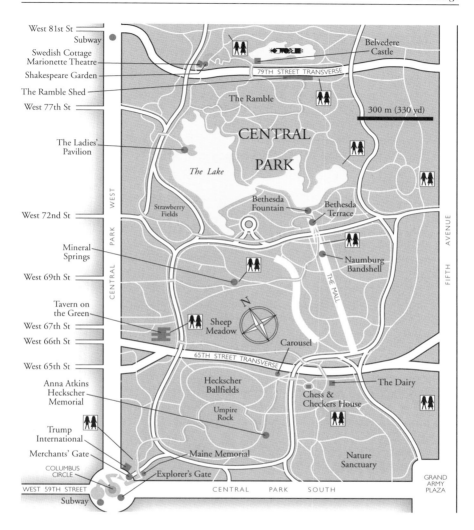

Crossing Pretty Bridges

Soon you encounter a fork in the path; take the left-hand tine. On your left as you go down toward a little valley is an extremely grand public toilet. At the bottom of the hill is Greyshot Arch, one of the many pretty bridges scattered throughout the park. Go through it, and afterwards follow the path around to your left and over another little bridge, Pinebank Arch. On your right are the big gray mass of Umpire Rock and the open space of the Heckscher Playground, named for the mining industrialist and real-estate owner August Heckscher (1848–1941), who donated this and the Heckscher Ballfields, which lie just ahead; confusingly, the philanthropist's grandson, Parks Commissioner in 1967–72, was another August Heckscher (1913–1997).

On the other side of the bridge you come to a T-junction; turn right here, walk downhill for a little way, and then turn left. Follow the path around the base of Umpire Rock, passing on your left a couple of the Heckscher Ballfields, which are used for softball. After passing the one marked Heckscher Field #2, take the path on the right into the open area of the playground. The small, pretty building ahead of you is a memorial to Anna Atkins Heckscher, wife of the philanthropist, but is in fact used as a toolshed. There are toilets here.

The Carousel

Go to the left of the Anna Heckscher Memorial building and then swing around to your left. Soon you'll see on your right yet another attractive bridge, this one called Driprock Arch.

Walk straight ahead to reach the Carousel. The building you see was put up in 1951. The original carousel here was built in 1871 and powered by a blind horse and a mule. It was replaced around the turn of the century by a steam-powered one, which was destroyed in a fire in 1924. A replacement was likewise destroyed by fire, in 1950. The current carousel, one of the biggest in the country, was manufactured in 1908 by the Stein & Goldstein Company of Brooklyn for a trolley terminal at Coney Island, and then was moved here when the old one burned. It is claimed that this carousel features the largest hand-carved carousel figures ever made; certainly it is true, as you can see, that the larger of its 58 hand-painted horses are up to three-quarters the size of a real horse. The Ruth Sohn band organ, playing Wurlitzer 150 music rolls, is original to the carousel. Rides are only a dollar for adults and children alike.

Chess & Checkers House

From here go under the immediately adjacent Playmates Arch, which takes you beneath Center Drive. On your right as you emerge from under the bridge is a rock outcrop, the Kinderberg (children's rock), on which the octagonal, oriental-looking red-and-cream-brick Chess & Checkers House perches. The outcrop, like most of the other outcrops in the park, is made up of Manhattan schist, an Ordovician (*c.* 450 million years old) metamorphic rock that forms the bedrock for the vast majority of the island. There are fissures of igneous rock within the schist, as well as plentiful minerals of the quartz group. About 30,000 years ago, during the last major glaciation of the current Ice Age, the glaciers covered Manhattan, and the evidence of their residence here is visible on the surface of this and other outcrops (e.g., Umpire Rock, which you passed a little while ago) in the form of striations and grooves. Elsewhere in the park there are other signs of glaciation, notably isolated rocks called erratics: These are boulders that were carried from far afield on or in the glaciers and were then left high and dry when the glaciers melted.

Assuming the surfaces aren't wet and slippery, you can climb up the Kinderberg to the Chess & Checkers House; otherwise you have to go around the rock to reach the main entrance. The first thing you'll sense on seeing the house, which dates from 1952, when it replaced a huge rustic summerhouse designed for kids to romp in, is that you've been here before: It has been the setting for countless scenes in the movies. The roughly circular area contains benches and concrete tables into which have been inlaid chess- and checkerboards, and there are further games tables inside; pieces can be borrowed from the Dairy nearby, and in summer the benches are full as young and old match wits.

The Dairy

You'll already have seen straight ahead of you a building that looks as if it's been wrenched from the top of a Swiss clock. This is the Dairy, now a visitor information center but originally a place where milk brought in from approved farms outside the city could be made available for New York's children at minimal cost. When the Dairy and the park around it were built, hundreds of New York's children were dying annually through drinking contaminated milk. The clean milk was tremendously popular, and soon the establishment was selling not just milk to the children but also coffee and beer to accompanying grownups. By the end of the 19th century, however, it began to fall into disuse as the obtaining of clean, fresh milk ceased to be a difficulty, and by midway through the 20th century the Dairy had closed and the building, now in occasional use as a toolshed, had been very comprehensively vandalized, so that only the core of the stone cottage remained. As part of the general cleaning up of the park that began in the late 1970s, however, the Dairy was reclaimed: The roof was reslated, the ornamental carved carpentry replaced, and the loggia rebuilt, so that by 1981 the structure was functional once more, although now as an information center and tourist store. It is very pleasant indeed in good weather to rest here on the loggia and enjoy a cold soda while looking out at the Manhattan cityscape, especially at the Plaza Hotel on Central Park South, and at the Wollman Memorial Rink. This latter opened in 1951 and is named for the philanthropist Kate Wollman, after whom the rink in Brooklyn's Prospect Park is also named.

The store itself doesn't have a great deal to offer, although it has a useful selection of guidebooks to Central Park and to other children-oriented aspects of the city; incredibly, the Dairy doesn't take credit cards, so unless you've come into the park with a reasonable amount of cash on your person (something you might think twice about doing, especially if on your own) you can't buy the books! Inside the building there are also exhibits related to the park, and you can join a guided tour.

Sheep Meadow

Coming out of the Dairy, follow the path that takes you to your right toward the summit of a low hill. Walk over the bridge across the 65th Street Transverse to Center Drive; cross this carefully because, even if there aren't motor vehicles around, there are certainly horse carriages, rollerbladers and cyclists. Keep going in the same direction as before, up and over what looks somewhat like another bridge but is in fact merely a hill.

On your right as you crest the hill you get a good view of the 6 ha (15-acre) Sheep Meadow. In the original plans for the park this was, at the insistence of the authorities, designated as a military parade ground, but Olmsted and Vaux, while obediently incorporating the requirement, were in the forefront of those who protested that the park was not a suitable setting for such activities, especially since military parades might attract unruly members of the populace. The area was left as a meadow while the attention of the authorities was quietly not drawn to the fact that the promised parade ground had not yet materialized, and in due course a flock of sheep was introduced in a successful attempt at *fait accompli*. In 1870 matters were formalized when a sheepfold was built on the other side of West Drive—on the current site of the Tavern on the Green (see below)—and each evening the sheep would be herded there for safety: There was (as there still is) a lot of poverty in the city, and a sheep represented temptation on the hoof.

The sheep were moved out in 1934, and the area became the site for large-scale performances. In the early 1980s the lawn was restored as a recreation area, and nowadays during the summer months (it's closed in winter) Sheep Meadow is full of sunbathers, frisbee-throwers, and strollers.

The Tavern on the Green

You're approaching the Tavern on the Green, to reach which you have to cross West Drive at the lights. Built around the converted sheepfold—Vaux's original building is still evident—this restaurant has six dining rooms of various sizes. Although extremely expensive, the Tavern on the Green is phenomenally popular: some half a million patrons dine here each year, and it is rare to find no line. The restaurant, a pet project of Robert Moses, was opened in 1934 by Mayor Fiorello La Guardia (1882–1947). In 1974, however, it had so much fallen out of popularity that it was closed down, but then in stepped entrepreneur-supreme Warren LeRoy. At huge expense he completely overhauled the restaurant, bringing in the mirrors, glass, and all the rest of the paraphernalia, and building the glass-enclosed Crystal Room and Terrace Room. The restaurant reopened in 1976, and with each passing year its interior decor seems to become more elaborate, so that now the various rooms are a riot of chandeliers, antique prints and paintings, Tiffany glass, and much more besides. Since 1992 the Tavern's Chestnut Room has served also as a music venue.

Outside during the summer you can have a drink at a 12 m (40 ft) bar made in 1996 out of hewn trees pruned from Central and other New York parks, but at any time of the year you can admire the imaginative topiary, done in 1993 by the same topiarists employed for the movie *Edward Scissorhands* (1990). The bushes have been expertly shaped into the semblances of various animals, some of them impressively large, such as the figures of King Kong and My Little Pony—described in the guidebooks as just "a gorilla" and "a horse," but it's perfectly obvious who they are. At night the shrubs and trees are illuminated by thousands of tiny lights to create a genuinely beautiful effect that can be admired to great advantage from nearby Central Park West.

Heroes and Villains

From the Tavern on the Green, come back out onto West Drive and turn left. As you reach the next set of traffic lights along you discover on your left a statue of Fred Lebow (1932–1994), the Romanian-born marathon-runner and -organizer who was largely responsible for turning the annual New York Marathon (inaugurated 1970, and initially run entirely within Central Park) into the major international event it now is. He dropped dead of a heart attack, so it is too easy to jeer at his achievements.

The running track that goes around the Jackie Onassis Reservoir (see page 40) is named in his honor, and the New York Road Runners Club, of which he was a celebrated long-time president, is very active in the park.

Further along you discover a bronze statue of Giuseppe Mazzini (1805–1872), the Italian patriot, political agitator and colleague of Garibaldi (1807–1882); the statue, created in 1876 by Giovanni Turini (1841–1899), was presented to the city in 1878 by the Italian community. Yet further along is a memorial erected in 1873 in honor of the 58 members of the Seventh Regiment National Guards of New York who died defending the Union in the Civil War. The statue, erected in 1869, is by John Quincy Adams Ward (1830–1910).

Just after the war memorial, cross West Drive at the lights and carry on along the path ahead of you toward a low-slung red-brick building with a dainty white spire. This is the grandly titled Mineral Springs, and here you can get light refreshments during the summer months; the building also houses facilities for the Central Park Lawn Sports Center, and has toilets.

Keep going, crossing over the long rollerskating area—once again, be wary of high-velocity rollerbladers—to find a statue of a pair of eagles doing nasty things to a mountain goat. It is hard to see quite how this, *Eagles and Prey* (1860) by Christophe/Christian Fratin (1801 or 1810–1864), was intended to edify the romping children and loving parents Olmsted and Vaux envisaged as the prime users of this region of the park.

Naumburg Bandshell

Pass *Eagles and Prey* and then turn left. Over on your right is the Naumburg Bandshell, the park's main venue for concerts, erected in 1922. It used to be the site for the free Summerstage concerts, inaugurated in the late 1980s and held during the summer months, but after a few years these shifted to the area just beyond the bandshell from where you're standing, the Rumsey Playfield. These free concerts (there's a "suggested donation," but many New Yorkers ignore the suggestion) are heartily recommended: Ranging from rock through opera to folksong, they cater for all tastes, and the atmosphere among the audience, seated on tiered wooden benches or lounging on astroturf, is extremely convivial and relaxed.

Literary Walk

You now come to the top end of The Mall, a long, formally laid-out, elm-lined promenade which Olmsted and Vaux intended to be a place where all sorts and conditions of New Yorkers could mingle and pass the time of day. You'll appreciate why the promenade is alternatively called Literary Walk (it was also at one time called The Promenade): at either end of it are various statues of literary figures (mainly at the lower end) and other creators. This concentration came about because Olmsted and Vaux were concerned that, with donations of statuary coming in from all directions, the naturalistic ambience of the park as a whole might be eroded: much better, they decreed, to restrict the sculptures to an already formalized area. In fact, there came eventually to be sculptures scattered everywhere and they seem in no way to detract from the ambience.

The first you see here is of Victor Herbert (1859–1924), not a literary figure at all but a composer best known for his comic operas. The statue was done by Edmond T. Quinn (1868–1929) and unveiled in 1927. Beyond him Ludwig van Beethoven (1770–1827) scowls at passersby thanks to sculptor Henry Baerer (1837–1908); the statue was installed in 1884. And beyond Beethoven, in a little lawn of his own, stands the great German poet, historian, and dramatist J.C.F. von Schiller (1759–1805). By C.L. Richter, this was the first statue to be installed in the park, being placed in The Ramble in 1859 and moved here in 1953.

Upper Bethesda Terrace
The magnificent structure you now encounter is Terrace Bridge. From where you are standing, on the Upper Bethesda Terrace, you can look through the underpass, between two tall stone poles carved respectively with symbols of Night and Day, at the further glories of the Lower Terrace. This terrace was Calvert Vaux's creation, and he persuaded the Park Commissioners to pay handsomely for its construction: The ornamentation of all the stone surfaces was commissioned from the eminent Jacob Wrey Mould (1825–1886) and the stone itself is costly New Brunswick sandstone.

Walk down the stairs under the bridge and you find yourself in an arcade that's pretty spectacular in its own right—it's more like a banqueting hall than a pedestrian subway. On both sides of you are blind columned arches, and the area abruptly doubles in width as you walk on. Inside the arches are pseudomedieval paintings, and the ceiling is done in Minton tiles. The entire arcade was restored in Spring 2000.

The Lower Terrace is another exquisite space. Before wandering around it, however, you might like to make a quick circle back up one of the outer sets of stairs to the Upper Terrace and down the other. Here you see Mould's artistry at its most magnificent: so detailed and accurate are the representations of birds and plants that naturalists can readily identify the species. Much of the carving is showing signs of the affectionate pressure of millions of hands; tempting though it might be, there's no need to add to the erosion.

Navy Terrace
Back on the Lower Terrace (also known as Navy Terrace in honor of servicemen who died at sea during the two world wars), walk across its admirable tiled surface to the Bethesda Fountain, the centerpiece of which is the dramatic sculpture *Angel of the Waters of Bethesda* (almost always known as *Angel of the Waters*), the only sculpture to be commissioned for the original design of the park. The fountain was restored in 1981 and the sculpture in 1988.

Once again, you'll recognize the scene, for terrace, fountain, and statue alike have all featured in scores of movies, and have also been much utilized for fashion and other photography. The statue is a splendid work in its own right. It was done in 1873 by Emma Stebbins (1815–1882) and was the first major work of New York public art to be commissioned from a woman. At the time wags mocked the fact that she was a sister of the President of the Central Park Board of Commissioners, but in the event this proved to be one of New York's finest public sculptures. A Neoclassical winged nude holds a lily, symbol of purity, in one hand while with the other blessing and celebrating the waters of the Croton Aqueduct, which supplied the fountain.

Terrace Drive

Take a fairly sharp left to follow the path up onto Terrace Drive, and turn right. As you look back from the top of the path you get a nice view of the eastern wing of The Lake, with the Loeb Boathouse on the far side. This was erected in 1954 to replace Vaux's original boathouse, built nearby in 1873, which had deteriorated beyond further tolerance. From the boathouse you can rent rowing boats to explore the lake or bikes to explore the land; in the evenings you can hire a gondola, complete with gondolier. Also you can eat there.

Keep going along Terrace Drive. On your right you pass Cherry Hill, a favorite picnicking spot around which grow, as the name implies, cherry trees. At its top is a pretty little fountain once used for watering horses. On your left as you reach the intersection with West Drive is the statue *The Falconer,* done by George Blackall-Simonds (1843–?) in 1875 and showing an Arcadian figure holding aloft his hunting-bird. In the 1970s vandals seriously damaged the piece, and the arm and falcon were lost. However, they were meticulously restored, and in 1982 this dramatic sculpture was reinstated. Further along, on the right, is a massive bronze statue of the great orator, lawyer, and statesman Daniel Webster (1782–1852), probably better known for the completely fictitious 1941 movie *The Devil and Daniel Webster* (aka *All That Money Can Buy*). This 1876 statue by Thomas Ball (1819–1911) impresses only by its size: it's ponderous and stodgy.

Strawberry Fields

Cross another arm of West Drive and enter Strawberry Fields. This landscaped Garden of Peace was funded for the park by Yoko Ono (b. 1933) in the wake of the assassination of her husband, John Lennon (1940–1980), on the sidewalk outside the Dakota, nearby on Central Park West (see page 15). In the light of her initiative, well over a hundred countries around the world expressed their official support; you can find a list of them on a plaque to the left of the path. Further along you'll find a big circular mosaic set into the path itself and containing the single word "Imagine," the title of one of Lennon's best-known songs, within a geometric surrounding; this was a gift to Strawberry Fields from the City of Naples. Actually, you may have difficulty finding the mosaic at first, because often it's obscured by the crowds who come to lay flowers and photographs (or even themselves) on it in an act of worship to the murdered rock star. The name of the 1-ha (2½-acre) garden—dedicated in 1985 by Mayor Ed Koch (b. 1924) and Parks Commissioner Henry J. Stern—refers to the Lennon & McCartney song, which itself refers to an orphanage near where they both grew up in Liverpool. There *have* been attempts to grow strawberries here but they've been largely unsuccessful thanks to birds. However, the garden is otherwise planted with 161 plant varieties, one for each nation of the world recognized by the United Nations. The opening of the garden was delayed because some members of the New York City Council felt it should be dedicated to all-American Bing Crosby (1904–1977) rather than a pinko Brit like Lennon.

The Ramble

After you've browsed in and around Strawberry Fields, and perhaps taken a look at the nearby Rose Hill and Woodland Wildflower Meadow, carry on in the same direction as before and cross one path to reach another that runs up the side of the park parallel with Central Park West. Follow this latter path northward. Over on your left as you walk are various expensive apartment blocks lining Central Park West, the Dakota among them; it's the squattish dirty-khaki building more or less level with Strawberry Fields.

When you come to a set of traffic lights, turn right to cross West Drive. Just as you make the turn you'll see a sign telling you that the promontory ahead is called Hernshead, a name derived from a fancied topographical resemblance, when seen from the other side, to the head of a heron. On Hernshead (and just visible as you start walking up the side of West Drive) is the Ladies' Pavilion, where ladies and others may sit and gaze out over The Lake. This pretty building started life as a bus shelter (for horse-drawn buses) where the *Maine* Memorial now stands; it was moved here about 1910 and was then left to rot. Vandals destroyed it in the 1970s and extensive restoration (virtually a complete reconstruction) was required.

After a few tens of paces more you're given the option of the high road, alongside West Drive, or the low road, veering to the right away from it; take the low road. A short way along it, cross a bridge, take a left-hand fork and then almost immediately turn right to climb a set of stairs. This leads you into The Ramble, an area of wild mountainous terrain, but all in fascinating miniature. You'll find yourself scrambling up hill and down dale, and after a short while you'll certainly be breathing hard. At one stage or another you'll cross the artificial stream called The Gill. All in all, this is a very exhilarating part of the park to be in.

There's no real set route through The Ramble—it's a complete maze—so you just keep heading in a generally northeasterly direction. In due course you'll find that the terrain flattens and that you're walking through small-scale woodlands. It's hard to describe the sensation here: it's as if *you're* the one who's out of scale, not the "countryside."

Belvedere Castle

Eventually you should emerge at a long, low and rather prettily quaint building called The Ramble Shed; it's actually a toolshed, and has toilets. Turn left along the front of this and follow the path until you come to an intersection, turning right to reach a steepish flight of stairs. Climb these to reach Belvedere Castle. It was designed in 1872 by Vaux as a folly, a pseudoantiquated shell in mixed historical styles—sort of Hollywood Arthurian— from which people could enjoy the view over Turtle Pond and the Great Lawn, in those days a reservoir. In 1919, however, it was taken over by the US Weather Bureau, which installed offices and then a weather station, in the process destroying parts of the architecture. After it moved out in the 1960s this vandalism was continued by enthusiastic amateurs, until in the 1980s, owing to public outcry, there was a major investment to restore the mock castle to its original state. It was reopened in 1982.

Belvedere Castle now houses the Henry Luce Nature Observatory, which displaced an environment-oriented Learning Center in 1996. Here you can look at wall displays on the natural history of the park or look through telescopes down into Turtle Pond (or even at the sunbathers on the Great Lawn). Upstairs from the main room there's one that's more specifically tailored for children, including child-sized furniture. Also housed in the castle is the New York Meteorological Observatory, an organization founded in 1868 by Daniel Draper (1841–1931) and taken over after his retirement in 1912 by the US Weather Bureau.

The Shakespeare Garden

Exiting the Nature Observatory, go straight ahead, passing a rusticated portico on your right. Go down the stone stairs on your right, noticing straight ahead of you, as you descend, the banked seats of the open-air Delacorte Theatre, created by the publisher George Delacorte (1894–1991) for the staging of Shakespearean and other plays. At the bottom of the stairs you find yourself in the Shakespeare Garden, 1.6 ha (4 acres) of sculpted landscape containing about half of the *c.* 200 plant varieties mentioned in the plays and sonnets. The ground was originally cleared for a rock garden, named the Garden of the Heart and established in 1913; just three years later, the tricentennial of Shakespeare's death prompted the name-change. It's a pleasantly quiet spot in which to pause—one of those places within the park where the traffic noise of Central Park West seems preternaturally distanced.

Swedish Cottage Marionette Theater

Once through the Shakespeare Garden, take another flight of stairs down to your right. At the bottom, take a left turn and walk down to the Swedish Cottage. This was actually built in Sweden in 1875 and shipped to Pennsylvania the following year for the US Centennial Exhibition in Philadelphia. In 1877 it was bought by the New York City Parks Department and moved here to serve first as a toolshed and then as a café and toilet. The local Swedish-Americans complaining bitterly that it deserved better, it became an entomological laboratory. During World War II it was used by the Civil Defense, and then in 1947 it was given for use as a workshop to the Parks Department's Traveling Marionette Theatre. In 1973 it was retrofitted as a marionette theater. Astonishingly, its first restoration was not required until 1997–1998. The marionette plays produced here are productions of the Citywide Puppets in the Parks program, and are generally well-tried classics like *The Reluctant Dragon* and *Hansel and Gretel*.

This is the end of the walk. To reach the nearest subway station, go around the back of the cottage, turn right on West Drive, go along to a set of traffic lights, cross West Drive to your left and keep going along a path that leads you to Central Park West. The 81st Street subway station is just outside the park exit.

From Frederick Douglass Circle to Grand Army Plaza

CENTRAL PARK WALK 2

Summary: As part of their Greensward Plan, Olmsted and Vaux imported to the area of the park some 590 species of shrubs and 815 of perennials and alpines, assuming that Nature herself would take care of stocking Central Park with birds and other wildlife. The most common mammal on view is the gray squirrel, and today you can often see little groups of people with cameras and telescopes observing the squirrels.

The first part of this walk takes you through the northern part of the park, the site of various military activities during, primarily, the War of 1812. In particular, the area known as McGown's Pass was of strategic importance. Because of the expanses of swamp in the region, travelers and soldiers were forced, unless they were prepared to make a long detour, to go through a narrow gorge when making their way north or south. In the War of Independence, once the British had in 1776 driven the troops under George Washington back out of the Central Park region into Harlem and beyond, they established a garrison at McGown's Pass. Much later, during the War of 1812, when New York feared a British attack from the north, McGown's Pass was refortified and the strongholds of Nutter's Battery, Blockhouse Number 1, Fort Fish (not on the route) and Fort Clinton were built. Of these, only the blockhouse still stands. In fact, the fortifications and strongholds never saw action, because the war was cut short by the Treaty of Ghent in December 1814, barely months after they were built.

Start:	Frederick Douglass Circle.
Transportation:	Subway lines B and C to Cathedral Parkway (110th Street).
Finish:	Grand Army Plaza and the Pulitzer Fountain.
Transportation:	Subway lines N and R from Fifth Avenue.
Length:	About 8 km (5 miles).
Time:	About 3 hours.
Refreshments:	There's not much on offer apart from the occasional snack counter, but of course the park's an ideal place for a picnic. Note that alcohol, beer included, is banned from the park.
Which day:	Any day, although weekends are best.
Highlights:	Blockhouse Number 1
	Harlem Meer
	Site of Nutter's Battery
	McGown's Pass

Site of Fort Clinton
Site of McGown's Tavern
Conservatory Garden
John Purroy Mitchel Memorial
Jacqueline Kennedy Onassis Reservoir
Cleopatra's Needle
Cedar Hill
Alice in Wonderland
Hans Christian Andersen statue
The Pilgrim
Waldo Hutchins Memorial
Tisch Children's Zoo
George Delacorte Musical Clock
Central Park Zoo/Central Park Wildlife Center
The Arsenal
Doris C. Freedman Sculpture Plaza
Grand Army Plaza
Plaza Hotel
Pulitzer Memorial Fountain
Sherry–Netherland Hotel

Frederick Douglass (1817–1895), for whom the circle is named, was born a slave, as Frederick Augustus Washington Bailey, in Tuckahoe, Maryland. He changed his name after escaping from a Baltimore shipyard at the age of 21, settled in New Bedford, Massachusetts, and worked for the Massachusetts Anti-Slavery Society. In 1847, by now at Rochester, New York State, he started the famous abolitionist journal *Frederick Douglass's Paper*. In later years he rose through various public offices, culminating in 1889 with his appointment as US Minister to Haiti.

From the subway station, cross to the northwest corner of the park. Enter the park directly at the corner of 110th and Central Park West and walk up the central walkway of three (crossing the little 110th Street Bridge) to reach East Drive.

From Blockhouse Number 1 to Harlem Meer
Up on your right is a rather forbidding rocky mass called The Cliff. From the road you can see the blockhouse crouching dourly and alone, a somewhat forlorn flag atop it; you can clamber up to have a look if you like, but it's not recommended, especially if you're on your own: This is one of the few areas of the park which, because of their loneliness and remoteness, are still regarded as problematic.

Keep strolling eastward along East Drive, being wary of the cyclists and rollerbladers and, of course, of motor traffic should you be here at one of the times when cars are allowed in: they are barred 10.00–15.00 and after 19.00 on weekdays and all weekend from 19.00 Friday to 06.00 Monday. Ahead of you are the waters of Harlem Meer and, as you begin to round the bend to the right you see the tiny Duck Island and, in winter, hear the sound of music—more usually, rap—

from the Lasker Rink. In the summer the rink becomes a swimming pool and is much quieter.

Cut down to your left to the edge of Harlem Meer. Across this little lake is the cheerful, colorful, slightly ecclesiastical-seeming Charles A. Dana Discovery Center (see page 47). Harlem Meer is the largest body of water in the park after the Jackie Onassis Reservoir. This once was an area of salt marsh, but Olmsted and Vaux drained it and built the meer in its place. This is one of the most attractive and popular places in the park for strollers and nature-lovers, not to mention kids.

Follow the edge of the water around to the rink/pool (more properly called the Loula D. Lasker Memorial) and cut over to the left in the lee of its ugly and controversial wall. Just after the end of the rink there's a flight of stairs going up on your right. Ignore it, and keep going just a little longer to reach a fork; take its right-hand, uphill tine toward a different flight of stairs. On your left at the top of the stairs is the site of Nutter's Battery. There's nothing much left of this military installation, but the site is marked with a low stone circle inside which are some benches.

McGown's Tavern

Return from the benches to the main path and carry on in the same direction as before; don't go off to the left and down the stairs. Over on your left as you walk is McGown's Pass. Further along, still on your left, you can see a distinctive stony area of cliffside that marks where Fort Clinton used to be. The Clinton in question was De Witt Clinton (1769–1828), Mayor of New York throughout the period of the War of 1812.

Nearby on your right as you ascend a hill is East Drive, so keep to your left, heading progressively away from it and veering around a bulky mound of rock, The

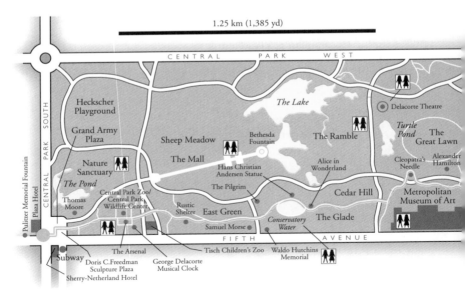

Mount. Around here was McGown's Tavern, a building that was finally obliterated in 1917 after a long and mainly illustrious career. The first tavern was erected in about 1750 by one Jacob Dyckman. In 1759 he sold the business to a widow called Cathy McGown; the establishment became McGown's and the nearby pass was named for it. The McGown family were still operating the tavern nearly a century later, when it was sold to the Sisters of Charity of St. Vincent de Paul. They converted it into a significant convent and girls' school called Mount St. Vincent. When the Central Park terrain was appropriated by the city in 1856, the Sisters were given notice. A couple of years later they were evicted (they moved, with the school, to the Bronx) despite the Park Commissioners not knowing quite what to do with the buildings. The Civil War covered their embarrassment through use of the buildings as a military hospital; ironically, some of the ousted nuns served here as nurses. After the war, in 1865, the place became a tavern once more while the Mount St. Vincent Chapel was converted into a sculpture gallery. The tavern catered to the illustrious during the day while in the evenings degenerating, as far as one can gather, into something little better than a bordello. In 1881 it burned down, but it was swiftly replaced by a bigger one, and well into the new century this was a popular watering hole for the well-to-do. It fell out of favor with the chic set in the period antecedent to World War I, and in 1915 the city decided to shut it down. All of its accumulated artworks were sold off and, in 1917, the building was destroyed.

Conservatory Garden

By now you'll find the path is leading you down toward the neat, orderly arrangements of the Conservatory Garden. You reach a side gate which is, unfortunately, usually closed; if you want to go inside the garden you must go out onto Fifth Avenue at 102nd

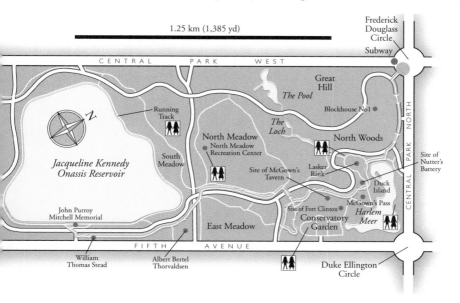

Street (see below) and walk a few blocks back up to its main entrance, the Vanderbilt Gate. There are really three gardens within this fenced-off 2.4-ha (6-acre) area: the North Garden, in formal French style; the Central Garden, in classic Italian style; and the South Garden, in an English style. In the North Garden is the Untermeyer Fountain, named for its donors and circled cavortingly by the sculpture *Three Dancing Maidens*, by Walter Schott (1860–1938). The Central Garden has a plain, unnamed fountain. The South Garden has the Burnett Fountain, named for the children's author Frances Hodgson Burnett (1849–1924) and embellished with a sculpture by Bessie Onahotema Potter Vonnoh (1872–1955), depicting the two central characters of Burnett's classic novel *The Secret Garden* (1909).

Toward the Reservoir

Turning away from the Conservatory Garden, walk uphill, taking the left tine of the fork and climbing a few stairs. At the top of this small hill you find yourself standing over a branch of East Drive that exits onto Fifth at 102nd. A path parallels the drive; follow it if you'd like to explore the Conservatory Garden. Otherwise, follow the path in the opposite direction to this to reach the main stem of East Drive at a set of lights signed North Meadow. Cross here to reach the bridle path on the far side; there's a footpath as well, but it may be fenced off as part of the effort to conserve the grass of North Meadow.

Turn left along the bridle path. This very pretty stretch of the route has few specific landmarks to offer. After perhaps 500 m (600 yards) the bridle path curves to the right while East Drive (and in theory another branch of the bridle path, but it's not visible) goes left. Go up to the road, cross at a set of lights again signed North Meadow, and take the footpath just beyond the road's edge toward your right. This takes you over the 97th Street Transverse.

On your left, in an island between two limbs of the transverse, stands a lonesome statue of the Danish sculptor Bertel Thorvaldsen (1770–1844) in a suitably arty stance. Keep along the path, staying to the right of the children's playground. In due course you reach an access road that enters the park from Fifth at the level of 90th Street. You see a bright New York Road Runners Club kiosk that marks the start and finish of the Fred Lebow Running Track, which completely encircles the Jackie Onassis Reservoir and is 2.54 km (1.58 miles) long. Fred Lebow (1932–1994) can be regarded as Manhattan's father of what is a phenomenally popular sport in the city, road-running (see page 30).

Cross to your right at the lights here to reach the astonishingly grandiose John Purroy Mitchel Memorial. Mitchel (1879–1918) was Mayor of New York City 1914–1918; losing the election of 1917, he patriotically joined the US Air Corps. The memorial by Adolf Alexander Weinman (1870–1952) was dedicated in 1926. Despite the fulsome inscription, Mitchel died not in combat but in a training accident.

The Jackie Onassis Reservoir

Go up either the stairs or the ramp beside the memorial to reach the running track and the edge of the Jackie Onassis Reservoir. Amble southward. A few of the

Plate 1: Angel of the Waters of Bethesda, *the centerpiece of Central Park's beautiful Bethesda Terrace, was the only sculpture of the park's many scores to be commissioned as part of the original plan (see page 32).*

Plate 2: *Instigated by Yoko Ono in memory of her husband, John Lennon, who was gunned down on the sidewalk nearby, Strawberry Fields draws millions to this small section of Central Park (see page 33).*

Plate 3: *The Lincoln Center, whose various institutions are figureheaded by the Metropolitan Opera House, is the main focus of the city's "establishment" performing arts (see page 22).*

Plate 4: *Standing in Central Park, it can sometimes be hard to remember that the teeming metropolis of Manhattan is only a short distance away (see page 24).*

Plate 5: *The memorial to Christopher Columbus at Explorer's Gate, outside the southwestern corner of Central Park (see page 26).*

Plate 6: *José de Creeft's statue* Alice in Wonderland *is one of the most popular of Central Park's attractions for children, who tend to use it as a climbing frame (see page 42).*

Plate 7: *Designed by Frank Lloyd Wright to be a new kind of museum, the Guggenheim's exterior architecture has brought both brickbats and bouquets (see page 52).*

Plate 8: *People come from all over the United States and even from abroad to sample the stores on Fifth Avenue (below left; see page 39).*

Plate 9: *Housed in what was previously the Felix Warburg Mansion, the Jewish Museum is one of the "distinguished elder gentry" of the Upper East Side's Museum Mile (see page 50).*

runners may give you disdainful glances, resenting the fact that you are intruding on what some regard as their exclusive territory. You'll very soon notice that you're actually walking faster than some of them are running, so hold your head high!

Officially renamed the Jacqueline Kennedy Onassis Reservoir shortly after the death of Jackie Onassis (1929–1994), a tireless campaigner for conservation within the city—and universally known as the Reservoir or the Jackie Onassis Reservoir—this is in fact no longer a genuine reservoir. Completed in 1862, while the park as a whole was still under construction, it was originally the distributing reservoir for the Croton Aqueduct, the major engineering project, completed in 1842, that brought a reliable supply of fresh water to Manhattan. However, this system was progressively phased out during the 20th century, and in 1991 this reservoir, the last relic, was cut off from Manhattan's water supply.

Toward the southern end of the Reservoir, tend to your left (away from a structure on the waterside called the South Gate House) and come down off the running track to join what looks like (but according to the maps isn't) a further stretch of bridle path. The cliff of glass panels you can see ahead and leftish is the side of the Metropolitan Museum of Art (see page 53).

Cleopatra's Needle

Continue to follow the path—there's a very attractive ornate cast-iron bridge—until you reach a set of traffic lights. Here cross to the left to take the path that leads along the back of the Met. From this side you get, if anything, even more of an impression of the Met's colossal scale than you do from Fifth Avenue. As you walk you'll find that, if you keep an eye out to your left, you can get a free viewing of the Met's sculptures, visible through the plate glass.

Soon you'll see on your right, on the far side of East Drive, the very distinctive shape of what is almost universally called Cleopatra's Needle but should officially be called The Obelisk. It is an approximate twin of the Cleopatra's Needle that stands in London. Cross East Drive and go around the other side of the hillock on which it stands for a closer look. Almost its entire surface is covered with hieroglyphics and other decorations. These sing the praises of the pharaohs Thothmes III (15th century BC), in whose time the two obelisks were made, and Rameses II the Great (1304–1237BC). They were first erected at the Temple of the Sun in Heliopolis in 1443BC. The Persians sacked the city and toppled the pillars in the 6th century BC, and there they lay for about 500 years until Caesar Augustus (63BC–AD14) salvaged them and took them to Alexandria. It was at this time that little bronze crabs were manufactured and inserted into crevices at the obelisks' bases to help hold them upright. In 1301 an earthquake in Alexandria felled one of the two, and in 1877 the Egyptian government gave this one to the British, who removed it to the bank of the Thames in London. If Britain could have one, could not also the USA? The Egyptian government readily granted the request, but that was where the problems started, for the actual fetching of the obelisk required a major engineering and navigational effort. Lieutenant-Commander Henry Honeychurch Gorringe (1841–1885), who masterminded the entire operation, excavated the monument in Alexandria, got it aboard the specially purchased steamship *Dessoug*, shipped it through the

Mediterranean and across the Atlantic, landed at Staten Island, towed it to the Hudson River end of West 96th, and thence transported it to Central Park (this seemingly trivial phase alone took 16 weeks) and finally, got it upright again. It was finally re-erected on January 22, 1881. It's depressing to record that Gorringe, whose achievement this had been, died only four years later, in his mid-40s.

The Glade

Recross East Drive and carry on along the path on its left-hand side. When you reach the bottom of a minor slope there's an underpass, Greywacke Arch, that leads to the Great Lawn. Detour there if you want to; otherwise keep going as before as the path veers to the left. When it splits, take the route on the right and go over a bridge above the 79th Street Transverse. On the other side of this bridge you descend into the Cedar Hill region. Particularly over on the right, you can admire the cedars that give this region its name; during the summer months you can walk around among them, but in winter the area is fenced off to allow the lawn to recover.

Go through Glade Arch and then tend slowly to the right. A branch of the path goes off to the Levin Playground, but keep on your course. You're now in the area called The Glade, and you can see ahead, at the center of a quasi-amphitheater, the famed statue *Alice in Wonderland*, by José de Creeft (1884–1982), commissioned and donated by the publisher George Delacorte (1894–1991). Dedicated in 1959 to the "memory of my wife Margarita Delacorte, who loved all children," it has been used as a climbing frame by kids from all over the world ever since—the high polish of the bronze is testament to this. The uncharitable might remark that it is in fact better as a climbing frame than a sculpture, because Alice is hardly the dainty little girl of the Sir John Tenniel (1820–1914) illustrations. Around the outermost ring of the statue's base are plaques containing lines of verse by Lewis Carroll (1832–1898), Alice's creator. The group shows Alice, the Dormouse, the White Rabbit, the Cheshire Cat, and others; the Mad Hatter may be a caricature of Delacorte himself and Alice may be based on the sculptor's daughter.

Another Children's Favorite

Just past the statue is Conservatory Water, a formal pond that is much used in the summer months for model boating. For a modest sum you can rent model boats from the Kerbs Memorial Model Boathouse, on the pond's eastern side. During the winter the pond is empty.

Go to the right of the pond, following its edge. About halfway around this side of the perimeter you encounter, set back a little from the path, another children's favorite: the statue, installed in 1956, of Hans Christian Andersen (1805–1875) by Georg J. Lober (1891–?). Two things will strike you immediately about this hefty bronze piece, assuming you can see it through the swarms of eager youngsters who treat it much as they treat Alice. First is the Ugly Duckling, standing looking quizzically up at the great but somewhat wearied-looking storyteller; the second is that … well, surely Andersen's nose wasn't *that* big and sharp? A pleasing tradition is that, in summer, storytellers come here to entertain eager young audiences in front of the statue.

Statutes and Memorials

At the south end of Conservatory Water, take the path that leads initially straight ahead and then curves to the left up the hill. This is called Pilgrim Hill because of the 1884 statue atop it, *The Pilgrim* by John Quincy Adams Ward (1830–1910). It shows a Pilgrim Father looking suitably dedicated. Ascend a couple of short flights of stairs and you find on your left a fungally white semicircular marble bench, which is a memorial to Waldo Hutchins (1822–1891). He was one of the driving forces behind the creation of Central Park. The bench is pretty hideous, but at its rear is an excellently enticing sundial, with a very vital little figure in bronze or cast iron acting as the gnomon.

Use the traffic lights to cross Terrace Drive. Off on your left you'll see a statue of Samuel Morse (1791–1872). Keep going straight ahead and, a little further along, once again on your left you'll see the back of the memorial to Richard Morris Hunt (1827–1895), one of the architects of the Metropolitan Museum of Art. He stares out over Fifth Avenue. Just after a flagpole the path splits in three; take the central course. Pass along below a quaint little rustic-style gazebo; its deliberately crude architecture is matched by that of the climbing artifacts in the Billy Johnson Playground, just beyond. Follow the path down a slope toward and through the impressively chunky stone Denesmouth Arch.

The Children's Zoo

On the other side you come to the Tisch Children's Zoo, up on a bank on your left. Beside each animal pen there's a small bronze model that emits the appropriate noise when touched. There are also big-scale educational models as well as more stylized ones for clambering on and in. In one of a pair of mini-theaters there are daily performances of educational plays. Perhaps most popular of all is The Enchanted Forest, where live animals intermingle with giant models of forest items. The zoo was reopened in 1977 after massive reconstruction funded by the philanthropist Laurence A. Tisch. Admission to the children's zoo comes with that to the Wildlife Center (better known by its old name, Central Park Zoo), whose ticket counter is just a little further along on the right.

Before you reach that ticket counter you pass through an elaborate red-brick gateway. On the right of the opening is the amiable statue *Honey Bear* (1935) by Frederick George Richard Roth (1872–?). But the big attraction is, atop the archway, the George Delacorte Music Clock, another gift from the publisher–philanthropist. The clock itself, housed in a white stone block, is not overly fancy, but on top of the block is a big bell that a pair of animated bronze monkeys beat with hammers to mark every hour and half-hour between 08.00 and 18.00. Beneath the clock is a minstrels' gallery where, as the monkeys ring the chimes above, a half-dozen animated instrument-playing bronze animals—a kangaroo blowing a horn or a hippo scraping at a violin—dance around in a circle to the strains of any of a variety of popular children's tunes. The figures are by Andrea Spadini.

The Central Park Zoo

Beyond the gate is the Wildlife Center itself. This is a lovely area: there's a marvelous feeling of air and light to it, and it's filled with the sounds from the aviary. (The ticket booth is on the right about two-thirds of the way along, and to the left there's a gift shop.) The Central Park Zoo really began through happenstance, as people got into the habit of leaving their unwanted exotic animals at the Arsenal (see below), whose officers perforce started housing them in cages. By 1870 things had got out of hand, and some wooden, cage-filled buildings were erected and called the Menagerie. From about this time the collection became a public attraction, and more organized efforts were made to display unusual creatures. One of these was "Mike Crowley," the first chimpanzee ever put on display in the USA. In 1935 the then Parks Commissioner Robert Moses (1888–1981) built a new zoo that was widely praised both for the amenities it offered visitors and for the humane conditions in which the animals were kept. However, over the succeeding decades these conditions deteriorated until public awareness of animal welfare prompted the Parks Department to do something about the problem. From 1982 the zoo was totally renovated, and it was reopened in 1988, with various additions and improvements since. Here and there are still a few relics of the Wildlife Center's forerunner in the form of limestone animal reliefs, again by Roth. Even if you don't go in, you can see a sample of the animals over the fence: The astonishingly clean-looking, glass-sided sea-lion pool is in the middle of the central courtyard.

More Military Matters
On your left, soon after you come through the gateway bearing the Delacorte Musical Clock, you can see the squat, red-brick rear of the Arsenal. This was built in 1848 (renovated 1934) to store the city's munitions as a replacement for a recently demolished precursor in Madison Square. The entrance is on Fifth Avenue, so if you want to explore the building, your best plan is to do so after you've finished the walk, in a few minutes' time. It is of interest as the second oldest surviving building in the park and one of only two in fact to predate the park; the other, and older, is Blockhouse Number 1 (see page 37). Much of the building is now filled with the offices of the Parks Department and the Wildlife Center, but on display inside, on the third floor, are exhibits related to New York in general and the park in particular; most notable of all is the display, under glass, of Olmsted's and Vaux's original Greensward Plan for Central Park.

You exit the Wildlife Center through a far smaller and less grand gateway than the one by which you came in. Straight ahead of you through the trees you can see the green-roofed, white-faced Plaza Hotel. Keep following the path down to the corner of the park and to Scholars' Gate and Grand Army Plaza. Just through the gate is the Doris C. Freedman Sculpture Plaza, where there are changing displays of modern US sculpture. Freedman was one of the champions of New York's Percent for Art campaign, which attempts to persuade companies, when they commission new buildings, to commission also public art to go alongside them.

Grand Army Plaza
Grand Army Plaza was created in 1912 by architect Thomas Hastings (1860–1929), and the colossal equestrian statue in it of General William Tecumseh Sherman (1820–1891) by Augustus Saint-Gaudens (1848–1907) has become an internationally

recognized symbol of New York City almost to rival the Empire State Building. The statue has been recently regilded, and its aggressive shininess may jolt the eyeballs a little, but its bright appearance is in fact in accord with Saint-Gaudens' intentions and is how it looked when first unveiled in 1903. You have to cross a small curve of 60th Street to reach it; here you'll find parked numbers of the horse-drawn carriages that ply their trade through Central Park. The horses are housed at night in various stables in the region of 35th/45th streets and Tenth/Eleventh avenues.

The other half of Grand Army Plaza is on the far side of 59th Street/Central Park South, and is overshadowed by the elegant, Renaissance-style Plaza Hotel, designed in 1907 by Henry J. Hardenbergh (1847–1918) and widely considered one of his masterpieces. Staying here can be less expensive than you would expect, because some of its *c.* 800 rooms are distinctly smaller and less favored—and cheaper—than the exterior elegance would suggest. The central feature of this part of Grand Army Plaza is the Pulitzer Memorial Fountain, designed in Italian Renaissance style in 1916 by Hastings after he'd completed the rest. Above its several tiers stands a bronze statue by Karl Bitter (1867–1915), *Pomona*. As Pomona was the Romans' minor deity who had responsibility for fruit trees, it's not easy to infer quite why she should be so honored.

To reach the subway station you have to cross Fifth, recross 59th, and then turn the corner into 60th. As you walk up this block, admire the excellent clock standing on a pillar on the sidewalk outside the Sherry–Netherland Hotel (architects Schultze & Weaver; completely renovated 1993). One of only four landmarked sidewalk clocks in Manhattan, this was made by the E. Howard Clock Company and installed in 1927 at about the same time the hotel itself was built.

Museum Mile

EAST SIDE MUSEUM WALK 1

Summary: If you simply wanted to look at the outside of museums and carry on, then in theory you could treat this and the next two walks as a single long walk—from the top of Central Park at 110th Street to St. Patrick's Cathedral between 50th and 51st—and do it in an afternoon. If you determined to do a full visit to every museum, on the other hand, you might still not have finished within a week. We've assumed you'll opt for a middle course, visiting some but not all of the museums, and we've therefore divided the route into three, so that each segment can reasonably be tackled in a morning or afternoon.

Museum Mile is actually a commercial organization of nine major museums rather than a geographical name. Each year in June there is a Museum Mile Festival: the relevant stretch of Fifth Avenue is closed to vehicles, so visitors can stroll down the middle of the road to the strains of live music, popping into any of the nine institutions (free admission during the festival) as the whim takes them.

Start:	Central Park North (West 110th Street) and Lenox Avenue.
Transportation:	Subway lines 2 and 3 to Central Park North (110th Street).
Finish:	The Metropolitan Museum of Art on Fifth Avenue at 81st–84th streets.
Transportation:	The nearest subway stations (line 6 at 77th Street and lines 4, 5 and 6 at 86th Street) are some distance away, so your best option is probably a taxi.
Length:	About 3 km (2 miles).
Time:	About 1 hour, plus visiting time.
Refreshments:	There's surprisingly little on offer, so it might be best either to take picnic makings (there are access points from Fifth Avenue into Central Park) or to make use of the various hot-dog stands.
Which day:	Not Monday or Thursday if you want the full range of museums. Not Friday or Saturday if you want to visit the Jewish Museum, and not Sunday if you want to visit the Goethe-Institut.
Highlights:	Charles A. Dana Discovery Center El Museo del Barrio Museum of the City of New York International Center of Photography The Jewish Museum Cooper–Hewitt/National Design Museum

Church of the Heavenly Rest
National Academy of Design
Solomon R. Guggenheim Museum
Goethe-Institut New York/German Cultural Center
Metropolitan Museum of Art

The exit from the subway station brings you out on the north side of 110th Street (Central Park North). Along to your left are some traffic lights; cross here to the south side of the street. There's a nice view of the 3.5-ha (11-acre) Harlem Meer, now a pretty little lake but until the early 1990s—when Central Park Conservancy, in partnership with various Harlem organizations, set about reclaiming it—a scum-topped, garbage-filled mess.

The Charles A. Dana Discovery Center

On your left you'll see a smallish green building. Take the path down to it from the street just a little way along from where you're standing. This is the Charles A. Dana Discovery Center, and inside it you'll discover an exhibition on aspects of the park's natural history and the conservation efforts being made to preserve it. The Center opened in 1993 and was a gift of the Women's Committee of the Central Park Conservancy and Charles A. Dana. It runs year-round children's workshops as well as musical performances and park tours. It has public toilets.

Once you've investigated the Center, take the lakeside path that initially parallels 110th Street. This offers a pleasant short stroll which, after leading you rightwards, eventually discharges you onto Fifth Avenue opposite the end of East 106th; if you're lucky, small flotillas of optimistic ducks will come swimming over the Meer to have a look at you. Cross over Fifth and turn right.

El Museo del Barrio

A couple of blocks down you find on your left El Museo del Barrio, whose entrance is set back a bit from the sidewalk at the rear of a little courtyard. There are strong links between the museum and the Boys' Harbor Inc. project, a charitable organization which operates out of the same building.

The museum was founded in 1969 in Harlem by a group of Puerto Rican parents, educators, artists, and community activists, partly in response to the then-current drive by New York's museums to decentralize, both geographically and in terms of their subject matter, and partly also in the context of the Civil Rights movement: it would have been one thing merely to take white culture to what was then regarded as a ghetto; what was more important was to make the Latin-American kids of Harlem more aware that they had a historical culture of their own, one that was worth appreciating on its own terms. Initially the museum was housed in a public school; it then led a peripatetic existence in various storefronts on Lexington and Third avenues before coming here to its permanent home in the Heckscher Building in 1977. (The neo-Georgian building was erected in 1925, the architects being Maynicke & Franke, by the Heckscher Foundation for Children and the New York Society for the Prevention of Cruelty to Children.) In 1978 El

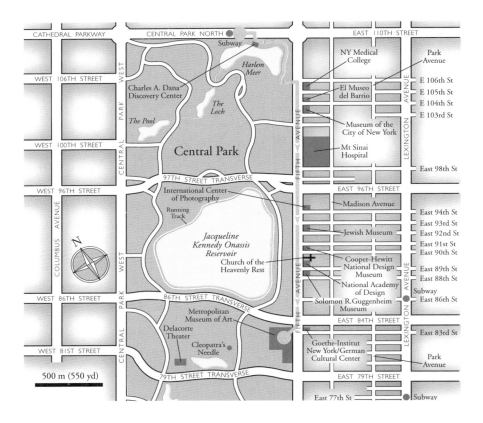

CATHEDRAL PARKWAY
CENTRAL PARK NORTH · Subway
EAST 110TH STREET

Harlem Meer
NY Medical College
Park Avenue

WEST 106TH STREET
Charles A. Dana Discovery Center
The Loch
El Museo del Barrio
E 106th St
E 105th St
E 104th St
E 103rd St

The Pool
Museum of the City of New York

WEST 100TH STREET
Central Park
Mt Sinai Hospital
East 98th St

97TH STREET TRANSVERSE

WEST 96TH STREET
International Center of Photography
EAST 96TH STREET
Madison Avenue
East 94th St

Running Track
East 93rd St
East 92nd St
Jewish Museum

Jacqueline Kennedy Onassis Reservoir
East 91st St
East 90th St

Church of the Heavenly Rest
Cooper-Hewitt National Design Museum
East 89th St
East 88th St

National Academy of Design
Subway
East 86th St

86TH STREET TRANSVERSE
Solomon R. Guggenheim Museum

WEST 86TH STREET
Metropolitan Museum of Art
EAST 84TH STREET
East 83rd St

Delacorte Theater
Cleopatra's Needle
Goethe-Institut New York/German Cultural Center
Park Avenue

WEST 81ST STREET

500 m (550 yd)
79TH STREET TRANSVERSE
EAST 79TH STREET

East 77th St
Subway

Museo was one of the nine museums that together founded the Museum Mile Association. The feel of the museum, as you wander among its exhibits of Latin-American art and artifacts, is predominantly lighthearted: it's a cheerful place to be, and the items on display are beautiful and fascinating by turns, and often both at the same time. One of the arts it fosters is music; the constant gentle background of music makes a pleasant change from the austere hush or the bland muzak of other museums.

El Museo del Barrio has an important permanent collection of Pre-Columbian artifacts (about 2,000 items) as well as significant collections of Caribbean and South American prints, paintings, sculptures, and photographs. There's a slightly chaotic aura to the organization, but don't let that, the friendly, informal staff, or the fact that you're enjoying yourself so much mislead you: this is a major cultural center.

The Museum of the City of New York

Come out of El Museo del Barrio, turn left, and cross 104th Street. Immediately, you find on your left the Museum of the City of New York, whose entrance is at the top of some white marble stairss.

Step through the revolving doors and you find polished wood everywhere. The museum was incorporated in 1923 and at first occupied space in Gracie Mansion. It soon started searching for a permanent site of its own, a quest hampered by the sudden diminution in public generosity following the Crash of 1929. Finally, in 1932, it found its current home, a Georgian colonial-style building, scaled down, because of financial exigencies, from the original grandiose plans done by architect Joseph H. Freedlander (d. 1943).

About half the museum's exhibition space is taken up by changing exhibitions; the rest is permanent display. The collections contain about 1.5 million items that between them comprise an absorbing social history of the city over the centuries. Possibly the most fascinating of the collections are the Toy Collection (over 100,000 items, from puppet theaters to simple dolls as well as several hundred children's books from all periods) and the Theater Collection, whose heart is the John Golden Archive (whose 40,000 or so folders comprise an almost complete documentation of New York theater since the late 18th century).

A Statute and a Plaque

Emerge from the museum and turn left at the bottom of the stairs to continue down Fifth Avenue. Opposite the end of 103rd Street you'll see on the other side of the road a statue of J. Marion Sims (1813–1883), an eminent figure in the history of gynaecology. His particular importance for New York, to which he came from Alabama in 1853, is that he founded (1855) the Woman's Hospital of the State of New York at 83 Madison Avenue. Opposite the statue, between 103rd and 102nd, is the imposing Romanesque building that houses the New York Academy of Medicine, which was founded in 1847 and came here in 1926; the building was designed by architects York & Sawyer and was a gift to the institution from the Carnegie Foundation. It was cited for the merit of its architecture by the Municipal Art Society and the Society of Architectural Historians in 1957.

You'll see on your left for the next few blocks as you go down Fifth that the name of the Mount Sinai Medical Center keeps turning up; these are annexes to the main building, which you come to just after you cross 101st Street and which stretches for several blocks. Before you get there, do pause at 1200 Fifth Avenue to look at the plaque commemorating the contralto Marian Anderson (1897–1993):

> *In 1939, after the contralto was refused the use of Constitution Hall by the D.A.R. because of her race, she sang at the Lincoln Memorial for an audience of 75,000. The first African-American to perform at the White House (1936), and to be a permanent member of the Metropolitan Opera Company (1955), lived here from 1958 to 1975. During that time she served as an Alternate Delegate to the United Nations (1958).*

The Mount Sinai Medical Center

The Mount Sinai Medical Center was incorporated in 1852 as the Jews' Hospital, and from 1855 was sited on West 28th between Seventh and Eighth. Soon afterwards it adopted the policy of treating all comers, regardless of creed, and in 1866 changed its name to the Mount Sinai Hospital. By 1872 it had grown out of its accommodations and moved to a site on Lexington Avenue between 66th and 67th; by 1898 these premises were likewise becoming cramped, and a new hospital was built here on Fifth, opening in 1904. Now called the Mount Sinai–NYU Medical Center, the establishment has an international reputation for both treatment and research. Its various "pavilions" are named for the major benefactors who have contributed to the hospital's growth.

International Center of Photography
You finally leave the Mount Sinai behind at 98th Street. For the next few blocks you pass some attractive but not noteworthy buildings until you come to the corner of 94th and the International Center of Photography (entrance on 94th Street). This institution, which now has another branch at 43rd and Sixth, was founded in 1974 by the photojournalist Cornell Capa (b. 1918), brother of the even more illustrious photojournalist Robert Capa, originally called Endro Friedmann (1913–1954), and is a museum, a school, and a center for photography and photographers. The main emphasis of the works you will see on display is photojournalism and documentary photography. The museum's major holdings include the archives and collections of Robert and Cornell Capa. The building is the former Willard Straight House. Willard Dickerman Straight (1880–1918) was a diplomat and financier, and the co-founder, with his wife Dorothy Whitney Straight, Herbert Croly (1869–1930) and Walter Lippmann (1889–1974), of *The New Republic* in 1914. Dorothy Whitney Straight was herself of some considerable interest. After Willard's death she was the first president (1921) of the Association of Junior Leagues International and, with her second husband, Leonard Elmhirst, progenitor (1925) of the Dartington Hall Trust in Devon, UK. Willard commissioned Delano & Aldrich to design this building as his family residence, and he and Dorothy moved into it in 1913. As a nearby plaque tells you, William Adams Delano (1874–?) was the prime mover in the architecture. He was much influenced by Georgian and Federal architectural styles, and incorporated elements of both in his design. After the Straights' time the house was the home of the socialite Mrs Harrison Williams. It was the headquarters of the National Audubon Society 1952–74, before the International Center of Photography arrived.

The Jewish Museum
Continue your progress down Fifth. Just a couple of blocks down, with its entrance on 92nd (wheelchair access via the Staff & Service entrance, just down from the main one), you find the Jewish Museum. This building used to be the Felix Warburg Mansion. It was designed in French Gothic style by C.P.H. Gilbert (*c.* 1861–1952) and completed in 1908 for Felix and Frieda Schiff Warburg. Felix Warburg (1871–1937) was a financier, art collector, and leader in the Jewish community. In 1947 his widow donated the mansion to the Jewish Theological Seminary of America as a permanent home for the Jewish Museum.

The Jewish Museum was founded in 1904 through the gift by Judge Mayer Sulzberger (1843–1923) of 26 objects of fine and ceremonial art to the library of the Jewish Theological Seminary, and was for over four decades, until Mrs Warburg's generous donation of the house, housed in that library. A sculpture court was added beside the current building in 1959 and an annex (the Albert A. List Building) in 1963. Between 1989 and 1993 there was major renovation, the net effect being to double the museum's gallery space, improve public amenities, create new space for educational programs and allow for the addition of a new permanent exhibition, *Culture and Continuity: The Jewish Journey*, which is essentially a challenging history of Jewry. The museum's permanent collection is claimed to be the largest and most important of its kind.

The Cooper–Hewitt

Exit the Jewish Museum and once more head down Fifth, but this time for only a few metres, because the Cooper–Hewitt/National Design Museum is just across 91st Street (entrance on 91st; wheelchair access on left of main entrance). The building in which the museum is housed dates from 1901 and is one of the mansions built for his own use by the plutocrat Andrew Carnegie (1835–1918).

The Cooper of the museum's title is Peter Cooper (1791–1883), the inventor and philanthropist (see page 118). One of his benefactions was the Cooper Union for the Advancement of Science and Art, which he founded in 1859. This absorbed the Female School of Design, which had been founded in 1846 to give women the option to educate themselves out of menial employment. A long-time director of the Union was Cooper's son-in-law, Abram S. Hewitt (1822–1903), and it was he who in 1896 implemented, on the Union's premises, an idea that his daughters Eleanor and Sarah had come up with and raised finance for: the Museum for the Arts of Decoration. Soon renamed the Cooper–Hewitt Museum, the institution grew and grew thanks to the enthusiasm of the Hewitts until it came to be recognized as of major importance. It became part of the Smithsonian Institution in 1969, and moved to its current premises in 1976. It now has a truly amazing number of items in its various collections in the Department of Applied Arts and Industrial Design, in the Drue Heinz Study Center for Drawings and Prints, the Textile Department, and in the Wallcoverings Department. There are no permanent exhibitions (you can in fact access the permanent collections, but only if you phone in advance), with all effort being put into temporary ones. This means, of course, that you can never be certain quite what you're going to see when you go to the Cooper–Hewitt, but we have never been disappointed.

The National Academy of Design

Return to Fifth and turn left to continue downtown. Just after you cross 90th Street you see the white frontage of the Episcopal Church of the Heavenly Rest, built in 1929 and done in stripped-Gothic/Art Deco style by Mayers, Murray & Philip; the church is open to the public during the week (not Saturdays), and you can find a printed walking guide to its interior in the rack near the door. It's well worth a visit.

Just beyond the church is the National Academy of Design. This building was gifted to the Academy in 1940 by one of the most interesting couples in a city whose history is littered with interesting couples. Archer Milton Huntington (1870–1955) was a railroad heir who was not content simply to spend his life as one of the idle rich. He traveled extensively in Spain as a young man and became an ardent hispanophile and a notable scholar. In 1904 he founded the Hispanic Society of America, a scholarly foundation which maintains a free museum and library on Audubon Terrace and which sponsors art exhibitions, expeditions, and learned journals. In about 1907 he produced an acclaimed translation and critical edition of the medieval *The Poem of the Cid*. Even more eminent was his wife, Anna (1876–1973), *née* Hyatt, a noted sculptor; the big bronze statue of Joan of Arc (1918) at Riverside and 93rd is one of hers, as is the one (1958–59) of the Cuban poet and revolutionary José Martí (1853–1895) at Sixth and Central Park South. She married Archer in 1923. In 1932 she was the first female artist elected to the American Academy of Arts and Letters. The Huntingtons commissioned the prominent interior architect Ogden Codman Jr. to redesign this house to accommodate their personal art collection as well as Anna's studio. Incidentally, Codman was co-author with Edith Wharton (1862–1937) of her first book, *The Decoration of Houses* (1907).

The National Academy of Design itself was founded by a group of 30 artists in late 1825 as the New York Drawing Association. They were concerned that the American Academy of Fine Arts was more interested in catering to its wealthy patrons than in the needs of the artists themselves. In January 1826 the name was changed to the grander National Academy of the Arts of Design. The academy's first president (and also one of its founder members) was Samuel F. B. Morse (1791–1872), then renowned as a portraitist and painter of historical subjects, and only later to become better known as the inventor of the telegraph (*c.* 1832) and the associated code. In 1877, because of internal ructions, a breakaway group set up the Society of American Artists in competition, although the two organizations had sufficiently reconciled by 1906 to merge in that year.

Today the academy has three components: an artists' association, a museum, and a fine arts school. The museum has the nation's fourth largest public collection of 19th- and 20th-century US art. Of special interest are pieces by the American Impressionists, the early Modernists, and the artists of the Hudson River School.

The Solomon R. Guggenheim Museum

As you prepare to cross East 89th it is difficult (despite the visual lure in the middle distance on the other side of Fifth of the colossal sprawl that is the Metropolitan Museum of Art) to see anything other than, on the far side of the street, the corner of one of the most controversial buildings in New York. Loathed by many ("the Big Toilet Bowl"), loved by many, and a source of bemusement to most, the specially created (1959) building that houses the Solomon R. Guggenheim Museum, designed by Frank Lloyd Wright (1867–1959), is either a triumphant redefinition of Modernist architecture or an eyesore.

Solomon R(obert) Guggenheim (1861–1949) was one of the younger sons of the self-made Swiss immigré billionaire Meyer Guggenheim (1828–1905). In collaboration with Baroness Hilla Rebay von Ehrenwiesen (1890–1967), his art adviser, from the late 1920s Solomon amassed a huge collection of abstract painting, and in 1937 he set up the Solomon R. Guggenheim Foundation with the express purpose of creating a museum. That establishment opened as the Museum of Non-Objective Painting in 1939 in a former automobile showroom on East 54th Street, receiving its current name in 1952. As early as 1943, however, Guggenheim and Rebay realized the museum's premises were inadequate, and they commissioned Wright to design them somewhere new. Guggenheim and Wright were neither of them entirely diffident men, and Rebay had a will as well, so it was not unnatural that there were clashes throughout the design and construction phases. It is perhaps ironic that both men died before the building was completed, so that neither could, as it were, have the last laugh. In fact, although the building opened in 1959, it cannot really be said to have been completed until 1992, when extensive restoration hugely increased the exhibition space. At this stage it was renamed the Thannhauser Building—a name that hasn't caught on— to honor the bequest in the early 1970s of the Justin K. Thannhauser Collection.

Whatever your opinion of the exterior, there can be no denying that the interior is a superb testament to Wright's vision. If you're interested in nonrepresentational art and the giants of 20th-century art, then this is another museum where you might choose happily to spend an entire day.

Goethe–Institut New York/German Cultural Center

Keep on down Fifth Avenue until you reach 83rd Street and the last stop on this walk. The object of the next, the Metropolitan Museum of Art, is now a vast and looming presence on your right. Before crossing the avenue to reach it, however, try to spare some time for the Goethe-Institut. This is in fact the New York branch and US headquarters of an organization, likewise called the Goethe-Institut, that has 126 institutes in 76 countries and which is dedicated to promoting the German language and "international cultural cooperation." Since it's a promotional enterprise, however stately, admission is free (except for some of the special events) and you can go in and browse through the library and around whatever exhibitions may currently be in place.

The Metropolitan Museum of Art

Almost opposite is the vast Metropolitan Museum of Modern Art, usually known as the Met. Cross Fifth to it. Just before you do so, have a look at the facade, which is one of the great landmarks of New York architecture. A plaque on the wall outside describes the architecture:

> *Founded in 1870, the museum originally opened at 681 Fifth Avenue, moved to 128 West 14th Street in 1873, and to this site in 1880. The first building on Central Park faced west and was designed by Calvert Vaux [1824–1895] and Jacob Wrey Mould [1825–1886]. It was later enlarged by Arthur Tuckerman [1861–1892] and Theodore Weston [1832–1919]. In 1902 the Beaux-Arts addition by Richard Morris Hunt [1827–1895], including the Great Hall, established the main entrance on Fifth Avenue. McKim, Mead & White added wings north and south between 1911 and 1926. In 1971, Kevin Roche, John Dinkeloo & Associates prepared a comprehensive plan, completed with six major additions between 1975 and 1989.*

Hunt's entrance hall (the Great Hall) with the beautifully elegant yet grandly massive staircase at the rear and its superbly graceful domed ceilings, is another architectural masterpiece. Even though littered with information desks, this huge, superbly proportioned space retains a sense of dignity and tranquility that it's hard to define—rather like the best of the British cathedrals. And there's a sort of cathedral feeling, too, to the first artwork that meets your eye as you enter: a massive green malachite and gilt bronze urn, made in Paris in 1819. This is the Demidoff Vase, made by Pierre-Philippe Thomire (1751–1843) for the Florentine palace of Count Nikolai Demidoff or Demidov (1773–1828).

The guidebook, a substantial volume of permanent reference value, is well worth its price.

This walk ends here. The nearest subway station is some distance away (cut along 83rd for three blocks to Lexington Avenue and turn left: uptown three blocks is the 86th Street Subway station, serving the 4, 5, and 6 lines), so you may opt for a taxi.

The Metropolitan Museum of Art to St. Vincent Ferrer Church

EAST SIDE MUSEUM WALK 2

Summary: If you've already tackled the previous walk you might be coming to the conclusion that it'd be almost impossible for Manhattan to contain any further wealth of museums. You would of course be wrong. Although there's no other museum to compete with the Met for sheer concentration of cultural treasures in a single spot, there are still large institutions like the Whitney and the Frick.

Start:	The Metropolitan Museum of Art on Fifth Avenue at 81st–84th streets.
Transportation:	The nearest subway stations (line 6 at 77th Street and lines 4, 5, and 6 at 86th Street) are some distance away, so your best option is probably a taxi.
Finish:	St. Vincent Ferrer Church on Lexington Avenue at 66th Street.
Transportation:	Subway line 6 from 68th Street.
Length:	4 km (2½ miles).
Time:	About 1 hour, plus visiting time.
Refreshments:	Not a huge amount on offer along the way, although you have a better chance toward the end of the walk.
Which day:	Not Saturday or Sunday for the Whitney, and not Monday for the Frick.
Highlights:	Owen Gallery
	Whitney Museum of American Art
	St. James' Church
	Frick Collection
	7th Regiment Armory
	China Institute
	St. Vincent Ferrer Church

From the Met walk in a downtown direction on the right-hand side of Fifth, then cross Fifth at 79th and keep going, past the imposing facade of the French Embassy. On the northern corner of 78th is the New York University Institute of Fine Arts, the James B. Duke House. There are other pretty buildings (mainly apartment blocks, some with offices on the ground floors) as you progress down Fifth. This is an area where the extremely wealthy dwell; nannies abound.

At 75th turn left. Look up and to your right just after you turn and you'll be able to see trees and bushes at the edge of the roof garden atop number 14 East 75th. Keep walking along 75th until, on your left just before you reach Madison Avenue, you come to the Owen Gallery at number 19. This is an upmarket commercial gallery; if you want to go in for a look at what's on offer you have to ring a bell for admission.

The Whitney Museum of American Art

Across Madison Avenue, on the opposite corner, is the Whitney, whose specialty is 20th-century US art. The exterior of the building, designed in 1966 by Marcel Breuer & Associates and Hamilton Smith, is truly hideous. A core of reinforced concrete is clad in gray granite; tiers of increasing size loom vertiginously over the sidewalk and—although it's difficult to see—a sunken sculpture garden. The entrance is on Madison, just a little way down from the corner of 75th. You enter via a bridge over the sculpture garden into a shabby outer lobby. As you penetrate the museum further, however, you discover that the building's exterior belies its interior: the galleries are a delight to be in.

The museum was founded in 1931 by Gertrude Vanderbilt Whitney (1875–1942), who at the age of 25, in 1900, shocked the establishment by becoming a sculptor—even more so, as the years passed, by becoming a highly successful one, The Washington Heights Memorial (1921) at 168th and Broadway is one of hers. From 1907 she had a studio in MacDougal Alley, Greenwich Village. In 1908 she made her mark as a serious art collector by buying four paintings from that year's exhibition by The Eight. From 1912 she rented a townhouse at 8 West 8th Street which she converted by 1914 into an exhibition space, the Whitney Studio, run in conjunction with Juliana Rieser Force (1876–1948), who remained a lifelong collaborator. In 1918 the two set up the Whitney Studio Club to cater for those (usually young) artists who couldn't find a market among the established galleries; and in 1928 they founded the Whitney Studio Galleries, which offered artists not only exhibition space but patronage. In 1930 Whitney offered her personal collection to the Met, which rejected it. She and Force therefore set up at 8–14 West 8th Street the Whitney Museum of American Art. Initially it contained about 700 items, mainly from Whitney's personal collection but with a fair number of special purchases. Her own preference was for the Ashcan School and for realist painters, but this did not stop her from ensuring that the early Modernists, such as Max Weber (1881–1961) and Charles Demuth (1883–1935), were also represented. For the succeeding two decades the increase in the museum's collection came about almost entirely as a result of her generosity. After first Whitney's and then Force's death, Hermon More (1887–1968) took over as director. He moved the premises to 22 West 54th Street. His successor, Lloyd Goodrich (1897–1987), realized the museum required larger and specially designed space, and it was he who was responsible for commissioning the current building, to which the museum moved in 1966.

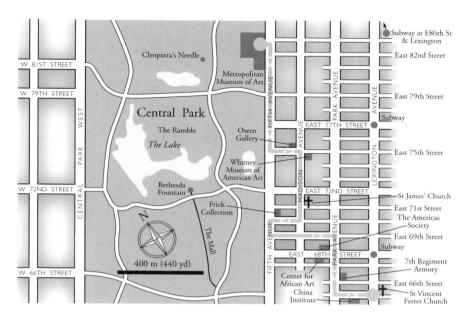

Although the Whitney doesn't offer the same overwhelming experience that the Met does, it's certainly a first-rate, if far smaller, complement to it. How very foolish of the Met to have turned down Gertrude Whitney's offer back in 1930!

St. James' Church
Exit the Whitney and turn left down Madison Avenue. On the far side of the street, at 940 Madison, the building of the United States Mortgage & Trust Company is worth a moment's admiration. All down this stretch of Madison you'll see lots of small galleries, boutiques, design stores, and so forth, all very chichi. At 925 Madison is a Christian Science Reading Room, and just beyond it is the Madison Avenue Presbyterian Church. This was under extensive renovation in early 2000, with no planned reopening date indicated. If hunger calls, cross at 73rd Street to see if there's any room at The Original Soup Burg Coffee House & Restaurant, which for all the grandness of its name and frontage is in fact a diner. Otherwise stay on the left-hand side of Madison and keep walking until you've nearly reached the corner of 71st Street. Here you find St. James' (Episcopal) Church, a vast and age-weathered red building of some distinction—an absolute beauty, in fact, both outside and in. Of particular interest is the reredos, *Christ and His Church*, done by Cram and Ferguson *c.* 1928, and regarded as one of the finer painted and gilded wooden altarpieces of the 20th century.

The Frick Collection
Come out, turn left, and continue down Madison to cross at 71st. Just off Madison is a pleasant Japanese confectionery and tea room called Toraya. Continue down Madison for another block, turn right on 70th, and walk along to Fifth Avenue.

Just before you reach Fifth you find on your right the Frick Collection. The building was designed in 1913–14 by Thomas Hastings (1860–1929), and was the home of Henry Clay Frick (1849–1919), who had become a self-made millionaire by his 30s by recognizing early that the introduction of the Bessemer process would greatly increase the demand for coke, and accordingly buying up coal lands, whose value rapidly rose. Frick willed that, on the death of his widow, his personal collection of fine art, his mansion, and a sizable fund for upkeep should go to New York City. Mrs Frick died in 1931 and, after appropriate renovation and expansion of the building by the architect John Russell Pope (1874–1937), the Collection was opened in 1935; since then it has been increased some 50% through acquisitions by the Trustees. It contains an art reference library of about 175,000 books, some 750,000 photographs, and nearly three million microfiche, but more important to the casual visitor are the artworks on display. There are world-class collections of 18th-century French sculpture and Renaissance bronzes, but what really make the Frick special are the paintings, especially the Old Masters.

Americas Society
When you come out of the Frick, go to Fifth Avenue, then left to 69th Street, and left again, walking back along to Madison. On your left as you reach Madison is a branch of the jewelers Cartier. Cartier, founded in Paris in 1847, came to the USA in 1909, opening its first store at 712 Fifth Avenue under Pierre Cartier (1878–1965). Cross Madison and keep along 69th a block to Park Avenue. Turn right and go down most of the length of the block to find the Americas Society at 680 Park Avenue. This was founded in 1912 as the Pan American Society of the United States with the aim of fostering a greater appreciation in the US public for the cultures of the other nations of the Americas. On the corner on the other side of 68th is the Council on Foreign Relations, a pretty neo-Georgian building erected in 1919.

7th Regiment Armory
Keep going down Park until you reach 67th, then cross Park to carry on down the avenue's left-hand side to reach the 7th Regiment Armory, a great squat red building. Nicknamed the Silk Stocking Regiment because of its many upper-crust members, the 7th was formed in 1847 from a distinguished voluntary militia that had been formed in 1806. Initially its armory was at Tompkins Square, down in the East Village, but when it outgrew this, by the late 1860s, the city allotted this block of land to the regiment for a new one. Unfortunately, it did not allot a sufficiency of funds for the actual building. The regiment's members therefore set up the New Armory Fund and succeeded in raising enough money for the place to open in 1879, albeit without interior decoration. Further fundraising paid for the interiors, completed in 1881 by Louis Comfort Tiffany (1848–1933) and Stanford White (1853–1906), and among the finest of their kind in the USA. The vast building is now used by the 107th Support Group of the New York National Guard, but its greater purpose is as a charitable center and shelter for the homeless. In the winter there's a major antiques show run here for the benefit of the East Side House Settlement.

Theoretically you can see around the armory only by appointment, but if you go in off the street you may be able to see something of the interiors by using a little genial persistence with any staff members you encounter. Remember, though, that this is a privately owned building and that its charitable concerns are more important than your tourist interest, so, if you're told to get out, do so.

The China Institute

Coming away from the armory, walk down to 65th and turn left. About two-thirds of the way along the block toward Lexington Avenue is the China Institute, founded in 1926 to promote understanding between the Chinese and US publics through cultural and educational programs, primarily lectures, presentations, and exhibitions. You can gain access only if there's an exhibition on.

St. Vincent Ferrer Church

Cross Lex and turn a little left to the imposing St. Vincent Ferrer Church. This Dominican church, done in the French Gothic style and on the Latin cross plan by Bertram Grosvenor Goodhue (1869–1924), was opened in 1916 and dedicated in 1918; it incorporates a convent in the northeast corner. The parish had been organized much earlier, in 1867, worshiping at a previous English Gothic-style church on this site from 1869 until that church's demolition in 1914. The building had done very well, since it had been intended only as a temporary structure. Particularly notable about the present church are its sculpture, by Lee Lawrie (1877–1963), especially the holy rood on the exterior (having it on the outside was an innovation, and even today the practice is rare), and its stained glass: The rose window and various others were by Charles Connick (1875–1945), an ex-newspaper cartoonist who became a leading light of the Neo-Medieval Movement in stained glass. The outside of the church is of random ashlar trimmed with dressed limestone; the roof is covered in copper.

The interior is stunning. Manhattan is full of beautiful churches, but this one lays fair claim to being the loveliest of them all. The focal point is the high altar, up to which lead five marble stairs. The centerpiece of the altar, which is shaped like a sepulcher, is the tabernacle, richly covered in gold and other precious metals. The striking reredos by Wilfrid E. Anthony (1877–1948). Among the various statues of saints and other holy figures scattered around the church, that in the Shrine of Our Lady of Fatima is of particular interest. It was sculpted at life-size by a priest, Fr Thomas McGlynn, working in consultation with one of the children who experienced the vision at Fatima. Also of note and also life-size is the statue of St. Vincent Ferrer (d. 1419) himself: clad in the black *cappa* of the Dominicans and with the flame of the Holy Spirit above him, he is visible from all parts of the church. The Stations of the Cross are marked not by the customary plaques but by oil paintings, by Mr and Mrs Telford Paullin. On a sunny day the inside is a riot of color, the strong blues and reds of Connick's windows washing across the dark wooden seating.

Once you've finished marveling at this gorgeous church, come out, turn right, and walk up Lex to the 68th Street subway station. Alternatively, if you've still got plenty of walking energy left, you could hook up with the start of the next walk. If you want something to eat before carrying on and aren't worried about your surroundings, try, despite its extraordinarily unprepossessing exterior, the Pastafina, more or less opposite the church, for some of the best pizza in town.

The Museum of American Illustration to the Museum of Television and Radio

EAST SIDE MUSEUM WALK 3

Summary: This is a fairly short walk, its latter part skirting the edges of the Rockefeller Center. The area of the Upper East Side in which it starts is sometimes (rarely nowadays) called the Gold Coast, because it used to be renowned for the numbers of the rich and famous living here. Today you're more likely to encounter such luminaries on the Upper West Side, but this is still a fashionable part of town. The museums you encounter on this walk do not (MoMA excepted) have the same sort of international repute as those on the previous few walks, but that's not to say they're not worth visiting; the first of them in particular is a gem. St. Patrick's Cathedral, at the walk's end, is one of New York's great landmarks.

Start:	The Society of Illustrators (Museum of American Illustration) on 63rd Street between Lexington and Park avenues.
Transportation:	Subway lines B and Q to Lexington Avenue (63rd Street).
Finish:	St. Patrick's Cathedral on Fifth Avenue between 50th and 51st streets.
Transportation:	Subway lines E and F from Fifth Avenue (53rd Street).
Length:	2 km (1¼ miles).
Time:	About 1 hour, plus visiting time.
Refreshments:	There are plenty of cheerful but undistinguished restaurants scattered around the area.
Which day:	Not Monday or Wednesday.
Highlights:	Museum of American Illustration
	Third Church of Christ, Scientist
	Central Presbyterian Church
	Christ Church United Methodist Church
	Asia Society at Midtown
	Spanierman Gallery
	F.A.O. Schwarz
	AT&T Building
	Trump Tower
	Museum of Modern Art (MoMA)

American Craft Museum
Museum of Television and Radio

If you're doing this walk as a continuation of the previous one, come out of St. Vincent Ferrer Church, turn left, and walk downtown along Lex to 63rd Street, crossing Lex to the right-hand side somewhere en route. Otherwise, emerge from the Lexington Avenue (63rd Street) Subway station and cross if need be to the western side of Lex.

The Museum of American Illustration

Almost as soon as you enter 63rd Street from Lex you find on the left-hand side, in the 1875 carriage house at number 128, the headquarters of the Society of Illustrators, which building also houses the affiliated Museum of American Illustration. It may initially look as if the premises are closed, because there are no windows—just a somewhat intimidatingly grand door. However, try the handle: inside is a small gallery that holds rotating exhibitions which are almost always superb. Part of the agenda of the Society of Illustrators is to counter the tendency of those in the art world to sneer at illustration as the tatty commercial poor sister of fine art, and these exhibitions generally provide emphatic support for the SoI's cause. In terms of sheer competence the works on display are likely to make most of the mimetic art you see in the other galleries look amateurish; more importantly, however, very often the pictures here are possessed of an artistry, affect, and aesthetic integrity that rival those of their more highly regarded (and priced!) cousins.

The SoI was founded in 1901 by a group of artists with a very modest manifesto:"The object of the Society shall be to promote generally the art of illustration and to hold exhibitions from time to time." In short, it was largely a social club. During World War I some members of the SoI worked creating poster designs for the Division of Pictorial Publicity while others were commissioned as captains and sent to France as war artists. The SoI was incorporated in 1920; a major by-product of this was that women were permitted to become full members. During the 1920s the SoI's artists and their models produced annual theatrical skits. The 1925 Illustrators' Show was held at the Shubert Theatre and the Shuberts were impressed enough that they bought the rights in the skits for the Broadway production of *Artists and Models*. Much later, it was the revenue from those rights that enabled the SoI to purchase its current building. During World War II, SoI members were again active in the poster campaign and also visited veterans' hospitals to sketch and console the wounded. After the war, in 1946, the society set up a welfare fund for indigent artists, and in 1948 issued its first Code of Fair Practice.

From 1954 the US Air Force has been employing the SoI members to paint various of its activities around the world. Today there are several thousand paintings by members in the Air Force Collection. The US Coast Guard later followed suit. In the early 1950s the first scholarship fund was set up. In 1959 there were two major developments: The Hall of Fame was established, with Norman Rockwell (1894–1978) as its first member; and the inaugural Annual Exhibition and

Illustrators' Annual were launched. The SoI was used as a setting for the 1969 movie *Loving*, in which George Segal played an illustrator.

The Museum of American Illustration opened in 1981 and today contains about 1,500 works of art in a collection unparalleled anywhere else in the world. There are also extensive archives of relevant historical and biographical material, and the Norman Price Library of books pertaining to the illustrative arts.

A Miscellany of Churches

Exiting the Museum of American Illustration, turn left, and continue along 63rd until you reach Park Avenue. Cross 63rd to your right and go up Park a way. The big red-brick building with massive white pillars is the Third Church of Christ, Scientist, and is dated 1895. A few steps beyond it is the Central Presbyterian Church, which looks older (the style is neo-Gothic) but in fact dates from 1922, the architects being Henry C. Pelton (1868–1935) and Allen & Collens. This is not normally open, but you can go in through the main doors and up on the left for a glimpse at the interior through a viewing window. As befits a Presbyterian church, the decor is in general somewhat austere, although the wood and gilt reredos is lovely. This church is a home for the New York Youth Theater and the 2nd Sunday Puppet Theatre, and holds distinguished choir concerts.

Return to the lights at 63rd Street and cross both it and Park Avenue. Turn left to walk down Park. In the block between 61st and 60th you find the Christ Church United Methodist Church; aside from service times it's open in the early mornings for prayer and meditation.

The Asia Society

On the corner of 59th Street is the Asia Society at Midtown, opened to the public on February 3, 2000. The main headquarters of the society is further uptown, at 725 Park Avenue; the 59th Street branch, housed in Florence Gould Hall, is theoretically only an interim location, although it has a look of permanency to it. There are exhibitions, film shows, and lectures. The Asia Society was formed in 1957 to promote good relations between Asia and the USA, and it now has one of the finest collections of Asian art in the world.

A Temple of Toydom

Turn right off Park at 58th Street. On your right almost immediately you find the Spanierman Gallery, a large commercial art gallery. At the end of the block cross Madison Avenue. On your right you see the rear entrance to F.A.O. Schwarz, which claims to be the largest toystore in the world. The business was founded in 1862 in Baltimore by the recent Westphalian immigrant Frederick August Otto Schwarz (1836–?). In 1879 he moved the business to New York, to 765 Broadway, where he opened up the Schwarz Toy Bazaar. He and his three brothers built up the business through importing choice toys from Europe. After operating from three other locations, the store moved in 1931 to 745 Fifth Avenue, where it stayed until November 1986, when it came across the street to its present location. It now has 17 stores elsewhere in the USA, but the New York headquarters remains the famous one, especially thanks to the movie *Big* (1988), directed by Penny Marshall and starring Tom Hanks as a young boy whose body has magically become that of a full-grown man. In one scene he visits F.A.O. Schwarz's flagship store and there dances with his boss (played by Robert Loggia) on a giant set of piano keys laid out on the floor. This scene brought countless extra customers to the store, and the management realized that its staff should, like those in the movie, concentrate on demonstrating and playing with the toys rather than just selling them. In consequence, you can now go into the store and enjoy what is in effect street theater, but with far better props and much more chutzpah.

Some Reviled Buildings

Assuming you don't make the detour to F.A.O. Schwarz, turn left and cross 58th Street to go down Madison. On the other side of 57th you see the IBM Building, which isn't of much interest except for the enigmatic red modern sculpture squatting on the sidewalk at its base; occasionally you'll see pedestrians pause and stare in puzzlement at this sculpture, as well they might. The building is basically just an anonymous black slab, as seen from this side, although there's a very pretty plaza on its diametrically opposite corner. It was erected in 1983 with architects Edward Larrabee Barnes & Associates.

Cross 57th and turn right. The building on the left that looks like some splendidly over-the-top movie emporium from the days when people had more gilt than taste is Niketown, a department store selling nothing but Nike products. The inside is not so much an experience to remember as one you'll never be able to forget. Continue along 57th to Fifth and turn left to find yourself beside one of the most vilified buildings in New York, the famous Trump Tower, erected in 1983 at the behest of real-estate developer Donald Trump (b. 1946) by architects Der Scutt & Swanken Hayden Connell. With its huge central court and its perpetual waterfall it does indeed display an ostentation at which it is easy to sneer; yet at the same

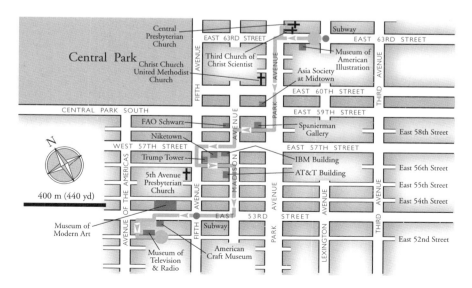

time there's something cheeringly foolhardy about it. The grandiloquent ostentation is somehow in keeping with a man who so happily parodied himself as the ruthless, cut-throat developer Daniel Clamp in the 1990 movie *Gremlins II—The New Batch*.

Turn left at 56th. Just before you do so, glance down toward where 55th Street joins Fifth on the far side of the avenue. The big dirty red building on that corner is the Fifth Avenue Presbyterian Church, founded in 1875 and now the largest Presbyterian church in the city in terms of membership.

Return to Madison Avenue along 56th Street and turn right. The edifice between 56th and 55th is the AT&T Building (now called the Sony Building). Cross over Madison to get a better look. The first thing that impresses is that the building, although it seems vast from street level, is not as huge as you at first thought; it's tall, but it has taller neighbors. The next thing you'll notice is that, for all its size, it has a certain delicacy of effect absent from those neighbors; run your eyes backwards and forwards between it and the IBM Building and you'll see the difference. And the third thing is that, despite its ostentatiously grand scale, the multi-story entrance arch is actually beautifully proportioned in terms both of itself and of the frontage as a whole. Erected in 1984, with architects Philip Johnson (b. 1906) and John Burgee (b. 1933), and clad in pinkish granite, this is regarded as Manhattan's first Postmodernist skyscraper, designating a retreat from the futuristic, technophiliac erections of the preceding two decades toward more approachable, humanistic conventions. Nevertheless, it is widely loathed by sections of the architectural fraternity.

Museum of Modern Art

Continue down Madison and turn right at 53rd. Cross Fifth and, on your right partway down the block to Sixth, you find the unmissable entrance to the Museum of Modern Art. As if it were not vivid enough, there are flags draped around the vicinity with "MoMA" in huge letters. The net effect is to make it easy for you to overlook the fact that there are two other museums of interest within a stone's throw, one of them just on the other side of the street.

MoMA's foyer can be a little intimidating—it's very bright and very large. There's a bookstore off on the right which is well worth checking out; in particular its basement level often has good clearance offers on art books that you're unlikely to see discounted anywhere else. The admission charge to the museum proper is pretty steep, and the toilets and eateries (except the Sette MoMA Bar & Ristorante, which can be entered from 12 West 54th Street) are on the far side of the entry barrier.

The museum was founded in 1929 by Lillie P. Bliss (1864–1931), Mary Quinn Sullivan—daughter of the collector and patron John Quinn (1870–1924)—and Abby Greene Aldrich Rockefeller (1874–1948), and claims to be the first art museum in the world devoted entirely to the modern movement.

There are now about 100,000 items on the museum's four floors. Film is not forgotten as a visual artform: Two small theaters on lower floors host various movie festivals and linked series of screenings. For some reason, however, a visit to MoMA is never quite the engrossing experience one would expect it to be—possibly because, for every stunning piece of work you see, there are about ten whose appeal at *any* level is hard to find. This effect is exacerbated if you've visited the Museum of American Illustration earlier in the walk (see page 61): after a visit there you come to expect as a given a certain level of technical mastery which far from all of the MoMA exhibits attain, and you can find it hard to judge the pictures *as pictures* because of the irritation of noticing subliminally their technical defects—rather as if you were listening to great music on a crackly transistor radio.

Exiting MoMA, cross West 53rd (be careful: you're crossing in the middle of the block) to the American Craft Museum, which is beside a large branch of the New York Public Library, the Donnell Library Center—there's a huge and distinguished collection of children's books upstairs. The museum was founded in 1956 by the American Craft Council, the building being specially designed for the purpose, and its permanent collection today contains many thousands of craft artifacts—from teapots to chairs to baskets to rugs—on four storys. There are also temporary exhibitions, either drawn from the permanent collection or specially curated. At the turn of the millennium, for example, there were two related exhibitions of beads and beadwork, the material being drawn not just from the USA but from all over the world. The three-story atrium/stairway just inside the main entrance is a wonder to behold, containing as it does the tallest interior museum wall in New York.

Once done with the American Craft Museum, come out and turn left to continue along 53rd Street. Before you get to Sixth Avenue, locally called Avenue of the Americas, there's an attractive little courtyard, Paley Park, through which you can cut to reach 52nd Street. Turn left on 52nd and, a little way along, you come to the Museum of Television and Radio. This opened originally as the Museum of Broadcasting in 1975 at 1 East 53rd Street; it moved to its current premises in 1991, at which time also it changed its name. The founder was William S. Paley (1901–1990), who was for a long time also president and trustee at MoMA, and the founder (1927) and first chairman of CBS. He also donated Paley Park, the little courtyard through which you've just walked. A tour around the museum is both fun and educational: You get to listen to some of the great voices of the past—listening to Orson Welles (1915–1985) at work is a particular thrill—and watch some of television's greats, such as Lucille Ball (1910–1989). The collection covers the full history of public broadcasting in the USA, and has over 40,000 programs in its archives, including commercials. This is a superb place to bring children.

Once finished with the Museum of Television and Radio, carry on along 52nd Street to Fifth, turn left, and walk up a block to the subway station. Alternatively, you could turn right to St. Patrick's Cathedral and start on the next walk.

St. Patrick's Cathedral and the Rockefeller Center

Summary: This entire walk takes place in a very small, tight area, but it's filled with interest, including a delightful little art gallery, the Dahesh Museum, that far too many tourists go right by without noticing. The walk starts off with St. Patrick's Cathedral, deservedly one of New York's major attractions for visitors. You may want to spend quite some time looking around the cathedral, and so you might prefer to go past it at the start of the walk and return to it again once you've finished with the Rockefeller Center.

An extra delight concerning this walk, especially if your wallet seems depressingly thin after the several walks preceding it, is that there's not a single admission charge to pay!

Start:	St. Patrick's Cathedral, on Fifth Avenue between 50th and 51st streets.
Transportation:	Subway lines E and F to Fifth Avenue (53rd Street).
Finish:	On Sixth Avenue near Radio City Music Hall.
Transportation:	Subway lines B, D, F, and Q from 47–50th streets (Rockefeller Center).
Length:	About 1.5 km (1mile).
Time:	About 1 hour plus, visiting time.
Refreshments:	There are plenty of cheerful but undistinguished restaurants scattered around the area.
Which day:	Not Sunday or Monday if you want to visit the Dahesh Museum.
Highlights:	St. Thomas' Episcopal Church
	St. Patrick's Cathedral
	Dahesh Museum
	Radio City Music Hall
	GE Building
	The NBC Experience
	Christie's New York
	Gotham Book Mart & Gallery

Exit the subway station and make your way the few paces to Fifth Avenue; you should find yourself on the south side of 53rd and the east side of Fifth.

The big gray Gothic building on the diametrically opposite corner of the intersection is St. Thomas' Episcopal Church. The congregation was formed in 1823 and this church, the parish's fourth, was built in 1911–1913 by Cram, Goodhue & Ferguson. Bertram Grosvenor Goodhue (1869–1924) was largely in charge of the interior, including the reredos, done by Lee Lawrie (1877–1963). The wood carvings are by Irving & Casson. Most of the windows are by Whitefriars of London. Although it doesn't seem nearly as big from the outside, this church is in fact not much smaller than St. Patrick's Cathedral, our next stop on the route. If the church is open, do go in to have a look. The interior is extremely handsome, and one of the many delights on show is, along on your left as you enter, a painting attributed to Peter Paul Rubens (1577–1640), *The Adoration of the Magi*.

St. Patrick's Cathedral

Go down Fifth Avenue on the eastern (left-hand) side. By the time you're preparing to cross 51st Street it's difficult to see anything other than the massive gray church on your left—this is, of course, the famous St. Patrick's. In fact, one of the best views of the exterior you can get is from here, on the northern side of 51st—from other directions you tend to be too close to the building to see it properly. Pause here to take a good look. For those accustomed to seeing cathedrals standing in solitary splendor, it can seem strange to find one of at least equivalent size occupying not a cathedral green but a city block, with other buildings close around it on all sides.

Having crossed 51st, look across to your right before turning to face the cathedral itself. The frontage on the other side of the street is of the International Building at the northeastern segment of the Rockefeller Center, with outside it the famous statue *Atlas*, by Lee Lawrie.

Entry to St. Patrick's Cathedral is not by the main doors but by a smaller door ontheir left. You'll have no trouble finding them because, whenever the cathedral's open, there's a steady stream of tourists going in and out. You might in consequence expect the inside to be crowded, with hundreds of people jostling each other to get a better look at the attractions, but in fact the cathedral is easily big enough (it can seat a congregation of over 2,400) that there's no sense of crowding at all.

The original St. Patrick's Cathedral was built in 1815 on what is now Mulberry Street, far downtown in Manhattan; see page 127 for a visit to it. It was the dream of Archbishop John Hughes (1797–1864) to replace it with a bigger and grander edifice. His intention was to create for the city's Irish Catholics a cathedral whose splendor could not be ignored. In August 1858 he laid the cornerstone of the present building. The architect was James Renwick (1818–1895). Almost immediately all work stopped because of the Civil War, but in 1865 work was resumed under Archbishop John McCloskey (1810–1885). (In 1875, incidentally, McCloskey would be elected the USA's first cardinal.) The cathedral was a long time in the building, not opening its doors until 1879, and there have been various significant additions since then. The Archbishop's Residence, again with Renwick as architect, was completed in 1880, and in 1888 Renwick, under Archbishop Michael Corrigan (1839–1902), added the towers on the West Front. Charles Thompson Mathews (1863–1934) was architect for the Lady Chapel, completed in 1906.

Renwick was charged with building a Gothic cathedral that would be as grand as Archbishop Hughes' dreams on a plot that was an awkward shape for the enterprise; picking elements from both French and English Gothic styles, he succeeded triumphantly, at least insofar as lay visitors are concerned. Architectural critics have persistently sniped over the decades, largely accusing the interior of blandness and kitsch. Whether these criticisms are justified or not is a matter for you yourself to judge. It is undoubtedly a splendid building, certainly well equal to take its place alongside the European models on which it was based.

On leaving St. Patrick's Cathedral, carry on down Fifth Avenue. You can see more of the frontage of the Rockefeller Center as you walk; this extends from 51st down to 48th.

Between 50th and 49th, on your left, you'll find the famous Saks department store. This was founded by Andrew Saks (1847–1912) in 1902 on 34th Street, near the current site of Macy's (see page 103). In 1923 Bernard Gimbel (1885–1966), director of the rival store Gimbel's, of whose founder he was the grandson, bought out the Saks store (it was in theory a merger) and with the proceeds Andrew's son Horace was able to open the current store. For some time now the store has been out of Saks or Gimbel family hands; it's currently owned by a multinational investment group. By all means pop your head in for a look around, but unless you actually want to shop (the service is among the best in New York) there's not really a lot to see.

The Dahesh Museum

Just before you reach 48th Street, look out for the doorway to 601 Fifth Avenue. This is a very unobtrusive entry, so you may well walk right past it and have to come back. It is in fact the entry to one of New York's most underestimated (because it's hard to find) attractions, the art gallery called the Dahesh Museum. It was chartered in 1987 and opened to the public in 1995, but its origins go back some time before that and are quite fascinating. The core of the collection was that of the Lebanese philosopher and writer Dr Dahesh (1909–1984). He had a passion for European academic art, and dreamed of opening a museum of it in his home city (since the 1930s) of Beirut. However, in 1975, during the Lebanese Civil War, Dahesh's collection was shipped to

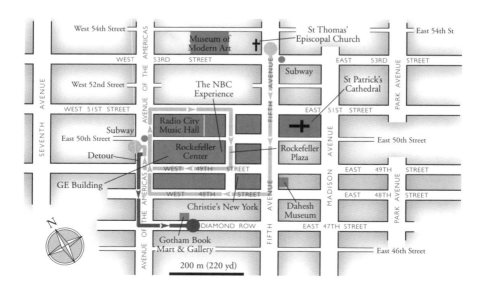

the USA for safety. But the fascination goes beyond that. Dahesh, born Saleem El-Ashi in Jerusalem and uneducated except for a few months at the American Mission orphanage in Lebanon, was from childhood a fairly well accredited miracle worker. Later he was the founder of the religio-philosophical spiritual movement known as Daheshism. He is today regarded by many of his followers as having been an unnoticed Second Coming of the Christ. Certainly he was a most remarkable man.

The museum itself is on the first (second) floor, so go in through the unassuming street entrance and along a short corridor to find the cramped elevator. The gallery is fairly small, but the artworks in its rotating exhibitions more than make up for that; they are never less than excellent. The gallery itself is so beautifully proportioned that it gives a great sense of tranquility.

Sixth Avenue

Exiting the museum, turn left down Fifth and cross the avenue at 48th. Passing the big branch of Barnes & Noble on the corner, stroll along 48th toward Sixth. About halfway along the block you come to the street called Rockefeller Plaza; if you look along it you'll see the area also called Rockefeller Plaza. But don't go there yet; the walk will bring you in from the other side.

On reaching Sixth Avenue (locally called Avenue of the Americas), turn right. Up and down the other side of Sixth is an array of archetypal New York skyscrapers, a representation in microcosm of what people the world over tend to think the whole of Manhattan looks like. Some of these skyscrapers are well known and in their day were architecturally highly lauded. The building of the McGraw–Hill Company, opened in 1972, and in 1990, for no apparent reason, designated a city landmark, is among the more famous. It was opened just in time for publishers McGraw–Hill to wish they hadn't spent the money, because they discovered that year that author Clifford Irving (b. 1930) had with bewildering (and in retrospect hilarious) ease swindled the company out of millions by claiming that recluse Howard Hughes (1905–1976) was willing to let Irving ghost his memoirs. More or less directly opposite McGraw–Hill is rival publisher Simon & Schuster, at 1230 Avenue of the Americas in a building that is part of the Rockefeller Center.

Go up Sixth, crossing 49th. At 1250 Avenue of Americas is the rear entrance of the GE (for General Electric) Building, also part of the Center; it is not to be confused with the General Electric Building, which is at 570 Lexington Avenue. Step into the alcove to have a look at the mosaic frieze, *Intelligence Awakening Mankind* (1933) by Barry Faulkner (1881–1966); its million-plus pieces of glass come in over 250 different colors. The theme is the benefits that radio (this used to be the RCA Building) spreads to humankind, and some of these are matched in strange-bedfellow fashion. One section reads: "Philosophy. Hygiene. Publicity."

Radio City Music Hall

Keep on up Sixth to 50th, on the other side of which is the famous Radio City Music Hall. It is one of the USA's largest theaters, seating 6,000. Opened on December 27, 1932 (the first of the Rockefeller Center's buildings), it was designed in Art Deco style by Donald Deskey (1894–1989), with Edward Durell Stone (1902–1978) as principal architect. Initially it was the home of the lavish productions by Samuel "Roxy" Rothafel (1882–1936); today its shows are mainly easy-listening concerts, although the famous Rockettes, who performed in that inaugural show in 1932 and were formed by Russell Markert (1899–1990) as the Missouri Rockets, are still going strong. There wasn't a black Rockette until 1987, which says something about the conservatism of lechery.

The exterior is in ripple-finished gray Indiana limestone, decorated with vertical aluminum spandrels. The three large panels on the 50th Street facade symbolize dance, drama, and song and are by Hildreth Meiere (1892–1962). The interior was extensively restored in 1979 and again by its new owners (from 1977), Cablevision, in 1999. You can see it either by purchasing tickets for a show or by going on one of the regular tours. For the moment, however, just go in to have a look at the Art Deco foyer, which will give you a good flavor of the rest.

The Time-Life Building

On the other side of Sixth from Radio City Music Hall is another famous member of the series of slabs lining the western side of the avenue: the Time-Life Building. *Time* was founded in 1923 by Henry R. Luce (1898–1967) and Briton Hadden (1898–1929) in New York, although in 1925–27 it briefly published from Cleveland for economic reasons. Luce started its more pictorially oriented sister magazine, *Life*, in 1936. *Life* ceased publication in 1972 but was revived, with only moderate success, as a monthly in 1978. It is still regarded with affectionate nostalgia by many Americans, and its picture archive is of preeminent international importance. This building opened in 1959; the former Time–Life Building, dating from 1937, was part of the Rockefeller Center—it was opposite the Dahesh Museum, on Fifth between 48th and 49th.

Continue up Sixth to 51st and turn right. You're now walking along the rear of the Radio City Music Hall, and if you're lucky one of the doors will be open so you can have a further peek at the Art Deco splendor within. You may be able to see a part of the mural *Fountain of Youth* by Ezra Winter, which rises above the grand foyer and depicts humankind in the search for eternal youth. It measures 18 m × 9 m (60 ft × 30 ft): the canvas was so large it had to be painted on a tennis court, then brought here in sections.

The GE Building

About halfway along the block, Rockefeller Plaza leads off to the right. Turn in here. On your right is the Associated Press (AP) Building's main entrance. AP was formed in 1848 by six New York-based newspapers: the *Courier & Enquirer*, the *Express*, the *Herald*, the *Journal of Commerce*, the *Sun* and the *Tribune*. They were joined in 1851 by the *Times*. After a corruption scandal in the early 1890s it reformed as the non-profit Associated Press of Illinois, then returned to New York in 1900 (still as a non-profit organization) as just the Associated Press. It is today one of the world's most important news-gathering and -dissemination services. It came here in 1937; by 1938 this was the first of the Center's buildings to show a profit. The stainless-steel relief panel above the doorway is *News*, done by Isamu Noguchi (1904–1988) in 1940; it shows journalism's traditional tools (such as typewriter and camera) as well as idealized newsmen.

As you come into the open part of the plaza you'll see on your left a large space with lines of flagpoles (and flags) along it. Cross over, and you find yourself looking down on a scene you'll recognize from having seen it before in countless movies—the Rockefeller Center ice rink. (In summer it may be in use as an outdoor restaurant; but it's recognizable nevertheless.) Across the street behind you is the main entrance to the GE Building, at whose other end on Sixth you saw Faulkner's mosaic. Over the entrance is yet another piece by Lee Lawrie, a triptych done in limestone and glass. The central panel, inspired by the famous William Blake (1757–1827) painting of Jehovah, depicts Wisdom; to Wisdom's either side are Light and Sound. The imagery throughout clearly relates to the building's former incarnation as the home of RCA and the idealistic notion that commercial radio would spread enlightenment rather than Howard Stern.

As you enter the GE Building the first thing you see is an information desk; there's an excellent free tourist leaflet available here. To your left, behind a pillar, there's an elevator down to the underground shopping/restaurant concourse; this was under renovation in 2000, with no reopening date predicted. All around the lobby are murals. The one above the information desk is by José Maria Sert (1874–1945) and shows Abraham Lincoln (1809–1865) and Ralph Waldo Emerson (1803–1882). Sert did most of the rest of the rather dull murals here, under commission from Nelson Rockefeller (1908–1979), a son of John D. Rockefeller Jr. (1874–1960) and the main person responsible for the art scattered around the Center. The Sert mural in the north corridor was not the first to be commissioned, which was by the Mexican socialist painter Diego Rivera (1886–1957): this idealized such figures as Karl Marx (1818–1883) and V.I. Lenin (1870–1924), and Rockefeller hit the roof when he saw it. At the building's inaugural ceremony the offending mural was shrouded behind a tarpaulin, and soon afterwards it was destroyed—although a copy by Rivera still exists in Mexico City's Palace of Fine Arts. The mural in the southern corridor, by the UK artist Sir Frank Brangwyn (1867–1956), is marginally better than Sert's efforts, although equally anodyne.

On your left and right as you come in through the main doors are flights of stairs. Go up either of these and take a promenade around the gallery to get a better appreciation of the lobby.

The famous Rainbow Room nightclub is on the 65th floor of the GE Building. Like the establishments in the underground concourse, however, it and the associated Rainbow Grill were closed in 2000 and no one was prepared to put a date on their reopening. Your best plan is to ask at the information desk or phone the number given on page 172. Opened in 1934, the club gets its name from its organ, which projects shifting patterns of multicolored lights in keeping with the music; from here there are fabulous views of the Manhattan cityscape.

Rockefeller Plaza

Come out of the GE Building and cross the road to take a clockwise tour around the outside of the sunken plaza. Go along between the flags to the far end, where two statues stand either side of a very large marble plaque. Glance for a moment toward Fifth Avenue to see what were christened in 1936 by the press the Channel Gardens, because the two buildings that they lie between are the British Empire Building (on your left) and La Maison Française (on your right); i.e., the gardens divide Britain from France much as the English Channel does. Around Christmas the Channel

Gardens are decorated with angels which, seen from Fifth, seem to frame the vast Christmas tree that is annually erected outside the GE Building.

The plaque, installed here in 1962, presents a declaration by John D. Rockefeller Jr. His father had been a curious combination of cutthroat, utterly unscrupulous businessman on the one hand and philanthropist on the other. Rockefeller Jr., as sole son, inherited a fortune of almost unimaginable scale. As a philanthropist he gave to New York land for public spaces, such as what is now Fort Tryon Park, at the northern tip of Manhattan. Also he donated to the United Nations the land for its headquarters, at the eastern ends of 42nd–49th streets. And, of course, the Rockefeller Center itself.

The notion for the Center began in 1928 when the Metropolitan Opera, seeking to move its premises uptown from 39th and Broadway, asked Rockefeller, a local resident, to help it to buy the rundown area between 48th and 51st, Fifth and Sixth. This help was forthcoming, but the Met very soon ran out of funds—not helped by the Depression—and had to abandon its grandiose plans. Rockefeller pressed ahead anyway, his vision now one of creating a communications "city," with NBC, RCA, and RKO as primary tenants; the Center's initial name was Radio City, which name of course survives in that of the Radio City Music Hall. Using three of the nation's foremost architectural firms—Corbett, Harrison & McMurray, Hood & Fouilhoux, and Reinhard & Hofmeister—he created during 1931–1939 the 14 buildings and the plaza, and incidentally provided a much needed source of employment during the grim Depression years. It was the architects' suggestion that the Center should be extensively adorned with specially commissioned thematic artwork.

From where you're standing in front of the plaque you can see several striking pieces of this art, most obviously the two directly in front of you on the far side of the sunken plaza: Lawrie's *Wisdom*, above the entrance to the GE Building, and, lower down, above the fountain at the opposite end of the rink area, the gilt-bronze statue *Prometheus* by Paul Howard Manship (1885–1966). The two statues that flank the plaque are by Manship also.

The NBC Experience

Continuing to circumnavigate the plaza, you pass a Metropolitan Museum of Art store on the corner. Facing you as you walk back between the flags you see directly ahead the side of the NBC Experience, NBC (National Broadcasting Company) being the only company still to remain here of the original three that Rockefeller regarded as essential occupants of his Radio City. Immediately in through the revolving door here you find yourself in a store selling NBC memorabilia. Stairs in the middle of the store take you up to more of the same but also to a few cases of exhibits that comprise the grandly titled NBC Museum. Many of its exhibits concern icons of popular US culture virtually unknown elsewhere, but some are of more general interest. From the top of the stairs, behind-the-scenes studio tours start every 15–30 minutes. These are expensive (a family of four can expect to pay $65) but offer a fairly fun-filled package, details of which vary according to what's actually going on in the studios at the time.

Alternatively, you can look at the museum and also enjoy a display in the NBC/Panasonic HDTV (high-definition television) theater, which is the garish ball occupying two storys just beside the museum display and covered with over 100,000 colored lights. Inside you can sit in comfort and watch three projectors display on a 130° screen a round-up of NBC's past, present, and future.

Descend using the stairs that spiral around the HDTV globe and come out of the store onto 49th Street. Turn right, toward Sixth, and a little way along is the door to the NBC studios proper. Go in and look at the lobby area, which is a fabulous piece of Art Deco, all done in black and bronze. Remember that this is a working building, not a tourist attraction: If you spot a famous face, bear in mind the person is probably on the way to or from work and may not appreciate being stopped for a fawning session.

Christie's New York

Coming out of NBC, cross 49th Street to the imposing facade of Christie's New York. The famous auction house, founded in London in 1766, opened up its first New York saleroom in 1977 at 502 Park Avenue, then in 1979 opened Christie's East, a smaller saleroom dedicated to less posh items such as rock memorabilia and animation art, at 219 East 67th Street; it also has a gallery on East 59th Street for private viewings. The new building here replaced the Park Avenue headquarters, and was opened in 1999; the facade is in limestone and bronze with a steel-and-glass canopy. From the outside you can also see a huge, specially commissioned mural by Sol LeWitt (b. 1928). The conceptual design and renovation of the exterior are by the architects Beyer Blinder Belle, assisted by the architectural company Gensler, who also designed the interior.

You can walk in and have a look around. Depending on the nature of the imminent sales, you can see spectacular, often museum-quality exhibitions of high and low art—and of course there's no admission charge. A store to the rear and right of the entrance hall sells catalogs of past auctions, and these are well-worth browsing.

Exiting Christie's, turn right and walk along to Sixth. Just on your left on Sixth is the B, D, F, and Q subway.

Detour: The Diamond District and Gotham Book Mart & Gallery

The walk ends here on Sixth, but you might like to go a little further. Walk down Sixth to 47th Street and turn left. You find yourself in the so-called Diamond District. All along both sides of the street are jewelers' stores, some of them household names.

Not far in from Sixth, on the left-hand side of the street, a sign declaring "Wise Men, Fish Here" announces the Gotham Book Mart & Gallery. This is one of Manhattan's legendary bookstores, and rightly; its policy is to stock only fine reading— no cookbooks, celebrity memoirs, etc. You will find a truly colossal selection of the best in books. Moreover, the assistants are genuine booksellers: rare in an era of chain bookstores, they know the books they stock and can usually find what you want quickly. The store was opened in 1920 by Frances Steloff (1887–1989), one of the great figures of the US book trade and of US literature. The list of her regular customers is a Who's Who of American 20th-century writing, and many of the writers became her friends and/or relied heavily on her (sometimes financial) support; moreover, over time she defied the censors to smuggle in books of importance during times of banishment from the USA, such as D.H. Lawrence's *Lady Chatterley's Lover* (1928) and Henry Miller's *Tropic of Cancer* (1934). Her successors keep up all the best of Steloff's traditions, and customers flock here.

Theaterland

Summary: Anywhere in the world, if you say the word "Broadway" to someone they'll assume you're talking about theaters. The difference between a Broadway and an off-Broadway production is largely a commercial rather than a strictly geographical one, although obviously there are further consequences through the greater prestige of the former by comparison with the latter. Geographically, some off-Broadway houses are closer to the street itself than are some of their Broadway rivals. This means that it's very difficult to make a count of the number of Broadway theaters that lie in the main theater area, which is bounded at north and south by West 53rd and West 41st, and at west and east by Ninth and Sixth avenues. Just to complicate matters, there are two smaller clusters of "Broadway" theaters well outside the main district: those associated with the Lincoln Center (see page 22)—as well as the Promenade, on faraway West 76th—and the group on 42nd and 43rd streets between Ninth and Eleventh avenues.

One little mystery is that some of the theaters use the spelling "Theatre" in their titles, while others prefer "Theater." This walk passes virtually every theatre *and* theater in the main district.

Start:	Broadway at West 50th Street.
Transportation:	Subway lines 1, 2, 3, and 9 to West 50th Street.
Finish:	Eighth Avenue and 44th Street.
Transportation:	Subway lines A, C, and E from 42nd Street, or by underground walkway from here to Times Square, served by the 1, 2, 3, 9, N, R and 7 lines, as well as by the S (shuttle) to Grand Central. You are advised not to use this walkway at night.
Length:	About 3 km (2 miles).
Time:	About 2 hours.
Refreshments:	There are eateries all over the place. The fast-food joints are generally all right. The restaurants are very variable; we recommend some at the end of the walk.
Which day:	On Mondays the theaters are almost all dark (i.e., closed), and this may be the best day. Steer clear of the whole area on matinee days (Wednesday and Saturday), as you're almost certain at some stage of the walk to get caught up in milling theater crowds. This may not sound too much to worry about: it is. Often encouraged by the theater managements, the crowds entirely block the sidewalks, refusing (sometimes aggressively) to let you pass, and their buses park illegally along the curbs, so that you end up having to dodge among the traffic. Why this state of affairs is permitted is a matter for the NYPD.

Highlights (aside from theaters):

Times Square Church
Times Square
Sardi's
Barrymores

When you come out of the subway you find yourself standing in front of an imposing but somewhat unsightly shiny black building. This slab is 1633 Broadway, and is
the home of offices including those of *George* magazine, founded by John F. Kennedy
Jr. (1960–1999), as well as part of Viacom/MTV, including the MTV animation studios, where such items as *Celebrity Death Match* are produced.

The Winter Garden

In the downtown direction you can see Times Square, while across Broadway is the
enormous Winter Garden Theater, where the Andrew Lloyd Webber (b. 1948) musical
Cats resided during its record-breaking 17-year run from 1982 to 2000; other notable
productions here have been *West Side Story, Mame,* and *Funny Girl,* but its most distinguished must be *La Belle Paree,* with which it premiered and which brought Al Jolson
(1886–1950) to the legitimate stage. Built originally around 1885 as a stable and auction
house, the building was taken over by the Shubert Brothers organization—Lee
(1875–1953), Sam S. (1876-1905), and Jacob J. (1880–1963)—in 1911 and converted to
a theater for them by architect William Albert Swasey (1864–?). It was further remodeled
in 1922–1923 by Herbert J. Krapp (1886–1973), an architect who did quite a lot of work
in theaterland and about whose name all the obvious jokes have already been made. The
exterior of the Winter Garden is not particularly special, but the interior, mainly by
Krapp, is; should the theater be open you could make your way warily across Broadway
at the lights to get a flavor from the foyer of the splendors of the auditorium.

The Broadway, the Virginia, and the Neil Simon

Turn to your left and walk up Broadway, away from Times Square. Cross 51st and
52nd, and turn left on 53rd. A short distance along you find the Broadway Theatre.
This was originally a movie house, but in 1930 was converted to become a legitimate
theater. It was renovated a few years ago when the hit show *Miss Saigon* came here;
other productions in its illustrious career have included *Candide* and *Evita,* another
Lloyd Webber juggernaut.

Continue along 53rd until you reach Eighth, then go down to 52nd and turn left
into it. On your left you find the Virginia Theatre. The long and creditable history of
this theater began when it was opened as the Guild Theater (it was the home of the
Theater Guild) in 1925 by President Calvin Coolidge (1872–1933) switching on the
floodlights. The Theater Guild was a collective venture founded in 1914 by various
amateur members of the theatrical community to present top-quality plays rather than
purely commercial ventures. Among its triumphs were the premieres of *Mourning
Becomes Electra* and *Ah, Wilderness!* by Eugene O'Neill (1888–1953). In 1943 the venture foundered. Between 1950 and 1981 the theater was owned and run by the
American National Theater and Academy and was called the ANTA Theater; among its

achievements was the US premiere of *A Man for All Seasons* by Robert Bolt (1924–1995). When it passed into commercial hands in 1981 the new owner renamed it the Virginia in honor of his wife. The architects were Crane & Franzheim; the facade they gave the theater was in conscious imitation of 15th-century Tuscan villas.

A little further along, on your right, is the Neil Simon Theatre. This was opened in 1927 as the Alvin Theater and was designed to be a showcase for the musical comedies produced by Alex Aarons and Vinton Freedley—"Alvin" for "Al/ex" plus "Vin/ton." The architect was the prolific H.J. Krapp. It debuted with the premiere of *Funny Face* by George (1898–1937) and Ira (1896–1983) Gershwin; two more hits by the Gershwins staged here were *Anything Goes* and *Porgy and Bess*. During the 1980s the theater was renamed in honor of the playwright Neil Simon (b. 1927).

Times Square Church

Keep walking until you reach Broadway. On the corner you find the curiously unchurchlike Times Square Church. Its secular appearance is no accident, for when the building was opened in 1929—architect Thomas White Lamb (1871–1942)—it was as the Hollywood Theater, one of the great Broadway movie houses of that era; all the rest have since been demolished. Just five years later it became a stage, the Mark Hellinger Theater, named for the producer Mark Hellinger (1903–1947), and in 1991 it became a church. The rather drab Modernist exterior is in stark contrast to the neo-Baroque interior, which has elaborate chandeliers, gilt galore, and big mirrors in all directions.

The Gershwin and the Circle in the Square

Cross 51st and turn left. About halfway down the block you come to the six-story Gershwin Theatre. Built in Art Nouveau style by the set designer Ralph Alswang on the site of the old Capitol movie plaza, this was opened in 1970 as the Uris Theatre, so named for the property developers Percy (1899–1971) and Harold (1905–1982) Uris. Among the many eminent musicals to run here has been *Sweeney Todd* by Stephen Sondheim (b. 1930); one that perhaps it's good to have missed was the 1981 production of *The Pirates of Penzance* starring Linda Ronstadt (b. 1946) and, fresh from *Grease*, Rex Smith (b. 1956). The Gershwin is one of Broadway's largest theaters and also claims to be the only one to have a permanent exhibition (a Theatrical Hall of Fame display of names painted on bas-relief inside a rotunda above the lobby), although the distinction between this and the situation at the Minskoff (see page 83) is a somewhat hairsplitting one. Unfortunately for the general magnificence, access to the lobby is shared with the entrance to an underground garage. Another unusual feature of the Gershwin is that it has, in place of the customary asbestos safety curtain, a water curtain.

Go under the building, through a little plaza, to reach 50th Street and the Circle in the Square Theatre, which is Broadway's only theater in the round and the only one not run for profit. Its productions have an excellent reputation and its ticket prices are a fraction of those demanded elsewhere on Broadway. It was opened in 1970 to house the theatrical company of the same name founded in Greenwich Village in 1951 by the directors Theodore Mann and José Quintero, and is best known for staging revivals of classic plays. Its Greenwich Village days were marked by classics like *Summer and Smoke* by Tennessee Williams (1911–1983) and *The Iceman Cometh* by Eugene O'Neill.

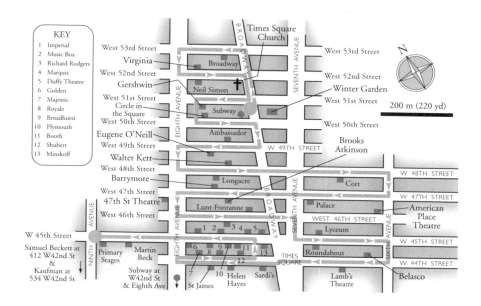

The Ambassador, the Eugene O'Neill, the Walter Kerr, the Longacre, the Cort, and the Palace

Walk along 50th to get back to Broadway; cross 50th, go down to 49th and turn right. On your right you find the Ambassador Theatre, opened by the Shubert brothers in 1921 with H.J. Krapp as architect; Krapp did the interior in imitation of the style of Robert Adam (1728–1792).

Further down the block, on the other side of the street, is the Eugene O'Neill Theatre. Another building commissioned by the Shuberts from Krapp, this was opened in 1926 as the Forrest Theater, in honor of the actor Edwin Forrest (1806–1872), then at some later stage became the Coronet before finally, in 1959, gaining its current name. Once considered an unlucky house because of its lack of hit shows—an exception was *Tobacco Road*, adapted from the 1932 novel by Erskine Caldwell (1903–1987), which was transferred here from the Theater Masque (now the John Golden Theatre; see page 85) in 1934 and proceeded to set what was then a Broadway record of 3,182 performances—it enjoyed a change of fortune for the better after Neil Simon bought it in the 1960s and began to present his own plays there. The interior was restored in 1994.

Continue on 49th until you reach Eighth; once again, pop down a block and turn into the next street, which is West 48th. On the left is the Walter Kerr Theatre. Originally built by the Shuberts in 1921 as the Ritz, with H.J. Krapp as architect, it spent years as a movie house before being restored in 1983 and returning to legit theater use; it was renamed in 1990, after further refurbishment, in honor of the drama critic Walter Kerr (1913–1996). The Italian Renaissance style of the interior is attractive, the real visual highlights being supplied by the murals framing the stage and the Art Deco chandeliers, sconces ,and other fixtures by Karen Rosen for the 1983 restoration.

More or less opposite the Walter Kerr, on the right, is the Longacre, designed in French Neoclassical style in 1913 as a musical-comedy house by the architect Henry B. Herts (1871–1933) for the producer Henry Frazee (1881–1929), who owned the Boston Red Sox and was known as "'the man who traded Babe Ruth." All through the 1940s the Longacre was used as a radio and television studio, but it returned to legit status in 1953.

Continue along 48th, crossing Broadway and Seventh. On the next block, on the right, is the Cort Theatre. This was built for the producer John Cort by architect Thomas White Lamb as a showcase for Cort's own productions. Lamb designed the building in imitation of the Petit Trianon at Versailles; inside there is a mural portraying a dance in the Versailles gardens, and the rest of the interior proffers a wealth of detail in the French Neoclassical style. In 1969 the theater, regarded as one of Broadway's most beautiful, became the home of television's *The Merv Griffin Show*, but in 1974 it returned to legit status.

At the end of the block, go right on Sixth until you reach 47th. Cross 47th and then turn right. Almost at the end of the block is the Palace, a landmark to a part of theatrical history that is dead. Built in 1913 by Martin Beck (1867–1940), this was possibly the world's most famous vaudeville venue until, in the 1930s, the talkies killed off vaudeville. It was bought and renovated in 1965 by James and Joseph Nederlander—whose Nederlander Organization owns several other Broadway theaters including, obviously, the Nederlander itself (see below)—and reopened the following year as a legit theater with Neil Simon's *Sweet Charity*.

Times Square

Carry on along 47th, recrossing Seventh and Broadway. As you do so you're crossing the top of Times Square; you'll be crossing the square again more than once before the walk is over, but here is as good a place as any to pause to have a quick look around it. When the ropelike intersection of Seventh and Broadway is full of traffic and pedestrians it's difficult to think of it as an open area. Defining Times Square precisely is not easy. Roughly speaking, it runs from where you are now down to 42nd Street, and is as wide as the intersection is wide.

Twenty years ago this used to be perhaps the sleaziest town center in the world. There were porn movies, porn bookstores, liquor stores, drunk panhandlers, muggers, pickpockets, and hookers; even by day you tended to be wary, and by night it was wise to be in a group. All that has now changed. The pickpockets are still there, of course, but the rest have been largely expelled, thanks to a concerted clean-up effort during the 1990s, so that now even at night you see families with small children exploring the area, gazing at the ever-changing neon advertising or going in and out of the Virgin Megastore, the Warner Bros Store, or the Disney Store. It's the Disney Store, one of the first pioneers of the "new" Times Square, that has been the particular target of those who dislike the changes—the "Disnification of Times Square," as they put it. In their view the old Times Square might have been sleazy, dangerous and miserable, but it had *vitality*. Yes, but it was also a center of human suffering and degradation. Perhaps the new illuminated frontages of the Chase Manhattan Bank and the ABC studios, and the kids jamming the sidewalk between 45th and 44th outside the Viacom Building screaming up at the windows of the MTV studios and any transient rock stars who might be there, are a small price to pay for clearing out what was, to be blunt, a cesspit.

If you are lucky there'll be street performers on view—the western corner of 45th is their main venue. If you're unlucky they'll be not musicians but a group of Bible-thumpers who have haunted the square for years, promulgating a hate-filled racism that is a vile as anything the Ku Klux Klan spouts. Many evenings a group of young men bring their huge tame snakes to the square and wander about, the reptiles draped around them like shawls.

The History of Time Square

The "square" got its present name just after the start of the 20th century when the *New York Times*, under the proprietorship of Adolph Ochs (1858–1935), moved into a new building here; before that this had been Long Acre Square. Much later the lower part of the intersection was named Duffy Square to honor Francis P. Duffy (1871–1932), a priest and, briefly, editor of the *New York Review* who became renowned mainly for his military service during World War I. There's a statue of Duffy in the central island near the ticket center TKTS. Ochs also introduced, as a publicity stunt, the spectacular annual New Year gathering in Times Square, during which upwards of a quarter of a million people pack into the "square" and the surrounding streets to see a huge, brightly illuminated ball lowered to the ground at the stroke of midnight. About the same time as the *Times* moved in, so did (one assumes coincidentally) the bordellos. These were initially discreet establishments, but as the decades wore on they became anything but. The mass immigration of theaters, vaudeville houses, and cabarets began a little later, in the years leading up to World War I.

The Brooks Atkinson, the Ethel Barrymore, and the Biltmore

Carry on along 47th. On the left is the Brooks Atkinson Theatre, another H.J. Krapp design—this time in Modern Spanish style. It opened in 1926 as the Mansfield Theatre, named for the actor Richard Mansfield (1854–1907), but was renamed in 1960 to honor the journalist and drama critic Brooks Atkinson (1884–1984).

On the other side of the street is the Ethel Barrymore Theatre, built by the Shuberts, yet again with H.J. Krapp, in 1928 and named in an attempt to lure the actress Ethel Barrymore (1879–1959) into playing there. She had become a Broadway star in 1925 through the production at the nearby Martin Beck of *Captain Jinks of the Horse Marines* by Clyde Fitch (1865–1909). The attempt was successful: the theater opened with her starring in *The Kingdom of God*. This theater has one of Krapp's most interesting facades: it takes the form of a Roman window with terra-cotta gridwork. Possibly the most notable premiere to be staged here was that in 1947 of *A Streetcar Named Desire* by Tennessee Williams (1911–1983).

Further along is the dilapidated Biltmore Theatre, long since dark, alas. H.J. Krapp was the architect once more for a theater commissioned by Irwin Chanin (1891–1988), one half of the Chanin brothers, who almost rivaled the Shubert brothers in their Broadway activities. It's slightly surprising that the Biltmore closed, because in the latter part of the 20th century it had shows like *Hair* and *Barefoot in the Park*. The theater is perennially scheduled for demolition, so catch it while you can.

The Richard Rodgers, the Lunt–Fontanne, and the Marriott Marquis

When you reach Eighth, turn left to reach 46th. On the corner of 46th is the Gaiety Bar—also known popularly as McHale's or Peggy's for its erstwhile husband-and-wife owners, whose son Jimmy now runs the place. It is much frequented by stage folk.

On the right-hand side of this block of 46th is the Richard Rodgers Theatre, Irwin Chanin's first, opened in 1924 as the 46th Street Theatre and renamed in 1990 for the composer Richard Rodgers (1902–1979), of Rodgers & Hammerstein fame. Not surprisingly, given its name, it has been the venue for some of the classic stage musicals, including *Finian's Rainbow* and *Guys and Dolls*.

Further along on the left is the Lunt–Fontanne Theatre, opened in 1910 as the Globe; it is the only known theater designed by Carrère & Hastings. Among its early highlights were *The Ziegfeld Follies of 1921*, starring W.C. Fields and Fanny Brice (1891–1951), and *The Cat and the Fiddle*, by Jerome Kern (1885–1945) and Otto Harbach (1873–1963), the last musical to play here before it was turned, in 1932, into a movie house. It remained thus until 1957, when Roger Stevens and Robert W. Dowling restored it to the legitimate theater, refurbishing it in an elegant 18th-century style. It reopened in 1958 with the new name in honor of the husband-and-wife acting team of Alfred Lunt (1892–1977) and Lynn Fontanne (1887–1983), one of whose best occasions was in the inaugural play of the restored theater, *The Visit* by Friedrich Dürrenmatt (1921–1990). Probably its big claim to fame in more recent years is that it was here *The Sound of Music* ran for many years from 1959.

Opposite is the Marriott Marquis, Broadway's newest legitimate theater (1986). The theater is on the third floor of the huge Marriott Hotel, popularly described as The Pen because its large, chilly, dark, internalized forecourt smacks of a penal colony. Conceived in the 1970s, this monolith was not built until 1985. The brainchild of architect John Portman, it has a revolving rooftop restaurant and an internal atrium that goes from the 8th floor all the way to the top, with tubular glass elevators; it is claimed to be the world's tallest atrium. The building has all the external visual appeal of a nightclub bouncer. The current theater replaced three earlier ones, including the original Helen Hayes Theatre, and got off to a flying start with the musical *Me and My Girl*, an imported (from London) revival of a 1937 hit; it ran for 1,420 performances.

The Lyceum and the Roundabout

When you reach Times Square again, cross over both Broadway and Seventh (it's as if you were crossing just one extra-wide street) and turn right to walk in front of the Virgin Megastore. Turn left into 45th.

Along the block, on your left, is the Lyceum Theatre, which has one of the most ornate theater facades in the city. This Beaux-Arts gem was built in 1903 by Daniel Frohman (1860–1915), with architects Herts & Tallant. Frohman had an apartment for himself above the theater which now houses the Shubert Archive. He was married to the actress Margaret Illington (1881–1934), who was well known for her occasional habit of lapsing into overacting. Still visible in the theater is the peephole through which he could watch his wife's performances and, when she started

Plate 10: Founded in 1862 in Baltimore by a Westphalian immigrant, the F.A.O. Schwarz chain now has 17 branches, with its flagship store here in Manhattan (see page 62).

Plate 11: Erected in 1983, the famous Trump Tower has been much derided by the architectural fraternity, but the average visitor can just enjoy its flamboyance (see page 63).

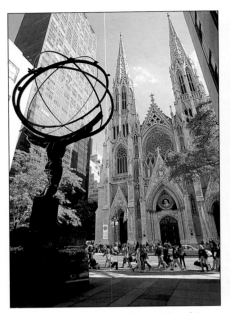

Plate 12: *The neo-Gothic splendor of St. Patrick's Cathedral and the equally splendid but contrasting Art Deco statue of Atlas outside the Rockefeller Center (see page 67).*

Plate 13: *Many of the sights of Manhattan seem intimately familiar because they have so frequently appeared in the movies, arguably none more so than the Rockefeller Center (see page 72).*

Plate 14: *The Rockefeller Center's Radio City Music Hall, home of the famous Rockettes—still going after all these years—has an auditorium that seats 6,000 (see page 69).*

Plate 15: *If 42nd Street represents the heart and soul of the city, Broadway is the city's spine (see page 86).*

Plate 16: *Night falls over Times Square and a neon battle commences as advertisers vie for public attention (see page 78).*

Plate 17: *UN Headquarters: The General Assembly Building is the lower structure in the foreground, whereas the Secretariat Building is the great black stone slab looming behind (see page 98).*

Plate 18: One of the wonders of modern Manhattan is the recently restored interior of Grand Central Terminal (see page 95).

Plate 19: Arguably the most beautiful Art Deco skyscraper of them all—the Chrysler Building on 42nd Street (see page 97).

hamming, signal to her by waving a handkerchief. Today the Lyceum is home to the National Actors' Theatre, run by Tony Randall.

Across the street to your right is the old Roundabout Theatre, deemed an off-Broadway venue because it is run on a non-profit-making basis. Nevertheless, it has staged some of the most successful Broadway-type shows, including a recent revival of *Cabaret*; its new home, opened in Spring 2000, is nearby, in the old Selwyn Theatre on 43rd Street, opposite the *New York Times* Building.

The Belasco Theatre and Lambs

When you reach Sixth Avenue (Avenue of the Americas), turn right and right again to go along 44th. To your right on this block is the Belasco Theatre, built in 1907 by the playwright, actor, and producer David Belasco (1854–1931), with architect George Keister, as Belasco's Stuyvesant Theatre; the name change came only a few years later. Belasco had the idea that this could be a more intimate venue than the other theaters of the day, and to this end he opted for a cosy Colonial Revival style of decor and design. Unfortunately, this theater has been dark most of the time since the 1970s, but if you do get a chance to attend a performance here be sure to enjoy some of the special details of the interior: There's Tiffany glass in profusion, and of note are the 18 murals done by the Ashcan artist Everett Shinn (1873–1953).

Further along on the left is the Lambs Theatre, considered like the Roundabout and perhaps more justifiably to be an off-Broadway venue. Affiliated to the Manhattan Church of the Nazarene next door, it stages evangelistic productions. The name comes from the Lambs Club, founded as a dining club in 1874 by various theatrical personages, among them the architect Stanford White (1853–1906), of McKim, Mead & White. He it was who in 1903 designed the new Lambs Club Building here at 128 West 44th Street, working in Colonial Revival style with lambs' and rams' heads as ornaments. In 1915 the premises were doubled in size by architect George A. Freeman, who virtually repeated White's design stone-for-stone at number 130. White is still glorified by the club, whose premises are now at West 51st and Fifth, although in fact he had a fairly checkered career which culminated in his being murdered by a (seemingly misled) jealous husband.

Sardi's

Carry on along the left-hand side of 44th. Cross Broadway and Seventh; as you do so, glance to your right at the statue of the singer, composer, actor, playwright, and producer George M. Cohan (1878–1942). The imposing black structure on the northwest corner of 44th is the Minskoff Building, named for its commercial proprietors; it's often called the Viacom Building because a major tenant is the media company Viacom. The building, designed by Kahn & Jacobs, also houses the Minskoff Theatre, whose entrance is on 45th; you'll come to it later.

Go straight ahead on 44th. On your left is Ollie's Noodle Shop, one of a small chain of Chinese restaurants that offer adequate food at reasonable prices. The building whose ground floor Ollie's partly occupies is the Paramount Building, done in 1927 by the architects C.W. & George L. Rapp, whose specialty was more along the lines of movie palaces; you can't see it from here, but atop the building is a vast (and famous) clock with a globe above it.

Further along the block are big blue doors that mark the back of the *New York Times'* current premises; the newspaper moved here during the 1920s, very close to the Times Square premises it had occupied but abandoned around the turn of the century. Beyond these is the famous Sardi's, a restaurant intimately associated with the Broadway theater scene. It was originally opened (in 1921) at number 246, where the St. James Theatre now is, but moved to its current position in 1926. The connection with the world of theater really began in 1946, when Vincent Sardi Jr. (b. 1915) took over the restaurant from his parents; there was a short interregnum in 1985–1990, but otherwise he has been running it ever since. It has been customary since the late 1940s for the cast of a newly opened show to come here after the first performance, receive a standing ovation from the rest of the diners, then wait nervously over their late dinner for the rushes of the next day's papers containing, for good or ill, the reviews. Another tradition at Sardi's is that there is a discounted menu for Actors' Equity members, a touch of grace from which many now extremely famous actors benefited in their early days—and because of which, of course, the restaurant now profits. The walls at Sardi's are covered in large, garish caricatures of theatrical personalities, and this is not entirely to everyone's taste.

The Helen Hayes and the St. James

Past Sardi's you come to the Helen Hayes Theatre, the second to be named after the popular actress Helen Hayes (1900–1993); the first was subsumed into the Marriott Marquis. The current house was renamed for her in 1983; originally it was the Little Theatre, commissioned by the producer Winthrop Ames (1871–1937) in Colonial Revival style from architects Ingalls & Hoffman and opened in 1912, and with the interior remodeled in the same style during 1917–1920 by the ubiquitous H.J. Krapp. Ames deliberately gave it a small auditorium in a gesture against what he regarded as the prevailing crass commercialism of the Broadway theater scene; its debut production was *The Pigeon* by John Galsworthy (1867–1933). More seating was added during Krapp's remodeling, and in the 1920s the house was leased to John Golden (1874–1955), Oliver Morosco (1876–1945), and others. In 1942 it was renamed the New York Times Hall and moved out of legit theater. In 1959 it became the ABC Television Studio, but in 1963 it returned to the legit-theater fold with a production called *Tambourines of Glory*, a gospel musical.

Further along, still on the left-hand side, is the St. James Theatre. Built in 1927 as the Erlanger Theatre by the producer Abraham Lincoln Erlanger (1860–1930), with architects Warren & Wetmore, this was renamed in 1932. The Beaux-Arts facade is worth admiring—something you can better do from the other side of the street. So walk along to the lights at Eighth and cross over, then return. Among notable shows to premiere here have been *Oklahoma!* and *The King and I*.

The Majestic and the Broadhurst

On this new side of the street the first theater you reach, roughly across from the St. James, is the Majestic, commissioned by Irwin Chanin, in what he referred to as Modern Spanish style, from H.J. Krapp. It opened in 1927. Here in 1928 the boxer

Jack Dempsey (1895–1983) made his Broadway debut in a sort of early version of *Rocky* called *The Big Fight*. This show flopped, as did an earlier production that year, *The Patriot*, despite having John Gielgud (b. 1904) in the cast—it lasted just twelve performances. The following year an adaptation of *Die Fledermaus* called *A Wonderful Night* did rather better, 125 performances; its star was a young UK acrobat, juggler, and actor called Archibald Leach (1904–1986), who not long afterwards went to Hollywood and changed his name to Cary Grant.

Next theater along the block is the Broadhurst, built by the Shuberts but opened under the aegis of dramatist and theater manager George H. Broadhurst (1866–1952). Yet again H.J. Krapp was the architect, and this time he produced a Neoclassical facade done in terracotta and brick. It has staged a long list of interesting items, but perhaps most fascinating of all has been Broadhurst's own play, *Tarzan of the Apes*, which he produced here in 1921 with the UK actor Ronald Adair (1900–1954) as the title character and real lions and monkeys in supporting roles. Alas, it closed within three weeks.

The Shubert

A little further along, Shubert Alley goes off on your left, linking 44th to 45th. Named for the three Shubert brothers, this is, presumably because of some aerodynamic peculiarity of the surrounding buildings, one of the windiest places in all New York: If there's a cool breeze elsewhere, you can expect a biting wind here. Although used as a public thoroughfare, it is in fact private property; to maintain its private status it is for one day in the year closed to the public.

The three Shuberts, born in Syracuse, NY, were theatrical producers, owners and managers of theatrical talent. In 1900 they acquired the lease to the Herald Square Theatre on Broadway and 35th, and from there they went on to found an empire that today encompasses over 60 theaters across the USA, including many in New York. The brothers produced over 500 plays and operettas and managed performers including Sarah Bernhardt, Al Jolson, and Eddie Cantor (1892–1964). The Shubert Organization's offices are located above the Shubert Theatre, which is the first thing you see on your left as you turn into the passage. This theater is named for Sam S. Shubert, the middle of the three brothers, and was done in a Venetian style by architect Henry B. Herts. It opened in 1913. The list of its productions reads like a history of the 20th-century popular stage: they include *A Chorus Line*, *A Little Night Music*, *Miracle on 34th Street*, *The Apartment*, *Paint Your Wagon*, *Can-Can*, *Babes in Arms*, and *The Philadelphia Story*.

The Booth and the Minskoff

At the other end of Shubert Alley, still on the left, is the Booth Theatre, named in honor of the almost legendary US actor Edwin Booth (1833–1893) and opened in 1913. Again the architect was Herts, this time commissioned by Lee Shubert in conjunction with Winthrop Ames. He built this and the Shubert deliberately as a pair, but here worked in early Italian Renaissance style. The Booth was designed to offer an intimate setting, primarily for straight drama and comedy. In 1979 the interior design, among the best-loved on Broadway, was refurbished by Melanie Kahane, who reasonably enough enlivened the old somber browns but also, more controversially, expelled various popular elements of the interior such as the delicate French chandeliers.

At the end of Shubert Alley, turn briefly right on 45th Street to take a look at the Minskoff Theatre. This is housed within the Minskoff Building, also known as One Astor Plaza in memory of the structure that was demolished to make way for it, the Astor Hotel, built in 1904 by architects Clinton & Russell for William Waldorf Astor (1848–1919). The new building was completed in 1970 by Kahn & Jacobs, by which time the local laws permitted buildings to be bigger than otherwise if they incorporated a legitimate stage—hence the inclusion of a new theater here, the Minskoff. The building itself is pretty hideous (it's even worse on the 44th Street side) but the theater inside it, which is reached through a covered walkway on your left as you face the building, is pleasant enough. The Minskoff also houses a branch of the Theatre Collection of the Museum of the City of New York, and its permanent exhibition space offers ongoing exhibitions.

The Duffy, the Plymouth, and the Music Box
On the far side of the street from the Minskoff is the other entrance to the Marriott Marquis, and just around the corner into Times Square is the Duffy Theatre, an off-Broadway venue housed in a renovated strip joint. From the outside it looks as if the Duffy hasn't changed its vocation, an impression hardly affected by your climb up a steep flight of stairs to reach the small lobby. However, the theater has been offering a significant hit play, Warren Manzi's *Perfect Crime*, since 1987—a *Mousetrap*-like mystery that's enjoying a *Mousetrap*-like run.

Retrace your steps along 45th, passing the Booth once more on your left. In the middle of the block, also on your left, is the Plymouth Theatre, built for the Shuberts by H.J. Krapp at the same time as the Broadhurst (see above) and opened in 1917. It's one of Broadway's most successful theaters, with *Dial "M" for Murder, The Caine Mutiny, The Odd Couple,* and *Equus* among its hits. On the other side of the street from it is the Music Box, built by the producer Sam H. Harris (1872–1941) and the composer Irving Berlin (1888–1989) specifically to showcase Berlin's work. Done by C. Howard Crane (1885–1952) and E. George Kiehler (1890–1961) in English Neoclassical style for the exterior (complete with a four-columned porch) and in Adam style for the interior, the theater opened in 1921 with the first of Berlin's many *Music Box Revues.*

The Royale and the Imperial
Next on the left-hand side of the street is the Royale Theatre. Built by Irwin Chanin at the same time as his Majestic (see page 82) and Theatre Masque (see below) and with architect H.J. Krapp, this was, like those two and various others of Krapp's theaters, done in Modern Spanish style. It opened in 1927, and in 1934 was for a short while called the Golden; sometime thereafter CBS took it over for use as a radio studio. In 1940 it returned to legitimate status, where it has remained ever since. Here it was that Julie Andrews (b. 1935) made her US debut in 1954 in Sandy Wilson's *The Boy Friend*; among many other plays to premiere here have been Tennessee Williams' *Night of the Iguana* (1961).

Across the street is the Imperial Theatre, again an H.J. Krapp building, this time for the Shuberts and specifically designed to stage musical comedy. It opened on Christmas night 1923 and has premiered a string of hit musicals ever since. Just along from the Imperial is Barrymores, another eatery (although its big attraction is as a bar) that's intimately associated with the Broadway theatrical scene. Every time a new Broadway show opens, Barrymores delivers a consignment of apples to the cast.

The John Golden and Martin Beck

There is one more theater before you get to the end of this theater-packed block: the John Golden, on the left. This was built by Krapp for Chanin as one of the trio with the Majestic and the Royale, and opened in 1927 as the Theatre Masque, the name changing in 1937 to honor the producer, playwright, and theater critic John Golden. It was intended to highlight plays of "artistic or intimate type," and this it has largely done throughout its history. If one had to pick any one item it would have to be the debut in 1956 of *Waiting for Godot* by Samuel Beckett (1906–1989).

Cross over Eighth Avenue and only a short further distance down 45th you reach the Martin Beck Theatre, opened in 1924 and named for the man who commissioned it, the vaudeville mogul Martin Beck; the architect was G. Albert Lansburgh (1876–?), and he gave the theater a Moorish–Byzantine style. It has since subsisted on a mixture of melodramas, comedies, and musicals, with—as for so depressingly many other Broadway theaters—revivals having been the main staple for the past decade or more.

Primary Stages

Well along the block, almost at Ninth Avenue, is an example of the type of theater that perhaps holds the key to Broadway's future salvation. Primary Stages, whose unassuming entranceway you could easily walk past without noticing, is a theater founded in 1983 with the aim of presenting the best new US plays by US playwrights (although it began to break the US-only rule in 1999). By the turn of the century it had presented over 70 such plays, by both new and established writers. In many ways it can—like others of the off-off-Broadway and off-Broadway venues around here—be regarded as a testing ground for future Broadway productions; of the five that have gone so far from here to Broadway, perhaps the best known has been Colin Martin's *Virgins & Other Myths*. The productions here also offer a breath of fresh air to those jaded by the revival-ridden, safe-investment-conscious atmosphere of modern Broadway.

The walk really ends here. For the subway, go back along this block of 45th to Eighth and turn right to the corner of 44th. However, you're very close to two quite exceptional and two very good restaurants, all four fairly modestly priced, so the option of finishing your walk with a meal is a very attractive one.

You've just passed one of the two exceptional restaurants: Moto, in the middle of this block. This is, although it doesn't have the largest of menus, perhaps the best Japanese restaurant in Manhattan. (Moto is closed on Monday. Kodama, on the other side of the street and closer to Eighth, also has good Japanese food.) Chez Suzette, on Ninth Avenue (cross Ninth and go uptown just past the corner of 46th), offers French country fare; the menu is not particularly diverse, but the food is consistently first-rate. The other gem of a restaurant is Lakruwana, on the southeastern corner of Ninth and 44th (stay this side of Ninth and walk down a block). Here the menu is Sri Lankan and the food out of this world. Especially recommended is coming here on a Sunday night, when you can help yourself from the generous buffet.

42nd Street—The Soul of Manhattan

Summary: If you were given just a single day of your lifetime to explore New York and wanted to capture the essence of the city during that time, this would be the exploration we'd advise you to undertake. A walk along 42nd Street will show you much of the best and a little of the worst of Manhattan but, more than that, it will give you an insight into the very soul of New York. You'll encounter people from every walk of life, from panhandlers to scuttling self-important executives with cell phones clamped to their ears, from ethnic New Yorkers who can trace their ancestry in the city back two generations or twenty to rich tourists from anywhere in the world or just from somewhere out of town. There are temples to God and to Mammon. Strip joints nudge against cultural centers, and works of great art jostle flamboyant kitsch. As Dr Johnson might have said, if you're tired of 42nd Street, you're tired of life.

Start:	Port Authority 42nd Street Bus Terminal.
Transportation:	Subway lines A, C, and E to 42nd Street. Also by underground walkway to here from Times Square, served by the 1, 2, 3, 9, N, R, and 7 lines as well as the S (shuttle) from Grand Central. You are advised not to use this walkway at night. Buses from out of town, particularly New Jersey.
Finish:	United Nations Headquarters.
Transportation:	Walk back to the subway at Grand Central or take a taxi.
Length:	About 4.5 km (2¾ miles).
Time:	Allow a full day if you want to visit all the attractions or drop into some of the many stores. Otherwise allow about 2 hours, or 1 hour on a Saturday or Sunday.
Refreshments:	There are numerous eateries and watering holes along the way, ranging from Burger King upwards. There's a whole nest of interesting places to eat and drink in the bowels of Grand Central Station, but you pay dearly for the locale.
Which day:	Any day, although the New York Public Library is closed on Sunday and the office buildings are generally closed all weekend.
Highlights:	Port Authority 42nd Street Bus Terminal
	Church of Saints Cyril and Methodius and Saint Raphael
	Theater Row
	Chez Josephine
	The old McGraw–Hill Building
	The Condé Nast Building
	Bryant Park

New York Public Library
Grand Central Terminal
The Grand Hyatt Hotel
The Chrysler Building
The old Mobil Building
The old *Daily News* Building
UN Headquarters

The subway station has a plethora of exits, some at a distance from the main Port Authority building, so the best plan to orient yourself is simply to find your way out onto the street by whatever exit is nearest, then, if you're not sure where you are, go to the nearest set of traffic lights and read the signs there. The route starts just outside Port Authority on the Eighth Avenue (main) side.

On the sidewalk, turn around and take a quick look (a quick look is quite enough) at the building itself. The original bus terminal was built in 1947–1950 by the Port Authority of New York and New Jersey, a public authority formed in 1921 and originally called the Port of New York Authority. The first bus terminal here became inadequate for the amount of traffic it was supposed to carry, and by the mid-1970s it was a rundown and rather intimidating dump where it seemed easier to buy drugs than bus tickets. From 1979, however, it was expanded and renovated, and nowadays it's about as pleasant as any bus terminal could hope to be—which is admittedly not very. The outside is an eyesore but, inside, the two concourses have plenty of stores, slightly overpriced cafés, and various toilets, plus more branches of the ubiquitous Hudson News than can readily be counted; there's a nice little bookstore, Book Corner, upstairs in the downtown section of the building.

West 41st Street

Depending on exactly where you are in front of the terminal, go either left or right to reach West 41st Street, and turn into it to walk westward between the two sections of the building. This block of 41st Street is pretty drab and dreary despite the efforts of a whale mural.

At the Ninth Avenue traffic lights you see signs directing you to the left toward the Lincoln Tunnel, a primary road exit to New Jersey. The first of its three passages under the Hudson River was opened in 1937, the others following in 1945 and 1957. Between them they carry some 40 million vehicles a year, making this the busiest tunnel in the world. During rush hours, progress through the Lincoln Tunnel can be very slow indeed; as you chug forward in fits and starts between the white-tiled walls, it's rather as if you were trying to drive through the longest public toilet in the world.

Cross Ninth and continue along 41st, keeping to the right-hand side. Cross Dyer Avenue. On your left, a little along, you see the rather dreary blue-green Hunter College, part of the City University of New York. Its windows seem last to have been washed in celebration of the Lincoln Tunnel's opening. Also on your left, on the southeastern corner of Tenth Avenue and 41st Street, is Covenant House, a rehabilitation center for teenagers.

Cross Tenth and keep going a few moments longer on 41st—here called Cardinal Stepinac Place after Aloysius Stepinac (1898–1960), the Yugoslav prelate imprisoned by Tito for alleged Nazi collaboration—to stand opposite the Croatian Roman Catholic Church of Saints Cyril and Methodius and Saint Raphael, run by the Franciscans. This is kept securely locked except during services, but if you're here very early in the morning you might be able to slip inside. Otherwise you'll have to be satisfied with looking at the highly decorated facade, which is topped by two spires highlighted in green. You'll notice there seems something a little odd about the decoration of the facade, but may at first be unable to put your finger on exactly what it is. It's the gray plastic owl perched jauntily there to frighten off the pigeons.

All around here there's a curious mixture of slum and elegant. The area is on its way up, so in a few years' time should look much more prepossessing than it does now, with derelict buildings scattered among the condos. If you were to carry on along 41st Street you'd soon find yourself in altogether a much rougher part of town, so go back to Tenth Avenue, cross over, and turn left (uptown), then turn right into 42nd Street, keeping to the right.

Theater Row

This part of 42nd is called Theater Row because of the proliferation along it of off-off-Broadway theaters, studio workshops, etc. It's often enough used as a testing ground for new plays, most of which never graduate to grander venues but a few of which emphatically do.

The first establishment related to the performing arts that you come across, just a few paces in from the traffic lights, is the National Video Center, whose studios comprise an important location for the making of music and other commercial videos. Immediately after the National Video Center you come to the John Houseman Studio Theaters; further along, behind the Pulse Ensemble Theatre, is a courtyard containing the Fairbanks Theater. A doorway just beyond the Pulse shows an impressive display of names of studio workshops associated with the surrounding theaters, of which there are many more in the area than can be listed here.

You've returned to Dyer Avenue, whose stark functionality is likely to inspire the obvious "by name and by nature" joke. Crossing hastily over it you discover the Theatre (*sic*) Row Theatre and further workshops, then Playwrights Horizons, which has both the Studio Theater and the Anne G. Wilder Theatre.

Chez Josephine: Josephine

Just after Playwrights Horizons is a delightfully unexpected surprise. Nestling behind an unassuming frontage is Chez Josephine, one of the city's most evocative restaurants. Unfortunately it's open only during the evenings, so for the moment you'll just have to press your nose against the glass to see the interior; the people inside are very friendly, however, so if they're here it's worth asking to be allowed in to look around.

Chez Josephine is owned and run by the extraordinary Jean-Claude Baker, the adoptive son of Josephine Baker (1906–1975), the black dancer and entertainer who, born in St. Louis, ran away from home at the age of 13 to tour with a vaudeville show. Her name is more associated, however, with France than with her native land.

She went to Paris in 1925 with a show called *La Revue Nègre* and, when the show failed, was stranded there along with other cast members. She got a job performing at the Folies Bergère, and was an instant hit as the totem of *le jazz hot*. For five decades she was a French heroine—she became a citizen in 1937, and during World War II assisted the French Resistance—and her reputation was international. US audiences were deprived of her performances, however: She declined to appear in her home-land where, at the time, blacks were still second-class citizens. As late as 1951, while in the USA to promote her beloved cause of world brotherhood, she was refused service at the Stork Club. During the 1950s she was active in the Civil Rights movement, forcing several nightclubs and theaters to adopt integrative policies; she was one of the speakers addressing the crowds during the famous 1963 March on Washington. As part of her personal crusade against racial disharmony she established a "world vil-lage" on her estate in France, where she raised a dozen children of differing races and religions whom she had adopted. When this enterprise collapsed financially in the early 1970s she made a comeback in order to raise money. For a long time during the 1950s she was regarded as a Communist and Nazi collaborator due to wholly bogus charges laid against her by the influential columnist Walter Winchell (1897–1972). No wonder she preferred France.

Chez Josephine: Jean-Claude

Jean-Claude is almost as kaleidoscopic a character as his adoptive mother. Born Jean-Claude Tronville near Dijon, he fled from an unhappy childhood to Paris. At the age of 14 he was working as a bellboy at the Hôtel Scribe when he was asked by the visiting celebrity to perform some errand, and the relationship between them blossomed. On her advice he moved to Liverpool to learn English, and there he got to know the Beatles. Later he went to Berlin and opened the enormously successful Pimm's Club—and was reunited with his adoptive mother. When she required a manager and MC for her comeback tour, he threw over his business and went with her. His arrival with her in Los Angeles signified the start of his love affair with the USA. He opened Chez Josephine in 1986 (on the site of a massage parlor called The French Palace whose win-dow promised "$10 Complete Satisfaction") and named it in tribute to his adoptive mother's first club in Paris, also called Chez Josephine. He tackled the decor first (mementoes of Josephine abound), only later hiring a chef to produce food that matched the environs. Everyone thought he was crazy to open a chic bistro in what was then virtually a no-go area of Manhattan, but today he has no shortage of patrons, who flock here to sample the ambience and particularly Jean-Claude himself as much as the food. In 1994 he published a book about his adoptive mother, *Josephine: The Hungry Heart*, which was shortlisted for a Pulitzer Prize. His anecdotes are legendary—and bril-liantly told. We would repeat some here, but have no space.

Today, just like Jean-Claude's adoptive mother decades ago, Chez Josephine has earned itself an international reputation.

Literary Connections

Keep along the sidewalk in the same direction as earlier. Pass the Harold Clurman Theatre, and then one of the more famous of these off-off-Broadway houses, the

Samuel Beckett Theatre. Cross Ninth and pass successively the 42nd Street Theater (which is concerned less with plays and more with dance and other musical arts) and the biggish, gray-fronted post office. The rather squat red-brick church directly across from the post office is the Holy Cross Church (Roman Catholic).

Just past the post office is the old McGraw–Hill Building, at 330 West 42nd. This has a very handsome Art Deco exterior and an equally handsome lobby in the same style. The publisher McGraw–Hill has long since departed to its somewhat less exciting headquarters opposite the Rockefeller Center, but there are still literary connections here: the Authors Guild and the Authors League of America have offices on the 29th floor. Designed by Raymond M. Hood (1881–1934) at the behest of the publisher James H. McGraw (1860–1948), the building opened in 1931; although it took in tenants, its main function was to house all the activities of the already major publishing and printing firm. The facade is done in horizontal bands of blue and green terracotta. At the time the building was a bit of a sore thumb: There were no other skyscrapers near it and so the public regarded it vehemently as an eyesore rather than as the astonishingly attractive building it is. (You might want to cross over 42nd to get a better look at the frontage.) In 1979, some years after McGraw–Hill's departure, the building was taken over by Deco Tower Associates in conjunction with Aaron Gural and George Kaufman, and they refurbished it, restoring it to its full elegance. It seems an odd juxtaposition that such an attractive building should be dedicated to the service of Mammon while the one across the street from it, the Holy Cross Church, dedicated to the service of God, should be so ugly.

Theaters

Go past the dreary northern face of the Port Authority Bus Terminal. At the Eighth Avenue crossing, look up and half to your right to see the top of the Empire State Building peeping through among the more recent skyscrapers. Directly ahead is another early landmark, the Chrysler Building.

Having crossed Eighth, keep going along the right-hand side of 42nd. Over on your left you see the adorably kitsch frontage of the newly opened (1999) Loews Theatres movie complex. As you walk on, you're approaching the downtown tip of Times Square, and most of the theaters you're passing are legitimate Broadway establishments. At least, they are now. Many of them went through a decades-long period as soft-porn houses before rediscovering their legitimate roots during the cleaning up of the whole Times Square region. You'll probably have noticed already, particularly while waiting to cross Eighth Avenue, various establishments that might look like small theaters (they have names like International Show Center) which are in fact surviving strip joints. Most of the "book stores" and "video centers" around here are equally seedy.

In complete contrast to these survivors of 42nd Street's "inglory days" is the New Amsterdam Theatre with, next door to it, the world-famous Times Square Disney Store. Indeed, some street maps give "Disney Square" as an alternative name for Times Square. (Most New Yorkers never do, except disparagingly and usually with a prefatory obscenity.) The New Amsterdam is a Disney establishment, where one can see the musicals based on the hit animated movies. Both theater and store were among the very first developments as Times Square cleaned up its act during the 1980s and 1990s.

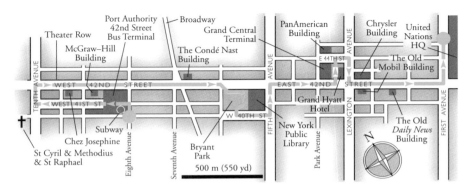

As you stand here on the corner of 42nd and Seventh you can see, diagonally opposite, the Warner Brothers Studio Store and, directly ahead, one of the several entrances to Times Square 42nd Street subway station, with a police station just beyond.

Cross Seventh and then Broadway; at this latter crossing, if you look left, you can get a sort of picture-postcard view of Times Square. Cross 42nd to your left and then continue along that side of the street.

A bit beyond Broadway you find the Condé Nast Building. Go inside for a look at the lobby, which is a symphony rendered in various shades of gray marble and which is, in a clinical way, rather splendid. As you walk further along 42nd, look up on your right to see a rather pretty skyscraper of the old school, Bush Towers.

Bryant Park

On reaching Sixth Avenue (locally named Avenue of the Americas), cross over the avenue and then turn right to cross 42nd Street. You're now at the northwest corner of Bryant Park.

This delightful little park is surrounded by plane trees. Although the traffic thunders all around, for some reason (either psychological or because of a trick of the acoustics) the noise seems further away than it actually is. The ground was originally laid out as a potter's field in 1823, then in 1847 was opened as a public park, named Reservoir Square for the Croton Reservoir, which lay right beside it. In 1853 the Crystal Palace, a splendid affair of glass and cast-iron that old photographs show bore some resemblance to its London namesake, was opened here to house New York's first World Fair. The Crystal Palace was advertised as fireproof; much as the unsinkable *Titanic* sank, the fireproof Crystal Palace burned down in 1858, just five years after its opening.

The area was renamed Bryant Park in 1884 after the then recently deceased William Cullen Bryant (1794–1878); there is a bust of him in the park. He was editor of the *Evening Post* from 1829 almost until he died and was also a poet of note; the renaming, however, primarily honored his efforts as a civic leader within New York, advancing causes such as public health and park creation. In 1899 the Croton Reservoir was drained to make room for the New York Public Library. In 1933 there was a competition for the redesign of the park. This was won by Lusby Simpson and, working largely to Simpson's designs, Gilmore Clarke remade the Sixth Avenue entrances, erected the stone balustrades, and created the side promenades and sunken lawn. The park went through a bad period in the 1960s and 1970s, becoming the territory of drug dealers and the homeless, but in the 1980s the Bryant Park Restoration Corporation took over. Since then the restaurant kiosk has been added and further landscaping has been done; beneath your feet and out of sight, extra storage room for the adjacent New York Public Library has been created. During the summer months there are free open-air recitals here, and of particular note between June and September is the Bryant Park Film Festival, which features Monday-night open-air screenings, again free, of classic movies.

Statues and Busts

Going clockwise around Bryant Park from the northwest corner you find various statues and busts. Toward the northeastern corner stands William Earl Dodge (1805–1883), notable in his time as a member of the House of Representatives. He is almost completely forgotten today aside from this statue and in the name of part of the northwestern Bronx, Dodgewood, where he owned land. The statue was erected in 1885. If you look across 42nd from here you get a nice view of the Grace Building, one of the more elegant of New York's recent skyscrapers. Opened in 1974, it has a curious concave curve to its frontage; the vertiginous effect this gives as you stand beneath it is delightful.

At the park's northeastern corner is one of Manhattan's few public toilets. On the Fifth Avenue side of the park, set back on a raised terrace that backs onto the Public Library, is a very grand statue of William Cullen Bryant. Further around is a bronze bust of Gertrude Stein (1874–1946); the original was done by Jo Davidson in 1923 and the cast in 1991. Almost more interesting than the artwork itself (of which Stein might have commented "a bust is a bust is a bust") is the superb gray-marble plinth. The *faux rustique* wood-and-glass structure on your left as you face the Stein bust is the Bryant Park Grill. The next piece of statuary you arrive at, on the downtown side of the park, is a bust of the German playwright Goethe (1749–1832). It was erected in 1932 by the Goethe Society of America.

The New York Public Library: The Beginning

Exit Bryant Park on its downtown side to emerge on 40th Street. Turn left toward Fifth Avenue. On your right as you walk toward Fifth, at number 50, is the very pretty Bush Towers; and at number 40 is the equally attractive American Radiation Co. Building, designed in 1924 by Raymond M. Hood, who also designed the old McGraw–Hill Building. Indeed, this whole stretch of 40th has some fine buildings; number 32 is another attractive piece.

As you go along the wall of Public Library you see a plaque to Wendell L. Willkie (1892–1944), who ran for the presidency against Roosevelt in 1940 and was soundly defeated; he earned the plaque for his good works within New York City.

Halfway up the block between 40th and 42nd, directly facing the continuation of 41st, whose course is interrupted by Bryant Park, you come to the New York Public Library. Indeed, with its broad stairs and imposing lions you can hardly miss it. This magnificent building opened its doors on May 24, 1911, but its story goes back quite a lot further than that, to 1886. In that year the one-time Governor of New York, Samuel

L. Tilden (1814–1886), died, leaving most of his fortune for the purpose of "establish[ing] and maintain[ing] a free library and reading room in the city of New York." The endowment was $2.4 million, no mean sum, but it seems that for a short while the city regarded it as one of those gifts which embarrass by not being quite enough for the purpose. Enter city attorney John Bigelow (1817–1911), one of the Tilden trustees. He pointed out that New York's two existing (although not fully public) libraries of note—the Astor Library, opened in 1849 thanks to a bequest from John Jacob Astor (1763–1848), and the Lenox Library, mainly the personal rare books, manuscripts, and Americana collection left by James Lenox (1800–1880)—were in financial difficulties. Why not, Bigelow proposed, unite the three under a single roof as a single entity, to be called the New York Public Library, Astor, Lenox, and Tilden Foundations?

The New York Public Library: Collections

In 1895 Bigelow's scheme, including full plans for the design of the building that would accommodate all this material, was agreed, and the present site (then occupied by the Croton Reservoir) was selected. The architects Carrère & Hastings were chosen after a competition. Draining the reservoir took two years, and it was 1902 before the cornerstone of the new edifice was laid. This was, in fact, after the library itself had been established (1901) and had joined forces with the New York Free Circulating Library, with John Shaw Billings (1838–1913) as the first director. The development of the branch libraries proceeded more rapidly than the building of the central headquarters, because, again in 1901, Andrew Carnegie (1835–1919) gave $5.2 million expressly for the setting up of a series of branch libraries throughout the city, providing the city supplied the sites and funded day-to-day operations; a few months later the New York Public Library and the city, in partnership, announced the establishment of 39 branches in Manhattan, the Bronx, and Staten Island. Today there are 85 branches containing 10.4 million books and other reference and leisure items, as well as four special libraries for research: the New York Public Library for the Performing Arts, the Humanities and Social Sciences Library, the Schomburg Center for Research in Black Culture—based on the collection of Arthur Schomburg (1874–1938), who sold it to the library in 1926 and himself was employed as its curator from 1932 until his death—and most recently (1995) the Science, Industry, and Business Library. Other specialist collections include the Rare Books and Manuscripts Division, the Carl H. Pforzheimer Collection of Shelley and his Circle, the George Arents Collection on the History of Tobacco and Tobacco-Related Literature, the Miriam and Ira D. Wallach Division of Art, Prints, and Photographs, the Berg Collection of English and American Literature, and the Spencer Collection of Illustrated Books, Illuminated Manuscripts, and Fine Bindings.

Back in the early 1900s, work continued slowly on the main building. The roof was finally completed in 1906, but the amazingly ambitious interior—including some 120 km (75 miles) of shelving to cope with an initial collection of over one million books—took a further five years. That all this effort was worth it was proved on the library's very first day of opening: estimates vary, but it seems that at least 40,000 New Yorkers visited, some for the purposes of serious research. Today an astonishing 180,000 or so readers make use of the library each week, and about 2.73 million people hold library cards.

The New York Public Library: Splendor

Climb the stairs between the two famous marble lions to enter the library; local wisdom has it that these stone creatures roar only when a virgin passes by.

Inside you discover splendor. The high-roofed main lobby is done in gray-white marble, and elegant stairs lead off to right and left. Before you venture up these, however, go to the back of the lobby to find yourself in a long, magnificently ceilinged gallery that stretches the full width of the building. Just on the left of the Library Shop is the D. Samuel and Jeane H. Gottesman Exhibition Hall, which houses changing exhibitions. Further along on your left is the DeWitt Wallace Periodicals Room, while along on your right are the Map Division and the elevators.

Go back toward the main door and take the stairs to your left. On the next floor there's another fine gallery, directly above the one on the ground floor. On your left are the Oriental Division and the Slavic and Baltic Division, and on your right is the Center for Scholars and Writers, among other things. Overlooking the main lobby is a permanent exhibition on the history of the library.

The New York Public Library: Refurbishment

Continue up the stairs to the next floor, where you'll find the General Research Division, whose two main rooms are the Bill Blass Public Catalog Room and the Rose Main Reading Room. Also of interest is the Edna Barnes Salomon Room, opened in 1986, which houses various, generally literature-oriented exhibitions and has some fine pieces of portraiture around the walls. As you reach the top of the stairs, take a look at the McGraw Rotunda, as this little central area is called; the ceilings in particular are spectacular, and the walls aren't much less so.

The Blass Room, reopened in January 1994 after extensive refurbishment, has a ceiling that puts even the ones you've already seen to shame. Next is the Rose Room, with, renovated during the 1990s, yet another stupendous ceiling—it's easy enough to get a crick in your neck while ambling around the Public Library. Divided into two halls, this large room is reminiscent of the old British Museum Reading Room, albeit outfitted with dozens of computer terminals. Whereas the BM Reading Room boasted that Karl Marx (1818–1883) did much of his work there, the New York Library could, but doesn't, boast that Leon Trotsky (1879–1940) did much of his work here. The south hall gives you access to the Miriam and Ira D. Wallach Art and Architecture Reading Room, the north hall to the Brooke Russell Astor Reading Room for Rare Books and manuscripts.

Go back through the Blass Room and into the central hall. Turn left along the corridor. Here, as elsewhere, the walls carry transient exhibitions of art or photographs; at the far end of the corridor, off to the left, is the Charles Addams Gallery, which has a rotating display of items from the Charles Addams Collection, the rest of which is housed in the library's Manuscripts and Archives Division.

Come back out of the Addams Gallery, turn right, and almost immediately on your right you'll see the elevators. Take a ride down to the ground floor, which is the level lower than the one at which you entered the building. Coming out of the elevator, follow around to reach the 42nd Street exit from the library. Any bags you're carrying will probably be checked by the security staff as you leave.

Grand Central

Emerging on 42nd Street, turn right to the traffic lights at Fifth Avenue, and cross. Keep going and cross Madison Avenue, then cross 42nd to continue along its left-hand sidewalk. Cross over the small Vanderbilt Avenue and walk on until you're in Pershing Square—you might not realize you were in a square at all were there not a sign to tell you so. Go under the iron viaduct that bears Park Avenue overhead and, on your left about 50 paces along, you find the main entrance to Grand Central Station, one of the great wonders of Manhattan.

Grand Central Station, often called GC and more properly known as Grand Central Terminal, opened in 1871 as Grand Central Depot. It was built for reasons that go back quite a few years earlier than that. The Common Council of New York (and indeed the people themselves) were concerned about the noise and dirt created by steam locomotives, and accordingly in 1854 banned them from approaching the city any further south than 42nd Street, which at the time was little more than a concept, the city proper not yet having extended this far north. Horses were used to pull the carriages southward from 42nd Street to the city. In 1869 Cornelius Vanderbilt (1794–1877), who by now had acquired all the railroads that came into New York, determined to build a central depot where the changeover could be made. With John Butler Snook (1815–1901) as architect, this facility opened a couple of years later, but almost immediately Vanderbilt began tinkering with it. His biggest change was to lower the lines progressively into the ground, so that finally there was a major tunnel that started at 96th Street and grew broader as it progressed southward, until by 57th Street it held 41 tracks on an upper level and 26 on a lower level.

This was the situation in 1889, by which time the city had extended northward. Now the Council demanded that the railroads should be electrified (again because of the dirt and noise of steam locomotives). The engineer responsible for much of the submerging of the tracks and their electrification, William John Wilgus (1865–1949), suggested to the New York Central & Hudson River Railroad that Grand Central should be rebuilt and that money could be raised by selling the ground above as building space. The architectural company Reed & Stern won a competition to solve the logistics of this, which they did by devising the ramp you can see that takes Park Avenue up and around the main body of the station. The splendid new facade of the building was designed by Whitney Warren (1864–1943). It is a triumphal triple archway in Beaux-Arts style, and is intended to be seen at its best on the uptown approach from Park Avenue. It's worth crossing 42nd Street and walking a block or so downtown, then turning back to have a look at this magnificent piece of architecture. The clock that forms the focus of the facade is 4 m (13 ft) across, and the figures surrounding it are of Minerva, Mercury, and Hercules. All around rear far vaster modern structures—including the Pan Am Building (1963)—but it is Grand Central itself that holds the attention.

Return to the main front and enter, then go down a short ramp to a second set of doors. Immediately inside these is Vanderbilt Hall, which contains frequently changing art exhibitions, craft fairs, etc. Pass through into the main concourse and look at the famous ceiling. This is marked out in the form of the constellations (with lights for the stars against a pale blue backdrop) but unfortunately, due to a mix-up at the drawing-board stage, the whole thing is mirror-reversed. When GC was being refurbished during the 1990s there was some debate about the possibility of turning the constellations the right way around, but luckily common sense prevailed over scientific rigor. The rest of the main concourse is equally magnificent, reminiscent of the era in which all the best old black-and-white movies were made.

Space does not permit a detailed guide to GC's interior, and also everything is in a constant state of flux. So why not just wander around, keeping in mind that the whole interior of GC is a maze of corridors and concourses containing all sorts of stores and that it's easy to get lost, particularly since the countless Hudson News outlets all look the same. Before you go exploring, then, take a good look at the circular information kiosk in the center of the main concourse—there's nothing else like it in the station, so when you find it again you'll know where you are.

Downstairs from the main concourse is the Dining Concourse, where there are 25 restaurants and eateries, none cheap, plus toilets. The famous Oyster Bar is just off the Dining Concourse up a short, wide ramp and through a vaulted area. This is generally regarded as one of the very best restaurants—and is almost certainly the best seafood restaurant—in Manhattan. Eating here is likely to put your credit card into catatonic shock but, if you've decided you can afford just one blowout during your stay in the city, then this is very probably the place to have it. The food really is superb and the ambience is not far behind. Not all the other eateries in the concourse are as expensive as the Oyster Bar, although if you've got money to burn you could try a take-out from the Caviarteria. Here, for example, you can pay $100 (at 2000 prices) for a single ounce of Caspian Caviar, although you can save money by buying in bulk: a full can (1. 8kg) sets you back a mere $5,995, or $84.66 per ounce. Oh, plus tax, of course.

The Grand Hyatt Hotel

Return to the main concourse and take the escalators up to the 45th Street exit. Before you actually reach 45th you pass through the pseudo-gilt extravaganza of the MetLife Building. Turn right on the 45th Street sidewalk and, on your way to the traffic lights at Lexington Avenue (often called just Lex; Madison Avenue for some reason is not similarly treated), pass the Post Office terminal associated with GC.

As you turn right on Lex you see, ahead of you and on the other side of the avenue, two interesting-looking skyscrapers. The nearer of these, a green and brown construction, is called Commerce Place; the more distant and more distinguished is the Chrysler Building. A block down Lex is 43rd Street, here called Archbishop F.J. Sheen Place; Fulton Sheen (1895–1979) was a controversial Roman Catholic prelate who served as Bishop of New York 1951–1966. Cross this street to reach 42nd Street and detour to the right to peek into the Grand Hyatt Hotel.

There is something splendidly kitsch about the design of the Grand Hyatt's huge foyer. Originally the Commodore Hotel (opened 1919) was here, but from 1976 Donald Trump (b. 1946) and the Hyatt Corporation rebuilt the hotel, retaining the Commodore's structural shell. It reopened in 1980 as the Grand Hyatt.

Come back out onto 42nd, turn left and go across Lex to reach the Chrysler Building; there are entrances on Lex and on 42nd, so pick whichever you like. Before you go into the lobby, look at all the Art Deco detailing on the outside. Also, if you're lucky with the angle, as you look up you can see, far above, one or more of the eagle-head gargoyles sticking out from the building's side. Inside, the lobby is pretty splendid. The floor is done in stunning orangy-brown marble and the walls in the same, but rather darker; the pictorial ceiling is in need of some renovation, but obviously has been and will be quite dramatic, and even in its current somewhat faded condition is fascinating. But the real highlights here are the wood-veneered Art Deco elevator doors.

The Chrysler Building is 319 m (1,046 ft) tall; its highly distinctive Art Deco top is almost as much a symbol of the Manhattan skyline as that of the Empire State. It was started as a speculative development sometime around 1920 by the developer William H. Reynolds (also responsible for Coney Island's amusement park, Dreamland), with William Van Alen (1882–1954) as the architect. In 1927 the project was sold lock, stock, and barrel to Walter P. Chrysler (1875–1940), the carmaker, and for his benefit new details were added to the plans that give the building its almost bizarre appearance, including the Chrysler radiator caps and the unique stepped vertex. At the time of its opening, in 1930, the Chrysler was the tallest building in the world, although it was overtaken just a few months later by the Empire State. Unfortunately, the lobby is the only part of it you're allowed to see and there's no observation gallery like the one at the Empire State.

Exit by the 42nd Street doors. Opposite you, at 150 East 42nd, is the old Mobil Building, opened in 1955. If you have the time, make a small detour via the nearest traffic lights to have a look into the vast, very bright lobby, otherwise just gaze at the outside from afar. The building's base is in blue glass; above it is a colossal structure clad in "self-cleaning" stainless steel. General opinion is that the building is ghastly, but to the unprejudiced eye a better description might be "differently splendid."

"Seven Little Pennies in the Newsboy's Hat"

Keep on walking down the left-hand side of East 42nd. Cross Third and then cross 42nd to walk on the right-hand side. Soon you see one of the Helmsley hotels, members of a chain that became notorious in the late 1980s when Leona Helmsley was convicted of a $1.2 million tax evasion and sentenced to four years' imprisonment. She gave the world a quotation: "Only the little people pay taxes."

Just beyond the Helmsley, at 220 East 42nd, is the old *Daily News* Building. Opened in 1930, this was another of Raymond M. Hood's designs, here done with John Mead Howells (1868–1959), and was the first Manhattan skyscraper not to have an ornamented top. The lobby was a major tourist attraction when first opened and, although it has been altered since, there is much of the original still to be seen. The floor's done in marble and anodized aluminum and has a general Art Deco air. The reflective faceted black-glass quasi-cupola above the lobby is of interest, but what immediately catches the attention is, in the middle of the floor and partly set into it, a huge globe of the Earth. On your left as you stand inside the doors is an excellent clock offering the time at 16 major cities around the world.

The *Daily News* was launched by Joseph Medill Patterson (1879–1946) as the *Illustrated Daily News* in 1919 (the "Illustrated" was soon dropped) in imitation of the London *Daily Mirror*: it was intended to be a tabloid that, despite the downmarket format, communicated news to the masses. Although the newspaper was widely regarded for its innovative presentation, its contents soon degenerated into the kind of sensationalist garbage one expects of the modern tabloid: plenty of sex and violence, and the melodramatization of the mundane. A highlight was the front-page photograph published in 1928 of the electrocution in Sing Sing of Ruth Snyder (1895–1928) who, with her lover, had succeeded on the eighth attempt in killing her unwanted husband; the photographer had smuggled a camera into the execution chamber by strapping it to his leg. The newspaper moved to the premises you're looking at in 1930, and stayed here until the mid-1990s.

Come out and turn right. Walk along to Second Avenue, this stretch of which has been recently renamed Yitzhak Rabin Way. Cross Second, then 42nd to go along the latter's left-hand side. About halfway along is the very dramatic facade of the Ford Foundation; inside is a big atrium filled with trees and bushes. From here the Ford car company issues grants to all sorts of needy and deserving causes.

UN Headquarters

Pass under the viaduct that carries Tudor City Place and keep on to the corner. From here you can see ahead, on your left, the UN Building. Cross Raoul Wallenberg Walk, as this bit of First Avenue is called in honor of the Swedish diplomat, born 1912 and who, "liberated" in Hungary by the Soviets after World War II, officially died in the Lubianka in Moscow in 1947, although persistent rumors suggest he lived many years longer. During the war he had been based in Nazi-occupied Budapest, and through considerable personal heroism succeeded in smuggling as many as 100,000 Jews out of Hungary.

The UN Headquarters was built in 1947–1953 on a site donated to the organization by John D. Rockefeller Jr. The tall (39-story) slab is the Secretariat Building; the unusually shaped lower-slung construction is the General Assembly Building. Both have their admirers and detractors. The lobby of the latter is a temple to 1950s camp, with curved balconies, marbleized glass panels, a parabolic ramp, and plenty of blue. The Secretariat Building is best seen from the other side of the East River; the wall facing the water is made of green sheet glass with narrow aluminum liners, and acts as a mirror to display constantly changing patterns of reflected light.

The visitors' entrance is on 45th Street, so walk up the avenue, passing the flags of all the nations (or just the flagpoles of all the nations, if the UN isn't in session) on your right. When you reach 44th, glance across the avenue to your left to see the All Faiths Church, created to serve all the faiths represented at the United Nations.

For most of the year guided tours of UN Headquarters depart from the visitors' entrance every 10–15 minutes and last approximately one hour; there's a charge for these. Otherwise, you are allowed into the Plaza to wander around during opening hours (see page 174), and indeed into parts of the building itself. However, there's not a lot to see in these open-access areas except for the General Assembly Building's grandiose lobby. But strolling around the Plaza is very pleasant, and you can go across to the far side of it to look out over the East River toward the western shore of Queens and, further upriver, Franklin D. Roosevelt Island.

This is where the walk ends. There's no sensible public transportation from here to more populous parts of the city and taxis are almost impossible to find, so your best bet is probably to amble back along 42nd to Grand Central.

From Penn Station to the Empire State Building

Summary: Of course, 34th Street—along which this short walk largely takes you—is the place where miracles are supposed to happen. One particular miracle, at least: the deservedly famous movie *Miracle on 34th Street* (1947) turned Edmund Gwenn overnight into a household name and introduced the young Natalie Wood to the world; strange to think that some movie executive somewhere thought a better title for it would be the bland *The Big Heart*. The walk's big attraction, at least in terms of global fame, is the Empire State Building, but there is much else to see, particularly at the walk's beginning.

Start:	Penn Station.
Transportation:	Trains from all over. Subway A, C, and E lines to 34th and Penn Station. (*Note:* There are two 34th and Penn Station subway stations, the other being served by the 1, 2, 3, and 9 lines. The description below assumes you've used the A, C, and E station.)
Finish:	The Empire State Building.
Transportation:	Subway B, D, F, and Q lines from 34th Street and Broadway (Herald Square). Subway 6 line from 33rd Street and Park Avenue South.
Length:	About 1.5 km (1 mile).
Time:	About 30 min (less at weekends) if you didn't visit any of the attractions, but then there'd be little point in doing the walk. Allow about 2 hours plus however long you want to spend in the Empire State Building's observatory.
Refreshments:	There are numerous eateries and watering holes along the way, ranging from Burger King upwards, but the highlight is the Tick Tock on 33rd.
Which day:	Any day.
Highlights:	Penn Station
	General Post Office Building
	Madison Square Garden
	Macy's
	Empire State Building

Penn Station—the busiest station in North America, with about 600,000 passengers going through each day—is something of a warren below ground. As you exit the subway to enter Penn Station proper you find yourself on a level that is two floors underground; here there are stores and little cafés, and at the far end there are the ticket booths and gates for the Long Island Rail Road (LIRR), which, opened in 1836, is the third oldest railroad in the USA. Unless you want briefly to prospect along there, follow the signs saying "Exit/Street/Taxis/Amtrak/NJ Transit/Mad Sq Gdn" up to the main level, directly below street level, where there are destination boards, lines of people wearily waiting to buy all the usual paraphernalia of a railroad station, and incomprehensible loudspeaker announcements. The exit you want is the one that's rather poorly marked for Eighth Avenue and 33rd Street. If you can't see the sign you should be able to spot the right exit anyway: it has two flights of stairs with an escalator in between. There are toilets near the bottom of the stairs.

The original Penn Station—more formally Pennsylvania Station—was created by the Pennsylvania Railroad as competition to Grand Central Terminal, which was the province of the New York Central Railroad. The architects were McKim, Mead & White, also responsible for the magnificent General Post Office Building on the other side of Eighth Avenue. As extant photographs show, it was a stunning piece of work, both inside and outside, and it covered the whole of the area bounded by (to north and south) 31st and 33rd streets and (to east and west) Seventh and Eighth avenues. How wasteful, thought the bean-counters of the Pennsylvania Railroad: We could put an anonymous slab there instead, incorporate offices and the relocated Madison Square Garden, and make a lot more money. Despite a huge and utterly justified uproar, there was no legislation in place to forbid this act of destruction, and in 1968 one of Manhattan's prime wonders was razed. The present structure is truly ghastly and is one of the most loathed in all New York.

The General Post Office Building

The Eighth and 33rd exit from Penn Station brings you out on a corner. Looking half-left you see the splendid frontage of the General Post Office Building, toward which you'll be heading in a moment. Just now, however, glance to your right up Eighth at the New Yorker Hotel. In the same general direction is the Tick Tock Diner (main entrance on 33rd), which serves exceptionally good burgers—perhaps the best you'll find during your stay in New York.

Either directly from Penn Station or via the Tick Tock, make your way to the General Post Office Building, opened in 1913 and built in Imperial Roman style. The entrance is at the top of an impressive set of stone stairs that stretches almost the length of the block; the (revolving) door you're aiming for is at the right-hand end of these. Inside there's a long, graceful hall that runs all the way across the building's front. It seems quite startling to see people performing such a mundane act as lining up to mail a letter in surroundings such as these! Look up at the ceiling—it's lovely, and there's an even lovelier one in the dome of the smaller chamber just on your right.

The General Post Office Building: Plaques and a Bicycle

Inside this chamber there are some fascinating items. The first to strike your eye is, of all things, an ancient, battered, red, double London-style pillar-shaped mailbox! This was presented by Royal Mail to the New York Post Office in 1985 as a token of respect. Further around is a fairly typical US mailbox of a similar vintage, and

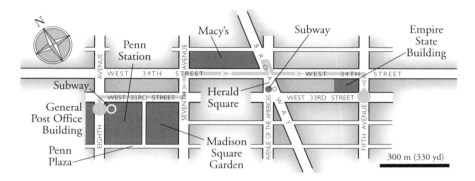

opposite is an old green Irish mailbox, again presented to the New York Post Office in 1985; in the fourth corner a French mailbox and a Greek mailbox stand side by side. In all four corners there are war memorials to employees of the New York Post Office killed in World War II, while behind a 1940s mailman's bicycle there's a World War I roll of honor; the latter memorial has as its background a painting by Louis Lozowick (1892–1973) dated 1935 and called *Manhattan Skyline*. Between the bicycle and the Irish mailbox is a display of various old postal scales, and above this there's a plaque (the Liberty Plaque) erected at the time of the Bicentennial. A further plaque, this one between the bicycle and the Greek mailbox, commemorates the sinking of the US *Maine* in Havana Harbor on February 15, 1898. This was one of the key events in the outburst of the short-lived Spanish–American War of that year: The *Maine*, anchored in the harbor, was blown up in the middle of the night and 266 lives were lost. This apparent sabotage was regarded as an act of war, although no one ever claimed responsibility and it has never been proved that the catastrophe was anything other than the product of carelessness aboard a ship packed with explosives. A couple of months later began what has often been described as the most useless war in human history. Its sole purpose, whatever the arguments of apologist historians, was to increase the sales of the New York newspapers owned by William Randolph Hearst (1863–1951), who had decided the only way to boost the circulation of his *Morning Journal* was to find a populist and bellicose cause. Anti-Spanish sentiment was as good as any, and so he seized on the supposed miseries of the Cuban people under tyrannical Spanish rule. A lot of puzzled Cubans were slaughtered defending the "tyranny," but Hearst got his profits and, as a by-product, Theodore Roosevelt (1858–1919) earned a national reputation that eventually brought him to the White House. The plaque itself is of some interest: it was cast from metal recovered from the wreckage of the *Maine*.

At Christmas time you can volunteer at the General Post Office Building to be, in effect, Santa Claus. Each year thousands of children mail letters to Santa, and these are gathered to this building; what you volunteer to do is pick up a letter and write back to the relevant child, if possible sending the requested present.

In early 2000 there were plans still current to revamp the interior. The idea was to shift all the functions of this bit to the Ninth Avenue (rear) side of the building, where they could have the benefit of modern amenities—the heart sinks— while the rest was to be gutted for conversion to an Amtrak station to go alongside the existing Penn Station. Again there has been a big public outcry.

Madison Square Garden

Exiting the General Post Office Building, go down the stairs and return to the traffic lights where you crossed Eighth, and cross back over. This time continue past Penn Station along 33rd Street. The big cylindrical building you shortly see on your right is Madison Square Garden; your next destination is its entrance on Seventh Avenue. On the left side of the street are lots of closeout stores, where the remnants of discontinued lines are on sale. You can get some tremendous bargains here if you shop carefully. Looking straight ahead along 33rd you can catch a nice view of the Empire State Building, the final destination of this walk.

Reaching Seventh Avenue, turn right and walk down it to reach Madison Square Garden, which, with Penn Plaza, straddles 32nd Street. the entrance, which is actually through the Plaza, is easy enough to spot because it has a big illuminated display advertising forthcoming attractions. Turn right and go up some stairs into the Plaza's huge lobby cum atrium, where there are the entrances to offices and stores. Madison Square Garden proper begins after you've gone up some further stairs: here you find the entrance to the theater. Keep going through a set of doors and you find the lobby associated with the sports arena, which is in fact five floors overhead, supported on a cunning pneumatically cushioned base. The seating capacity of the arena varies depending on the event that's being put on, from about 20,000 for something sober like a concert down to about 19,000 for a major sports contest. Normally there'll be lines of people out in the lobby at the ticket windows. Unfortunately, this is as much as you can see of Madison Square Garden without buying a guided tour (expensive); or you could attend one of the events (also expensive).

The present Madison Square Garden is in fact the fourth in a line that started in 1879, when William Vanderbilt (1849–1920) erected a structure at Madison Square on a site previously operated by P.T. Barnum (1810–1891) and Patrick S. Gilmore (1829–1892). Despite having the boxer John L. Sullivan (1858–1918) as a regular attraction, the enterprise lost money and so Vanderbilt demolished the building in 1889. The Horse Show Association put up a new building there (at the time it was the second tallest in New York and had the city's largest restaurant and the largest auditorium in the USA) to house its own and other sporting displays as well as cultural and political events. This venture likewise lost money. A salvage operation was mounted in 1911 when the building was bought by the F&D Real Estate Company, but this firm went bankrupt just five years later and the New York Life Insurance Company took over the building in lieu of payment. In 1920 they issued a ten-year lease of the building to the promoter Tex Rickard (1871–1929), and he soon started making a profit, largely thanks to the popularity of boxing. When in 1925 New York Life Insurance, despite the lease, took back the building and demolished it to make way for their new headquarters, Rickard kept the name for a new arena he built at 50th and Eighth, and this time the profits poured in from the start—again mostly from boxing. The Garden's basketball tradition began in 1931 thanks to a journalist called Ned Irish (1905–1982), who initially mounted hugely popular charity matches in it. In 1938 the venue was, accordingly, selected to host the National Invitational Tournament, and things have never looked back. The Knicks (more formally, the New York Knickerbockers) made it their home soon after World War II, and their matches are still a colossal attraction. However, in these postwar years the profits began to decline, partly because scandals in basketball turned people off the sport for a while but mainly because boxing was losing popularity and because the arena had never been particularly well designed for spectators—why, in the TV age, go to see a live contest, at not inconsiderable expense, and then find yourself stuck behind a pillar? A new building was required, and in 1968 the current Madison Square Garden opened its doors. In 1977 the enterprise was taken over by Gulf & Western, who rapidly escalated ticket prices but at least poured much of the profits back into improving the facility, which was completely renovated in 1992.

The Largest Department Store in the World

Come back out through Penn Plaza and turn left up Seventh Avenue. On this block there's some interest at number 450; now nameless, this building used to be called the Nelson Tower. It has a very pretty bronzed aluminum frontage and lobby, in Art Deco style.

When you reach the traffic lights at 34th Street, cross both the street and the avenue to reach the southwest corner of Macy's. More correctly R.H. Macy & Co., Inc., Macy's fills the entire block between Seventh Avenue and Broadway/Sixth Avenue and between 34th and 35th streets. It claims to be (and quite probably is) the largest department store in the world. Although there are doors on 34th, the main front door is actually around on Broadway, so keep going past the renowned Macy's windows until you get to the traffic lights, then turn left to find the entrance just a little way along. Usually the window displays on this face of the building are just a little bit more special than the others. The best time of year for seeing the window displays is between Thanksgiving and Christmas, when they feature animated mannequins; the theme for the holiday period of 1999 was the movie *A Miracle on 34th Street*—the 1947 original, a colorized version of which had just been issued, rather than the 1994 remake—and accordingly the windows showed animated scenes while strategically placed television screens displayed the movie itself.

Inside Macy's, although the scene varies through the year, it is generally true that the decorators are blessed more with vigor than with a refined aesthetic sense. In the spring there is a famous flower show in the store, and the smell can be deliciously overpowering. If you go around to the left after you come in through the store's main entrance and then turn right to parallel 34th Street, you find signs pointing you to the visitor center, which is on the balcony. Here you can obtain free printed literature about virtually every tourist attraction in New York except, oddly enough, Macy's itself.

Rowland Mussey Macy

The original Macy from whom the store derives its name was Rowland Hussey Macy (1822–1877), born in Nantucket to a family of seafarers and coastal traders. One of his ancestors was Thomas Macy, founder in 1659 of the first Quaker colony on

Nantucket. When he was 15, young Rowland enlisted for a four-year expedition aboard the whaling ship *Emily Morgan*. On returning he tried various landbound trades, after a few years marrying and moving to Boston. In 1858 he opened a small dry goods store on New York's Sixth Avenue and 14th Street. Some of his business practices were at the time unusual: He quoted prices in his newspaper advertisements, and the prices were fixed—there could be no haggling, as in other stores. Over the years the store thrived, and by the time of his death had become a genuine department store, occupying the ground space of eleven contiguous stores. After his death there were various changes in ownership and venue, but the most important change was probably the relocation in 1902 of the flagship store to its current site on 34th Street, then so far north of the fashionable shopping district that the company's owners, Isidor and Nathan Strauss, had to lay on a steam wagonette from 14th Street to bring hesitant customers northward. The tradition of illuminated Christmas window displays predated that move, as did the Macy's Santa; both were 1870s innovations.

Macy's Thanksgiving Parade

Macy's Thanksgiving Parade, a colossal spectacle that brings hundreds of thousands of watchers to the streets and millions more via television, was inaugurated in 1924. Dozens of floats are devoted to different themes, many of them to current Broadway musicals, whose casts perform numbers on the street outside the store as the climax of their promotional enterprise. College bands from all over the country come to perform in the parade; one of the delights of mid-Manhattan in the couple of days before Thanksgiving is to stroll around keeping an ear open for the sounds of these bands rehearsing, which sometimes they even do in the street outside their hotels. Santa Claus is the supposed focus of the parade (hence the movie), but the strongest and probably most popular image is that of the gigantic helium-filled balloons that are towed aloft. These show popular comic-strip and cartoon icons such as Snoopy and Garfield. There are no Disney characters, though, Disney being jealous of its copyright. The parade wends its way along Central Park West from 77th to 59th streets and then down Broadway to 34th. The evening before it you can go to the streets surrounding the Museum of Natural History (81st and 82nd between Columbus Avenue and Central Park West) to see the balloons being filled. Once a treat enjoyed by only the few, this has become an attraction in its own right, so be prepared for crowds. An odd fact is that, because of the balloons, Macy's is the USA's second-largest helium user after the US armed forces.

You may want to wander around for quite a while in Macy's, possibly even buying something. The prices are middling-high but generally not outrageous. The escalators are quite interesting: some are of the old wood-slat type. The toilets used to be marvelous affairs—spacious and impeccably clean, with attendants ever present. Alas, those days have gone, but past glories are still evident in such items of decor as the marble floors.

The Empire State Building

Once your senses have been thoroughly oversaturated by Macy's, go out by any of the doors and make your way to the traffic lights on 34th and Broadway/Sixth

Avenue (Avenue of the Americas). Cross Sixth and then 34th to continue along the right-hand side of 34th.

As you approach the end of the block you find you're passing the side of the Empire State Building, which for a long time was the tallest man-made structure in the world and still (even though the World Trade Center towers are taller and more massive) dominates the Manhattan skyline when you look at the island from the other side of either river. It is instantly recognizable, even if only from the iconic image of the giant ape perched on it from the 1933 movie *King Kong*. Of course, the one place where it's hard to see the building is directly beside it, which is where you are now. Continue to the end of the block and turn right to discover, perhaps 30 paces down, the main tourist entrance to the building.

Inside, you need merely follow the signs and the throngs in order to sample the various attractions on offer. The most significant of these are, of course, the two observatories (viewing platforms)—one on the 86th floor (320m/1,050ft up) and the other on the 102nd (373m/1,224ft up). After buying your tickets for these, you're escorted up in groups on a couple of elevators (there's a pause midway to change elevators) to the 86th floor, with a further elevator ride to the 102nd, which is closed on foggy days. The view of Manhattan and much of the territory beyond from even the lower observatory is stunning. It's very hard to rid your mind of the sensation that you're not on a building at all but in an airplane. There are barriers to prevent people from being tempted to jump off, but they barely obstruct the visibility. On the clearest days you can see for 130 km (80 miles), which means you're seeing parts of five states: New York, New Jersey, Connecticut, Pennsylvania, and Massachusetts. Over 3.5 million people visit the observatories each year; about 120 million visitors have come since the observatories' inception.

The other attractions are somehow more touristy. The New York Skyline, on the second floor, is a big-screen movie experience that takes you on a vicarious trip around the main New York landmarks; and the Transporter, located next to the ticket office, promises "a total immersion experience that whisks you to a futuristic underground world where danger and excitement lurk around every corner."

The Empire State Building: History

Although the Empire State Building is very much a 20th-century artifact, its story can really be traced back to 1799, when the land was bought from the City of New York by a farmer called John Thompson for the then princely sum of $2,600. He got a living from it for a quarter of a century before selling it to one Charles Lawton for a more than healthy profit: the price was $10,000. But if Thompson felt he'd done well, Lawton did even better: only two years later he sold it to William B. Astor, the second son of John Jacob Astor (1763–1848), for $20,500. In 1859 John Jacob Astor Jr. put up a mansion on the south of the plot; in 1862 John Jacob Jr.'s elder brother, William B. Astor responded by building a mansion of his own on the site now occupied by the Empire State. John Jacob Jr.'s son, William Waldorf Astor (1848–1919), in 1893 razed his father's mansion and put up the Waldorf Hotel; the widow of William B. Astor Jr. in 1897 permitted her late husband's mansion to be likewise razed, with the Astoria Hotel put up on the site, the new "double hotel" becoming known as the

Waldorf–Astoria Hotel. In 1928 the Waldorf–Astoria was sold to the Bethlehem Engineering Corporation, and in the following year it was pulled down to make way for the new building planned by the newly formed (1929) company Empire State, Inc. Excavation began on January 22, 1930 and actual construction began a couple of months later on March 17, 1930.

This immense feat of engineering was completed astonishingly quickly: the building was opened on May 1, 1931 by President Herbert Hoover (1874–1964). In the early days tenants were skeptical about the new skyscraper, however much it was regarded as a modern wonder of the world, and so the landlords kept many of the lights on at night in an attempt to persuade people that it was in fact well occupied. In due course it became a going concern, yet it has never been as hugely profitable as one might expect: It cost about $41 million to build, yet was most recently bought in 1954 for only $51.5 million—no great return on 20 years' investment.

A moment of drama occurred on July 28, 1945 when an Army Air Corps B-25 crashed into the building's 79th floor. Fourteen people died and about $1 million's-worth of damage was done, but the building retained its structural integrity. Do not think about this as you gaze out from one of the observatories!

The walk ends here at the Empire Sate Building.

From the Flatiron to the Strand Bookstore

Summary: There is no mistaking the Flatiron. There isn't another building in New York (and possibly in the world) that's quite like it. For this reason, and because of its dominating position pointing northward at the intersection of Broadway and Fifth Avenue, at the very heart of the city, it is the most immediately recognizable landmark in all Manhattan, the Empire State Building included. This walk starts at the Flatiron and takes in a stretch of old Broadway and the tackily picturesque Union Square Park before leading to the bibliophile's Mecca that is the Strand Bookstore.

Start:	The Flatiron Building.
Transportation:	Subway N and R lines to 23rd Street and Broadway.
Finish:	The Strand Bookstore.
Transportation:	Subway N, R, L, 4, 5, and 6 lines from Union Square, or subway 6 line from Astor Place.
Length:	About 1.5 km (1 mile).
Time:	1–1½ hours, although visits to the Old Town Bar, Pete's Tavern, and the Strand Bookstore may indefinitely extend this.
Refreshments:	Not so many fast-food joints as you'd expect, but there are eateries in the streets between Broadway and Park Avenue South and between Broadway and Fifth Avenue. Best of all is the fascinating Old Town Tavern.
Which day:	Better on weekdays.
Highlights:	The Flatiron Building
	The Theodore Roosevelt Birthplace
	The Old Town Bar
	Pete's Tavern
	The Strand Bookstore

The subway station has several exits, and there's no real telling which of them you'll come up at. In most instances you'll instantly recognize the Flatiron: The acute angle of this medium-height triangular skyscraper is utterly distinctive. There are, however, three places you can come up where the Flatiron seems at first to be unfindable, one on Broadway, one on Fifth Avenue and one on 22nd Street. At any of these you can stand staring around for quite a little while, wondering where in the world the Flatiron could have got to, before you realize the reason you can't see the building is because you're standing an arm's length from it!

Directly across from the Flatiron is Madison Square Park, and you may choose to stroll around in it for a while before starting the walk proper. It's a good place from which to take photographs of the Flatiron or to snack sitting on one of the benches, but otherwise there's not a huge amount of interest here. At one time the playing field of the Knickerbocker Baseball Club was just a block north of here, at Madison and 27th. The 2.75 ha (6.8 acres) of the park, opened as such in 1847, are all that remain of The Parade, a 97-ha (240-acre) piece of land designated in 1807. Soon after, in 1814, it was savagely decreased in size to 36 ha (90 acres), and named for President James Madison (1751–1836).

The Flatiron Building

If you're not already on the Broadway (east) side of this lovely skyscraper, make your way there. If you're starting on its Fifth Avenue side you can, assuming the building's open, cut through the small lobby.

Originally called the Fuller Building (the name didn't catch on), the Flatiron was erected in 1902 by the architect Daniel Hudson Burnham (1846–1912), one of the stalwarts of the Chicago School of architecture during the late 19th and early 20th centuries; but the real hero was designer Ernest R. Graham (1866–1936), also responsible for the Equitable Building (see page 152). The Chicago architects can be said to have invented the skyscraper, and certainly they developed an aesthetic for skyscrapers that regarded them not just as unusually tall buildings but as potentially artistic objects in their own right. The mode in which this one was designed has come to be known as Burnham Baroque; it was designed to be particularly stylish because at the time Madison Square was the stylish place to be. If you took the chance to look at it from Madison Square Park or as you came out of one of the more distant subway exits you'll have been aware of its tremendous presence—a presence the more surprising in that the building is only 20 storys tall, almost a bungalow by comparison with Manhattan's other famous skyscrapers.

If you didn't cut through the lobby to get here, take the chance now to have a quick look at it. Just press your nose against the glass if the building's closed. Quite small and unusually triangular, it has a slightly shabby class to it. This is a working building rather than a tourist attraction, and so there's no public access beyond the lobby—just as well, because the elevators are notoriously slow and cranky. Two publishing houses are located on upper floors, the historic St. Martin's Press and its much more recent sister company Tor. This gives the building a strong science-fictional association, for Tor is primarily an sf and fantasy house and St. Martin's has traditionally had an extremely strong sf list. If you were to be allowed into the Tor offices you might find them familiar: The set designers for the 1994 movie *Wolf* spent a few days at Tor, photographing and measuring, then reconstructed the offices in California, albeit placing them within a different architecture. *Wolf* is possibly the only movie in Hollywood history to show a publishing office that actually looks *right*, complete with untidy stacks of paper and filing cabinets that close only if you handle them *just so*. Indeed, *Wolf* gives a reasonably good picture of book publishing in general—unusual for Hollywood, which tends to glamorize the industry—and is said to be a movie *à clef*.

Go downtown along Broadway. Although this section of old Broadway doesn't have much in the way of highlights, as you look around you you'll keep seeing pretty pieces of architecture.

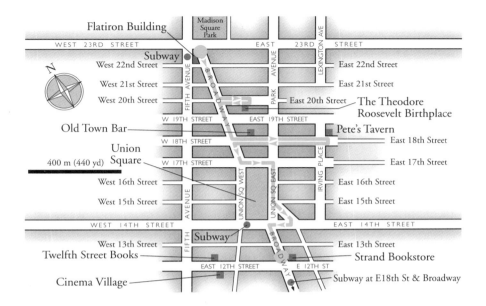

Theodore Roosevelt's Birthplace

Cross Broadway at 20th and then cross 20th itself. Go down 20th a way and you find a rather unobtrusive building with its entrance set back and down from the sidewalk. As the signs tell you, this is the Theodore Roosevelt Birthplace, designated a National Historic Site and now housing a small but interesting museum. There are (very cheap) tours every hour, but you can stroll around the gallery (off on the right as you enter) for no charge. Exhibits give a biography of Theodore Roosevelt (1858–1919), President of the USA for two terms from 1901.

Come out of the museum and turn right. A little further along 20th, still on the right-hand side, is the famous Gramercy Tavern. A sign in the door tells you that "Proper attire is requested" because this isn't just a tavern but a Historical Venue—as reflected in the prices. Having decided your attire is improper, return along 20th to Broadway, cross over and turn left to go down to 19th; the reason for crossing Broadway is to have a look up at the very attractive top of 874 Broadway, opposite. The building is now the home of a company selling mattresses and bedsteads, Kleinsleep, whose displayed slogan, the attemptedly alluring "Have More Fun in Bed," makes an astonishing contrast with the staidness of the store.

The Old Town Tavern

Walk down to 18th Street and turn left. A little along on the left-hand side of 18th is a genuine treat, the Old Town Tavern. From the outside it looks just like any other tavern, although somewhat quainter and more olde worlde than most, but the inside is like a throwback to some earlier era. The place was opened as Viemeister's in 1892, and by the 1920s (when the booze was hidden under the seats in the bar because of Prohibition, although Tammany Hall protection ensured the joint wasn't busted) had become Craig's Restaurant. During this era the trolley drivers would keep a lookout as they passed in case the bartender flashed a light to let them know they should stop to pick up passengers from the bar. In 1933 Claus Lohden reopened the establishment as the Old Town, under which name it continued to thrive in the hands of his descendants. An early landmark date in the tavern's history was 1910, because it was in this year that the magnificent Hinsdale urinals, now subject to a preservation order, were installed in the men's rest-room; it is sobering, as you use them, to think about what it is you're doing to a piece of history.

While supping a beer or chewing on a burger in the Old Town, you may have the familiar Manhattan feeling that you've been here before. Yes, this is yet another place you've seen in the movies. The interior has been used as a set in a number of them; a likely incomplete listing of recent ones is *State of Grace* (1990), *Q & A* (1990), *Bullets Over Broadway* (1994), *The Devil's Own* (1997), and *The Last Days of Disco* (1998).

Pete's Tavern

If you're in the mood for movie-oriented bars, you could venture a couple of blocks further along 18th to find Pete's Tavern, at the northeast corner of 18th and Irving Place. This is claimed to be city's oldest bar (1864), and the ambience would support this claim. Here were filmed parts of *Ragtime* (1981) and, less prestigiously, *Endless Love* (1981). Perhaps more significant in the cultural scheme of things, it is believed that it was in this bar that O. Henry (1862–1910) wrote *The Gift of the Magi* (1906).

Union Square

Coming out of either the Old Town Bar or Pete's Tavern, turn right and retrace your steps to Broadway. Go left down Broadway to 17th Street and the top of Union Square—more correctly, Union Square Park, because in the old days this whole area was called Union Square. The original park was opened in 1831, and soon became a fashionable place to be. Among the centers of culture that sprang up around it was the Academy of Music, erected in 1854 on a site now occupied by the Con Edison Building at the bottom of Irving Place, on 14th Street. Some of the more upmarket stores—including the famous Tiffany's, immortalized for the world by Truman Capote (1924–1984) in *Breakfast at Tiffany's* (1958), famously filmed in 1961—came to the Union Square area in the latter part of the 19th century and the early years of the 20th, but thereafter the region went downhill fast. Although the legacy of those days is the enduring tattiness of the square, in social terms this for some decades was no bad thing; around here gathered the headquarters of various trade unions and radical political groups like the American Civil Liberties Union; and Union Square Park was the site of the first Labor Day Parade, on September 5, 1882. The downside was that the notorious Tammany Hall, heart of one of the most corrupt political institutions the country has ever known, likewise moved in (1929). However, by the 1960s, even though Andy Warhol (1928–1987) moved his "Factory" here from 47th Street in the middle of the decade, the area had become dangerous, the haunt of destitutes and dope peddlers. In the mid-

1980s various groups came together to reclaim the area, and the central park area is now a reasonably attractive place of recreation—grownups can picnic on the benches or stroll around eyeing the statuary while kids can play on the swings and merry-go-rounds.

Go left along the top of Union Square to get a good view of the pretty, quasi-oriental arch that poses as the park's entrance. Directly opposite this is a big branch of Barnes & Noble; you can get a better view of the archway and the park as a whole from the windows on the first floor of this bookstore.

As you continue along the top of the park you'll see, almost facing you but on the downtown side of 17th Street, the banners of the New York Film Academy. From this location and at affiliated sites in California, Paris, Cambridge (UK), and elsewhere there are run film-making workshops for adults and young people.

Cross over Park Avenue South (taking care—it's a fairly complicated two-way nexus, and the WALK/DON'T WALK light changes very quickly indeed) and turn right to cross 17th. There's the usual collection of stores as you stroll down the side of the square—a nails store, a liquor store, and a rather tatty-looking CD/video store that merits a brief foray (limited stock but very good prices). When you reach the corner of 15th you find the building of the Union Square Savings Bank (American Savings Bank), formerly the Institution for the Savings of Merchants' Clerks, incorporated in 1848. This building is now the home of the Daryl Roth Theatre, a fringe-style theater that opened in 1998 and whose entrance is around on 15th.

Keep on down Park Avenue South (locally called Union Square East), passing on your left a branch of the Beth Israel Medical Center and the Phillips Ambulatory Care Center; neither building gives much cause for a break in stride.

The Strand Bookstore

Cross East 14th and cross to your right over what is now called Fourth Avenue although in fact it's just the continuation of Park Avenue South. Walk briefly along 14th Street at the bottom of the square and turn left down Broadway. Already you'll see, a couple of blocks ahead, the big red banner sticking out from the left that marks the site of the Strand Bookstore.

Before you get to the Strand, which is on the corner of 12th Street, you'll see on the corner of 13th the specialist bookstore Forbidden Planet. If you're an aficionado of the famous Forbidden Planet in London, which has an internationally renowned stock of sf/fantasy books, you're in for a big disappointment here. This is a pale imitation of its London counterpart and devotes almost all of its space to comics, games, cards and plastic toys, with a stock of sf/fantasy *books* smaller than you'd expect to find in a middle-sized mainstream bookstore.

Any book-lover who has ever been to New York will go misty-eyed at mention of the Strand, for this is a huge secondhand and (primarily) discount book emporium, reportedly the largest such in the USA. Outside it on the Broadway side you find bookcases containing special bargain items selling for a dollar, and around the corner on 12th Street the prices drop even lower; you can often find excellent books on these shelves, so it's worth taking a good look through them, just in case, before you plunge into the store proper.

Inside, you have to check your bags before passing through a turnstile into a ramshackle paradise. The Strand is not a good place to go if you're in a hurry to find a specific title; there are books everywhere, from floor to ceiling on shelves and stacked precariously high on tables and, although these are theoretically divided up into subject categories, the placement of particular books is haphazard, as is the alphabetical order in those sections that promise A–Z arrangement. The expression "floor to ceiling" is not used as hyperbole, and the ceilings are very high; to get to the upper shelves you have to borrow a stepladder.

Some people take a full day over a visit to the Strand. While you may not wish to go to quite that extreme, you will probably want to spend an hour or two here. If you do decide to make a day of it, there are toilets in the store and the nearest acceptable diner (it's nothing special) is the University Restaurant at 12th Street and University Place (go westward a block on 12th Street from the Strand and it's just around the corner to your right). A little further along, just opposite Cinema Village, the 12th Street Book Store, another excellent although much smaller discount/secondhand bookstore, benefits from significantly better organization than the Strand's.

The walk ends here, the nearest subway stations being at Astor Place (go down Broadway a few blocks to 8th Street) and back at Union Square; if you choose the Union Square option you connect with the start of the next walk, which takes you back to the Flatiron by a different route.

Plate 20: *It is astonishing to believe that the huge task of erecting the Empire State Building was accomplished in a mere 13 months. From its observation platforms you can see five states (see page 104).*

Plate 21: *Claiming to be the biggest department store in the world, Macy's was the focus of the classic Hollywood movie* Miracle on 34th Street *(see page 103).*

Plate 22: The most distinctive of all Manhattan's skyscrapers, the Flatiron is dwarfed but not intimidated by the more recent building around it (see page 108).

Plate 23: After a long period in the doldrums, Union Square is beginning to look up again— not least because of its regular Greenmarket (see page 113).

Plate 24: *Washington Square, with the various buildings of New York University scattered through the streets around it, has long been a center of counterculture (see page 120).*

Plate 25: *Crossing Lower Manhattan almost from one side to the other, Canal Street is a tremendous place for a shopping expedition in search of exotic foods and delightfully kitsch curios (see page 125).*

Plate 26: *New York's Chinatown used to be virtually a separate mini-nation within the city, but over recent decades the barriers have been eroded (see page 130).*

From Union Square to the Flatiron

Summary: This short walk encompasses a street market, some historic apartment buildings and the area around Gramercy Park, and finishes at New York's favorite skyscraper. It can be done as a continuation of the preceding one.

The subway station at Union Square has exits all over the place. The route assumes that you start at the southwest corner of Union Square.

Start:	The southwest corner of Union Square.
Transportation:	Subway N, R, L, 4, 5, and 6 lines to Union Square.
Finish:	The Flatiron Building.
Transportation:	Subway N and R lines from 23rd Street and Broadway. A block east on 23rd, at Park Avenue, is a 6 line station; a block west on 23rd, at Sixth Avenue/Avenue of the Americas, is an F line station.
Length:	About 1.5 km (1 mile).
Time:	1 hour.
Refreshments:	There are lots of eateries around Union Square and in the streets between Broadway and Park Avenue South, plus the renowned Mayrose Diner at the end of the walk.
Which day:	Any day. Wednesdays, Fridays, and Saturdays are best for the Greenmarket.
Highlights:	Union Square Greenmarket
	Green Arc
	Union Square Park
	The Samuel J. Tilden House
	Gramercy Park
	Brotherhood Synagogue
	34 Gramercy Park East

From the southwest corner of Union Square (on 14th Street between Broadway and University Place), cross over to the southwest corner of the park.

Union Square Greenmarket

You find yourself at the bottom of a pedestrianized area, the site of the famous Union Square Greenmarket that runs all the way up the western side of the park and around the top; quite how much of this area the market fills when you're here depends primarily on the day of the week, with Wednesday and Saturday particularly busy, Friday less so and the other days rather quiet, although it's rare to find no stalls here at all.

If you're here on a busy day you'll find stalls offering all sorts of items, from brightly colored batiks that stain all your underwear puce when you put them in the washing machine to expensively authentic handcrafted pottery that looks marvelous but falls to bits before you get it home.

Do not be put off by these, however, because they're just the rind on the cheese. The heart of the market is formed by the numerous stalls offering fresh produce from all over the New York hinterlands and even—notably in the case of the superlative maple syrup you can buy here at rock-bottom prices—as far as Vermont. If you're only on holiday in New York you may have little immediate use for the vegetables, but you should certainly think of picking up some fruit here, and perhaps also some flowers from the semi-permanent flower stalls at the northern end of the park. The produce is cheap by Manhattan standards and the quality is generally first-rate. Moreover, if business isn't too hectic the farmers who're selling their own wares here are often willing to talk with you—you may never before have had any great yearning to discover the details of mulching or manuring, but you'll find yourself fascinated by them as these friendly people talk about their jobs.

Working northward up the side of the park, take your time enjoying the market.

Green Arc

About halfway up the side of the park, on your right, you come across an open-air store called Green Arc. For many New Yorkers this store is the single good reason for coming to Union Square, aside from the Greenmarket. It sells used CDs and videos and some secondhand books—a bald description that gives little idea as to why the place is so special.

The point is that, while some of the stock is fairly general (prices moderate), much of it is determined by the personal tastes of the two brothers who run the establishment. Hence you have, among the music, a great preponderance of jazz and blues, including many specialty items—on CD, tape, or vinyl—that you could pay huge sums for, if you could find them at all, in more conventional collectors' arenas: they're here for people who like *music*, not for collectors of rare objects.

The videos are less interesting, but the array of secondhand books is likewise quirky. There's an extensive and fairly eclectic selection of books on esoteric philosophies, texts on the history of Sikhism or of Anthroposophy rubbing shoulders with the outpourings of some of the less pragmatic—shall we say—of the ufological mystics. There are also plenty of art books at good prices, and the science fiction/fantasy section is worth checking out. In addition to the books there are postcards old and new, either for collecting or for sending.

The store was originally located in Bryant Park, where it prospered for three or four years, but it had to move out of there and come here in 1986 because of construction work. In 2000, when Union Square Park as a whole is being reconstructed, Green Arc may be forced to move yet again or even to go out of business—the brothers were nervous about the future when we spoke to them. Let's hope the planners won't be so foolish and will pay heed to the staunch public support for Green Arc being allowed to remain exactly where it is—as noted, it's one of the main reasons why people come to Union Square.

Union Square Park

Further up from Green Arc you'll find one of several entrances into the middle of the park. Once a potter's field, the park owes its name to the fact that it lay at the intersection (union) of two major roads: Bloomingdale Road, now Broadway, and Bowery Road, now Fourth Avenue. The Commissioners' Plan of 1807, the blueprint for Manhattan's grid system, designated the field Union Place. It was declared a public place in 1831 and acquired by the City of New York in 1833. By 1839 it had been designed as an elegant park, oval in shape and surrounded by an iron picket fence. It was opened to the public, as Union Square, on July 19, 1839. A large central fountain was installed in 1842 to mark the opening of the Croton Aqueduct. In 1872 the park was redesigned by the architects Frederick Law Olmsted (1822–1903) and Calvert Vaux (1824–1895). Among the innovations for which they were responsible were the muster ground and reviewing platform, designed to cater for mass meetings. The park's statuary was added at various times.

During the construction of a new concourse for the subway in 1928–1929 Union Square was demolished, and the reconstructed park of the 1930s incorporated the new colonnaded pavilion and the Charles F. Murphy Memorial Flagstaff, better known as the Independence Flagstaff. You can see this on your right in the center of the park; the flagpole is impressively tall, and there's a suitably inspiring bas relief around the base. Murphy (1858–1924) was a powerful Tammany Hall boss who controlled the city's politics with an iron fist for approximately the first two decades of the 20th century. The memorial was erected in 1926, two years after Murphy's death. The bas relief is by the Italian-born US sculptor Anthony de Francisci (1887–1964), best known for having won a competition in 1921 for the design of the Peace dollar, a silver coin minted in 1921–1928, 1934, and 1935 in commemoration of World War I. It never really caught on, however. The portrait of Liberty on the Peace dollar was, incidentally, based on de Francisci's wife.

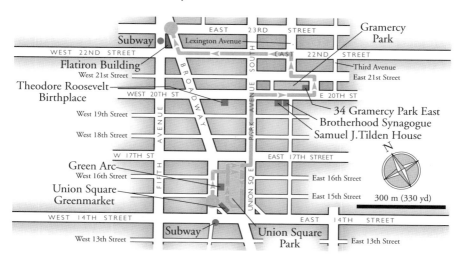

115

Union Square Park: Statuary

You can see the rest of the park's statuary, all predating the Independence Flagstaff, as you stroll clockwise around the area.

Almost immediately you find Abraham Lincoln (1808–1865), standing with his back to the pavilion. This imposing black statue (1869) is by Henry Kirke Brown (1814–1886). There's a wistful expression on the great President's face as he gazes toward the downtown end of the park and sees the Bradlees department store, a branch of the Odd-Job Closeout Centers, and the occasional homeless person sprawled on one of the park's benches. The next statue you come to shows, facing out over Park Avenue South and erected in 1876, the Marquis de Lafayette (1757–1834), and is by Frédéric-Auguste Bartholdi (1834–1904); the marquis was inspired by the American Revolution and gave military assistance to the rebels. At the bottom of the park, depicted dramatically on horseback, is George Washington (1732–1799), in another statue by Brown, this time dated 1856. Finally, on the Broadway side of the park overlooking Green Arc, there is the James Fountain, by Adolf von Donndorf (1835–1916) in 1881.

There's one further and much more recent item of statuary associated with the park, and you can see it on a traffic island as you look toward the southwest. This is a statue, erected in 1986 and by Kantilal B. Patel, of Mahatma Gandhi (1869–1948).

The Tilden House

Once you've finished your perambulation around Union Square Park, emerge at the northeast (17th Street/Park Avenue South) corner. Turn up Park Avenue South and cross it to the right at East 20th Street. A short way along East 20th you come to Gramercy Park on your left.

Facing the park on the right-hand side, at 14/15 Gramercy Park South, is the Samuel J. Tilden House (also called the Samuel J. Tilden Mansion), which houses both the National Arts Club and the Poetry Society of America. This building was originally erected on two adjacent lots by a merchant and a banker in the early 1840s. In the 1860s the two houses were bought by Governor Samuel J. Tilden (1814–1886), who a decade later commissioned Calvert Vaux to give the houses a single facade in Victorian Gothic style with sandstone bay windows. The interior was likewise redesigned, with stained glass by John La Farge (1835–1910). Tilden's library gained a now-famous dome, by the stained-glass designer Donald MacDonald. The building was acquired by the National Arts Club, which had hitherto been housed in a brownstone on West 34th Street, in 1906. The club's first public meeting was held in this house in October 1910.

Artists' Studio

Not visible from where you stand on 20th Street is the 13-story building behind the Tilden House and facing onto 19th. This was erected by the Arts Club soon after it had purchased the Tilden House and was equipped with studios for member artists, musicians, and writers. Those studios are still in use today. Another institution that had its genesis in the early 20th century and continues to this day is the permanent collection. The kernel was created when, around 1910, the artist and sculptor members of the club were invited each to contribute a piece of their work valued at

$1,000 or more, in return for which they would receive a Life Membership. Since virtually all the best artists in the USA at the time were club members, the collection got off to a flying start!

The Poetry Society of America was founded in 1910 as a non-profit organization supporting poetry and poets, and with the aim of promoting wider recognition for poetry. One of the means whereby it has done so has been, it boasts, the creation of the Pulitzer Poetry Prize. Ongoing programs have titles like Poetry in Motion, Poetry Today, and Poetry in Public Places.

Gramercy Park

The Tilden House is unfortunately open only to members of the two societies, so you can't go in and look around, and this principle of exclusivity is continued by Gramercy Park itself, as you'll discover when you cross the road. The park has been private, the property of the owners of the local buildings, since its inception in 1831. The only occasion on which nonresidents have been allowed to make use of it was in 1863 during the Draft Riots, when soldiers trying to restore the peace were permitted to encamp here.

The name Gramercy is a corrupted version of the Dutch *Krom Moerasje*, meaning "crooked little swamp." The story really starts when Samuel B. Ruggles (1800–1881) bought what was then Gramercy Farm shortly before 1831. He laid out streets around the drained swamp and divided the area into 66 lots, which he put up for sale. Ruggles's private urban development was a great success, and for decades this was a locality populated almost entirely by the rich. The list of New York's luminaries, particularly cultural ones, who have lived here is extensive, from writers like Eugene O'Neill (1888–1953) to politicians like Theodore Roosevelt (1858–1919), whose birthplace is only a little further west along East 20th (see page 109); Eleanor Roosevelt (1884–1962) was baptized at Calvary Episcopal Church, to the park's northwest. However, various developments served to pull the area downhill, notably the extension of the Third Avenue elevated railroad and, much later, the Depression. However, the apartments that were created in the 1940s in the grand mansions became over the years in turn exclusive residences, so once again the area is most definitely the domain of the well-heeled.

From outside the park you can appreciate its comeliness. The statue in the center is of Edwin Booth (1833–1893), a famous tragedian in his time, although his fame was later eclipsed—albeit for all the wrong reasons—by that of his brother, John Wilkes Booth (1839–1865). On the night of Friday, November 25, 1864, Edwin was playing the title role in *Julius Caesar* at the Winter Garden Theater when a Confederate terrorist called Ashbrook, one of a half-dozen who'd sneaked into the city to cause havoc in an attempt to destroy Union morale, hurled a bottle of Greek fire in through the window. Luckily the blaze was soon put out, with no loss of life.

Go back across 20th and carry on along its southern side. Just before you do so, glance up at the dark red-brick building on the park's southeast corner; you'll be having a closer look at it very shortly, but from here you can appreciate what an exceptionally pretty building it is. Certainly it is the prettiest in the immediate area and a gem in any context.

Along what is here called Gramercy Park South there are some buildings of interest aside from the Tilden House, especially after you've crossed the end of Irving Place. At number 28 is the Brotherhood Synagogue, which used to be, before being remodeled in 1975, the Friends' Meeting House, built in the 1850s—it seems an odd religious conversion.

Cross 20th to the east side of the park. Number 34 Gramercy Park East, with pink marble columns around its door, is the especially attractive Queen Anne-style apartment block we drew your attention to a moment ago. The pinkness of the columns is visually echoed by the sandstone facade of the first two storys and the brick above that. This was the first co-op ever to be built in the city.

To the Flatiron

Go up the side of the park, cross 21st, and go left along it to Lexington Avenue, into which you turn right. Pass the entrance to 7 Lexington Avenue, the Park Gramercy, and a little further along you find a plaque which tells you that

On this site Peter Cooper, inventor, philanthropist, founder of the Cooper Union and beloved citizen of New York, erected his house in the Fall of 1850, and he lived here until his death on April the 4th 1883.

Cooper (1791–1883) was a self-made man and a jack of all trades. He had no formal training, but received some education in business from his father. He made cloth-cutting equipment during the War of 1812, became a grocer afterwards, then really achieved prosperity through the manufacture of glue and gelatin. The ironworks he opened in Baltimore in 1828 built the first steam locomotive in the USA, the *Tom Thumb*, and, independently of Alexander Lyman Holley (see page 122), he introduced the Bessemer process for steel manufacture to the country. He was involved in the laying of the first transatlantic cable. Elected to the Common Council of New York in 1828 and later working with the Citizens' Association, he did much to improve life in the city, tackling the problems of poor sanitation and water supplies, providing better education for the poor, and ameliorating prison conditions. The Cooper Union, which he founded in 1857–1859, essayed to provide free education to gifted working-class adults in the arts and technology/science; the Cooper Institute, its descendant, still survives. He ran for the presidency unsuccessfully in 1876 under the banner of the Greenback Party. All in all, a remarkable man.

You now reach East 22nd Street. Cross it, and then turn left to cross Lex. Carry on along 22nd until you reach Broadway and the Flatiron. Since there have been few appealing eateries along this route, you may be hungry and/or thirsty. If so, you're close to the Old Town Tavern on East 18th (see page 109), just a little way down Broadway, or you could opt for the relaxed simplicity of the Mayrose Diner, just a block down from where you stand. There are more elegant establishments nearby, but in our experience these have been overpriced and are not exceptional—better to forage further up Broadway if it's a treat you're after.

A Ramble in Greenwich Village

Summary: The first written use of the name "Greenwich," as "Grin'wich," to describe this area of the island of Manhattan was in 1713, when it appeared in the minutes of a meeting of the Common Council. At the time Greenwich was a settlement somewhat separate from the main center of New York, much as its English namesake was from the center of London; this is presumably why the name was adopted. Much later, during the 20th century, "the Village"—as it's almost always now known—became New York's center for non-establishment art and culture, a development that owed its origins to attempts in the early 1930s to alleviate the worst effects of the Depression, which had hit the Village particularly hard. For the same reason the rents were cheap, and this provided an additional incentive for artists, writers, and musicians to move into the area. From the 1950s onward the Village was a counterculture center on a national and even international scale, with newcomers arriving from distant parts of the USA (notably California, the other focus of the country's counterculture movements) and from abroad. Allied to this was the growth of the gay community; the 1969 Stonewall Rebellion, when both gays and straights rioted against police harassment of gays, is regarded as the spark that kindled the national Gay Rights movement. The Village was also a hub of the national movement against the Vietnam War; allied to this was the protest song, which can trace its genesis to the clubs and taverns of the Village, where such singers and songwriters as Bob Dylan (b. 1941), Paul Simon (b. 1941), Joan Baez (b. 1941), Tom Paxton (b. 1937), and especially Phil Ochs (1940–1976) flourished, at the same time molding the future of popular music.

Of course, the effect of this prominence was to drive those once-cheap rents up, and the population moved from radical to radical chic and finally to just chic. Most of the music clubs have vanished. But there is much of the old Village still to be seen, and the area retains its bohemian atmosphere ... as you'll discover in the course of this relaxed, pleasant stroll.

Start:	Prince Street.
Transportation:	Subway lines N and R to Prince Street.
Finish:	Christopher Park.
Transportation:	Subway lines 1 and 9 from Christopher Street (Sheridan Square).
Length:	About 4 km (2½ miles).
Time:	About 1 hour.
Refreshments:	There are plenty of student hangouts in the earlier part of the walk. Later on, you have abundant choice on Bleecker Street or, more expensively, on Cornelia Street.

Which day:	Any day.
Highlights:	The Bottom Line
	22 Washington Place
	Washington Square Park
	Washington Memorial Arch
	Washington Mews
	Marie's Crisis
	Christopher Park

Come out of the subway station and turn up the left-hand side of Broadway to reach Houston Street, which you cross. On your left as you continue up Broadway is the New York HQ of *Time Out*. The weekly listings and what's-on magazine, which made its name in London, was launched here in 1995, and has been very successful. Its offices are located in what's called the NoHo Building—NoHo for *n*orth of *Ho*uston Street.

The next intersection you come to is with the famous Bleecker Street, immortalized in numerous 1960s neo-folksongs, notably including Paul Simon's "Bleecker Street" (1964). Almost all of the clubs around here that gave birth to the folk-rock movement of the 1960s and after have gone now, although the Bitter End still survives as a nightclub that also features up-and-coming musicians, while the cabaret-style Bottom Line, another survivor of that era, caters more for the fans of established artists.

The Bottom Line

Pass the end of Bond Street and cross Great Jones Street. You're now getting well into NYU (New York University) territory: Many local stores are designed with students in mind, while here and there are various university departments. Cross East 4th and then immediately cross Broadway to your left to walk along 4th. Cross Mercer Street and you find, right on the corner, the Bottom Line.

The outside of the club and its ticket area are almost beyond seedy, yet this is one of the premiere venues (with prices to match) for seeing live popular music. The staff are not noted for their friendly courtesy, but the sound system is rated among the best in New York. And, of course, you have the sense while there that you're sitting in the middle of an important piece of cultural history.

Further along West 4th, on the other side of the street, you see two rather disparate buildings joined at the corner—one white and modernistic and the other vintage dirty red brick, both belonging to NYU. In the plaza in front of them stands an artifact that looks like a particularly freehand version of the *Playboy* bunny; it is in fact by the French sculptor Jean Arp (1888–1966), is called *Seuil Configuration*, and is on permanent loan from the Metropolitan Museum of Art.

Just after you've crossed Greene Street you pass the Frederick Loew Theatre, which houses the New York University Musical Theatre Hall of Fame.

Washington Square Park

At the end of the block you come to Washington Square East, one of the streets that frame Washington Square Park. Nowadays this is *the* place in town to come to have your

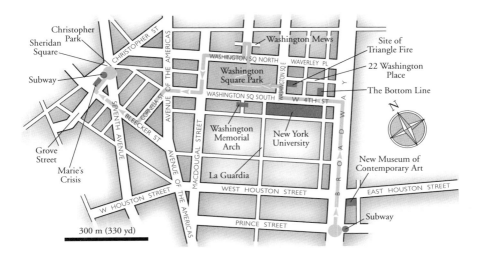

political riot or, perhaps just for now, to stroll around, sit and eat a picnic lunch, watch or listen to the performance artists, feed the pigeons, listen to the occasional political speech, or simply read a book. In the early 19th century it was a burial ground for paupers and was also used for public hangings, but in 1827 the city bought it and started to develop it as a public park. Until the 1960s Fifth Avenue went right through the middle of the park, but now the avenue stops at the square's north side. There are usually lots of NYU students around. In rather more restrained days, this was the square around which Henry James (1843–1916) wrote his famous 1880 novel *Washington Square*.

Go up Washington Square East to the corner with Washington Place. Today this looks a placidly residential site, but a plaque erected by the International Ladies Garment Workers Union commemorates that here, at 22 Washington Place, called with bitter irony the Asch Building, stood the infamous sweatshop that was the Triangle Shirtwaist Company. Here in 1911 a fire broke out on the building's upper floors, where the company operated. The owners had taken so many security measures—such as barring the doors—to ensure that their often child employees would not, *could* not stop work for even one minute during their inhumanely long working day that the teenagers were trapped. Mainly through jumping from the flames to the street, over 140 people died, of whom 125 were young girls. The owners were prosecuted for manslaughter, but got off scot free and were soon back in business nearby, inflicting the same medieval working conditions on other children from familes too poor to refuse *any* source of income. The fire did, however, have beneficial longer-term consequences. Before this the USA's fledgling labor movement had been reviled by almost all, and often enough its activities were ruthlessly and murderously suppressed by the "robber baron" industrialists, such as many of the men whose names are associated with parts of this city. Hereafter, because amid the widespread public horror (the Triangle Shirtwaist Company's owners were lucky to escape lynching) even the stupidest free marketeer could hardly brush off the disaster as of little importance—it became recognized both socially and legally that the labor unions had a valid case, and could be an important force in curbing the worst miseries the rapacious employers attempted to inflict.

Cross the street to enter the park, and go straight onward to reach the statue of the Italian freedom-fighter Giuseppe Garibaldi (1807–1882) just to the east of the fountain at the park's center. This memorial, by Giovanni Turini (1841–1899) in 1888, was a gift from like-minded Italians to the USA, acknowledging the fact that Garibaldi spent various periods living in the city between 1850 and 1853.

Move over to the big circular fountain, which isn't particularly distinguished. On your right from here you're looking at the vast Washington Memorial Arch, which is inside the park and serves as a punctuation point to the foot of Fifth Avenue. The arch was designed by Stanford White (1853–1906) in 1895, replacing a temporary wooden structure that White had put up a few years earlier, and whose massive popularity gave rise to a public subscription for something more permanent. The sculptural figures on the arch are by artists Hermon A. MacNeil (1866–1947) and Alexander Stirling Calder (1898–1976), and were not completed until 1918. The spandrels are by Frederick MacMonnies (1863–1937). In 1917 a group of young artists, including John Sloan (1871–1951) and Marcel Duchamp (1887–1968), famously climbed to the top of the arch and declared that Greenwich Village had seceded from the USA and was henceforth to be known as the Republic of Washington Square, thereby securing forever the Village's status in the eyes of the world as a center of artistic Bohemia.

Complete the semicircle around the fountain and, matching Garibaldi's statue on the other side, you find one of the "Father of modern American steel manufacture," Alexander Lyman Holley (1832–1882). He established in about 1863 at Troy, NY, the first US plant to use the Bessemer process. The sculptor was the prolific John Quincy Adams Ward (1830–1910).

The Foot of Fifth

There's an exit from the park on the far side of the Washington Memorial Arch; cut diagonally across to it. The WALK/DON'T WALK sign is a bit along to the right.

Start walking up the right-hand side of Fifth Avenue. Off to your right leads a little alley belonging to New York University (NYU). At the bottom of it is a statue of the Spanish writer Cervantes (1547–1616), of *Don Quixote* fame, that's worth making a quick sojourn to examine more closely. It was presented to the city in 1986 by the Mayor of Madrid, and for a short while stood in Bryant Park; in 1989 the city foisted it off onto NYU. Quite why it should have done so is a mystery, because it's quite a handsome piece.

A few steps further up Fifth Avenue, Washington Mews goes off to the right. The houses on the uptown side were converted in the 1920s and 1930s from the stables where the rich folk of Washington Square North used to keep their horses; those on the south were built to more-or-less match in 1939. It's closed to pedestrian traffic between 23.00 and 07.00, for reasons that are not immediately obvious. Just beyond the opening of the mews is 1 Fifth Avenue, a numbering which may cause you some perplexity because of course you've already passed several buildings that are lower down Fifth; go back and you'll notice that one of these is number ½!

The Heart of the Village

Retrace your steps to Washington Square North and cross Fifth. At the end of Washington Square North is McDougal Street, another to have been enshrined in the halls of fame through 1960s neo-folksong. Cross McDougal and turn left to cross Waverly Place, which is the continuation of Washington Square North. Go on down the side of the square, crossing Washington Place, to reach West 4th Street. Turn right to go along West 4th, passing the Washington Square United Methodist Church (1860), another of Manhattan's fine churches; it is by Gamaliel King (1800–1876).

When you reach Sixth, locally called Avenue of the Americas, cross over and then turn left to cross 4th. Continue not down Sixth but, half on your right, down the small Cornelia Street. On both sides here you'll find a selection of rather chichi restaurants, including Pó, owned by the famous television chef Mario Batali, and (opposite) Little Havana, an excellent restaurant serving a Cuban cuisine.

Taverns and Bars

At the end of Cornelia Street you arrive on Bleecker Street once more. This part of it, however, far more epitomizes the ethnically and culturally scrambled Village than the far end: Look in either direction at the countless stores selling anything from cut-price CDs and books on esoterica to items you've never heard of and whose function is unknown but looks painful. Turn right and cross Jones Street and then Seventh Avenue South. Continuing along Bleecker, cross Grove Street and turn right along it. There are two or three interesting taverns along here, notably Marie's Crisis, a gay bar (but not exclusively so) which has live music in the evenings; if you visit on a Friday night you can join in with the singalongs. Although the current building is more recent, philosopher Thomas Paine (1737–1809) lived on this site. The plaque claims that he also died here, but the history books disagree, saying that he died on his farm at New Rochelle.

Reach Seventh Avenue. This complicated junction is called Sheridan Square in honor of General Philip H. Sheridan (1831–1888), a cavalry leader during the Civil War who became commander-in-chief of the US Army in 1883, succeeding General William Tecumseh Sherman (1820–1891).

Cross Seventh on your right, and then cross to the left toward a little enclosed area, Christopher Park. This was created in 1837, but has become best known today because of riots here and elsewhere on Christopher Street on June 27, 1969, following a police raid on a popular gay establishment, the Stonewall Inn on Christopher Street. In the wake of the rioting the national Gay Liberation movement was born. How things have changed: In 1999 the Stonewall Inn, Christopher Park, and surrounding streets were put on the New York Register of Historic Places. The park was restored in 1983–1986—it had begun, despite its glory days, to get a seedy reputation—under the direction of the landscape artist Philip Winslow. The flagpole in the park dates from much earlier, having been erected in 1936 to commemorate several of the 1861 Fire Zouaves, an elite Civil War unit. That same year there was installed the bronze statue by Joseph P. Pollia of General Sheridan. The other statue in the park is *Gay Liberation* (1992), by George Segal (b. 1924), and is a duplicate of one at Stanford University, Palo Alto, California. Just opposite Christopher Park, the Duplex is another famous gay bar.

The subway station is hard by, on the south side of the square.

SoHo

Summary: The name SoHo comes from the fact that the northern boundary of this area is considered to be Houston Street—SoHo is *so*uth of *Ho*uston. The other boundaries of SoHo are less defined, although approximately they are Sixth Avenue and Lafayette Street to west and east, and Canal Street to the south. In the earlier decades of the 19th century this was the most densely populated and fashionable part of Manhattan, but later in that century the slide started as retailers, hotels and bordellos arrived, followed by factories and offices. The cast-iron mode of building construction, so evident in Tribeca, became very popular here as well. Through the first half of the 20th century the region became progressively more of a dump, earning itself the name Hell's Hundred Acres, but in the 1960s a populous artistic community took over, taking advantage of the peppercorn rents and converting—quite illegally at the time—the deserted warehouses into studios and studio apartments. The laws were changed in the early 1970s, and over the next couple of decades the area grew more fashionable once again, with the result that the very same artistic community that had made it so could now no longer afford to live here. SoHo lost more than perhaps it has ever realized in the process. Although there are lots of small art galleries, graphics studios and so on around its streets, the area has lost that atmosphere of true creativity it once had—really, its soul. It is still trendy, and is certainly not short of things to see but there is too much of the pseudo for the old vibrancy to survive; it's like the difference between art that is bad but about which someone has been passionate and art that is bad because it has no heart.

Start:	Canal Street and Varick Street.
Transportation:	Subway lines 1 and 9 to Canal Street.
Finish:	SoHo Museum Row.
Transportation:	Subway lines N and R from Prince Street.
Length:	About 2.5 km (1½ miles).
Time:	About 1 hour, plus visiting time.
Refreshments:	There are lots of eateries of various types and price ranges on Canal and on Broadway. You're likely to get a good meal at any of the Chinese establishments around Canal.
Which day:	Not Sunday, Monday, Tuesday, or Wednesday if you want to take in all the museums at the end of the walk. As this doesn't leave much of the week, consult pages 175–6 for their various opening times to decide which day is best for you.
Highlights:	Deitch Projects
	The Drawing Room
	Animazing Gallery
	Gourmet Garage
	Little Singer Building

St. Patrick's Old Cathedral
Puck Building
Museum for African Art
New Museum of Contemporary Art
Guggenheim Museum SoHo
American Primitive Gallery
The Alternative Museum

Come out of the subway station. On your right Canal Street leads straight to the Holland Tunnel, which goes to New Jersey. Turn left along the north side of Canal Street. On your left at the end of a very short block is Duarte Square, in which there stands a handsome statue of the nationalist politician Juan Pablo Duarte (1813–1876), founder of the Dominican Republic. Canal Street itself is primarily of interest for shopping, mainly clothes, though, as you're on the edge of Chinatown, there are also plenty of oriental restaurants.

Cross West Broadway. The big orangy-brown Art Deco skyscraper up to your right is the AT&T Headquarters (originally the Long Distance Building of the American Telephone & Telegraph Company), opened in 1932 with architects Voorhees, Gmelin & Walker. At the time it was the biggest long-distance communications center in the world. Nearer to you is a curious-looking pink-and-black post office.

Cross Wooster Street, glancing up it on your left to see the original cobblestones; here and there throughout this walk you'll see other examples of these, sometimes forming an odd juxtaposition with adjacent architecture of a much more modern era. All through the blocks north of this section of Canal Street there are art and design studios, clothing studios, and small art galleries.

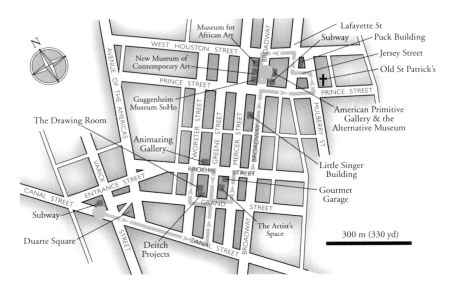

Little Galleries

On reaching Greene Street, turn left up it. Again there are the original cobbles. Once you reach Grand Street, turn left again, and about three-quarters of the way along the block you discover, with premises on both sides of the street, the two-part art gallery called Deitch Projects. These offer changing exhibitions of contemporary art.

On reaching Wooster Street, turn right. At number 40 a bunch of little galleries share a building and show mainly drawings and prints. The one likely to be of most interest is on the ground floor: The Drawing Room, an annex of The Drawing Center, opposite. Opening hours are—whatever it says on the signs—"informal," as is much else: We once discovered the gallery open but completely unattended, leaving potential thieves with a choice of the artwork on the walls or the portfolio of original drawings left conveniently on the table by the door!

Carry on up Wooster Street to Broome Street; cross over and turn right. About halfway along the block you come to the Animazing Gallery, full of art and memorabilia associated with animation. Hung around the walls are original cels and reproductions from countless different animated movies you may have seen—from *Snow White and the Seven Dwarfs* onward, including a great deal by master animator Chuck Jones (b. 1912)—as well as, sometimes, fine art by great animators like Ralph Bakshi (b. 1938) or, again, Jones. There are paintings associated with animation, notably a seemingly endless series by Tom Everhart based on the *Peanuts* characters created by Charles Schulz (1922–2000) and authorized by Schulz himself. All of this stuff is for sale, but there's no pressure put on you if you simply want to look around; be careful not to miss the basement, where much of the most interesting fine art is often to be found.

At the end of the block you reach Greene Street; turn right to walk down it, recrossing Broome Street. Halfway down the block on the left is The Artist's Space, up on the third floor of number 38; it can sometimes be worth a look. Turn left when you reach Grand Street and then left up Mercer Street. On the corner of Mercer and Broome is Gourmet Garage, a warehouse-like store selling nothing but gourmet foods. If you're not hungry before you poke your nose in here you certainly will be afterwards; the prices here and in the three sister stores around Greenwich Village are more modest than in the various competitors you'll see around the city, but even if you don't buy it's worth spending a few minutes looking around at the wares on offer.

The Little Singer Building

Cross Mercer Street on your right and continue to Broadway, where you turn left. At number 555, between Spring Street and Prince Street, is the very pretty Charles Broadway House. A little further up, at number 561, is the Little Singer Building, built in 1904 by architect Ernest Flagg (1857–1947). The "Little" is because four years later Flagg built the Singer Tower at Liberty Street and Broadway; that gem of a skyscraper was for a short time in 1908–1909 the tallest building in the world, but was demolished in the 1970s to make way for One Liberty Plaza, one of Manhattan's notable eyesores. The Frenchified Little Singer Building is, however, extremely attractive in its own right.

St. Patrick's Old Cathedral

When you reach Prince Street, turn right and, crossing Broadway, go along it. Go over Crosby Street, Lafayette Street, and Mulberry Street, then turn left to cross Prince Street.

The biggish, handsome, dark red church on this corner is St. Patrick's Old Cathedral, the first Roman Catholic cathedral in the New World to be named for Ireland's patron saint; it lost its cathedral status in 1878, with the completion of St. Patrick's Cathedral (see page 67) on Fifth Avenue. The foundation stone for the building here was laid in 1809 and the church was dedicated in 1815, the architect being Joseph-François Mangin (*fl*1794–1818); the cathedral was much restored in 1868 after a major fire. The complex in fact includes five other buildings aside from the church itself, of which the most notable are the still-functioning St. Michael's Russian Catholic Church—on the other side of Mulberry Street, built by James Renwick Jr. (1818–1895) and William Rodrigue in 1859 in Gothic Revival style as the St. Patrick's Chancery Office—and St. Patrick's Convent and Girls' School, originally the Roman Catholic Orphan Asylum, built at 32 Prince Street in 1826 in Federal style by an unknown architect and converted into a school in 1886. Inside the church itself (which is unfortunately rarely open to visitors) is an 1868 three-manual tracker pipe organ by Henry Erben, and under the church is a labyrinth of mortuary vaults; in one of these lies Anne Leary, the first US woman to be made a papal countess.

Anti-Catholic prejudice, usually walking arm-in-arm with prejudice against the Irish immigrants, who in turn expressed virulent anti-black prejudice, was commonplace in 19th-century New York. (By 1853 the city had the world's largest anti-Catholic library.) The cathedral more than once had to defend itself against the mob. In 1835 a drunken Protestant host organized by the grandly titled Native American Democratic Association marched on the cathedral, and Bishop (later Archbishop) John Hughes (1797–1864) had to assemble his parishioners to defend it. The following year the Ancient Order of Hibernians was formed (see page 134), and they supplied armed men for the cemetery walls in time of trouble. The height of the anti-Catholic fervor came a couple of decades later with the Know-Nothing Party, so christened by an implacably opposed Horace Greeley (1811–1872) because when anyone was asked if they belonged to such a subversive organization they always responded that they knew nothing about it. Mixing racism with anti-Catholicism and surrounded by thugs to defend them from retaliation, preachers stalked the streets, gathering all-too-gullible crowds. Of these hate-mongering hooligans—for that is really all they were—Abraham Lincoln (1809–1865) was moved to remark sorrowfully that "When the Know-Nothings get control, the Declaration of Independence will read. 'All men are created equal except Negroes and foreigners and Catholics.' " A Know-Nothing mob was repelled from the cathedral, but not before the stained-glass windows had been smashed.

The Cemetery

The cemetery is a beauty, but unfortunately you can't normally get into it to look around. However, there's a generous hole in one of the big black iron gates, and through this you can peer. Among those buried here are the Venerable Pierre Toussaint (1766–1853), brought to New York from Santo Domingo as a slave and eventually a philanthropist, currently under consideration by the Vatican for canonization, and Dominick Lynch (1754–1825), one of those who ratified the Constitution, a signatory of the Catholic Address presented to George Washington (1732–1799) at his inauguration in 1789, and the first president of the Friendly Sons of St. Patrick.

The Puck Building

Go a little way up Mulberry to Jersey and turn left to reach Lafayette. Turn up Lafayette to the right, and on the right you'll find the famous Puck Building, which currently contains miscellaneous offices but originally was the premises of the humorous magazine *Puck*, first launched in German in 1876 by cartoonist Joseph Keppler (1838–1894) and publisher Adolph Schwarmann. The English-language edition, which followed in 1877, edited by Henry Cuyler Bunner (1855–1896), soon became the USA's first widely successful humorous magazine. The building has a very ornate Romanesque Revival frontage, and there's a rather bizarre figure of Puck above the doorway, repeated around the corner. The original building of 1886 was extended in 1893, both times by Albert Wagner (1848–?). At this time Lafayette Street stopped further south, but in the later 1890s it was pushed northward, and the Puck Building required an additional frontage, the one before which you're currently standing. The architect for this extra bit was Herbert Wagner, a relative of the earlier architect. The Puck figure here was done by Henry Baerer (1837–1908); the earlier one is by Casper Buberl (1834–1899).

Three Museums, or is it Four?

Go to the corner of West Houston and turn left. This street is usually regarded as the dividing line between Greenwich Village/NoHo and SoHo. Cross Crosby Street and then Broadway, and turn left down the latter. This block of Broadway has been dubbed SoHo Museum Row, in an echo of the Upper East Side's Museum Mile (see page 46).

A short way down is the Museum for African Art, founded in 1984 as the Center for African Art, renamed in 1992 and today possessing what must be the most appealing museum store in the city: Most of the traditional-style artworks on display are so lovely that you might feel it hardly worth paying the museum's admission fee to see the stuff you *can't* buy. But worth it it is: Not only are the artworks themselves stunning but great attention has been paid to their mode of presentation.

A few doors further down is the New Museum of Contemporary Art, complete with a typographically confusing banner outside to make sure you realize its art is really, you know, yer actual *contemporary*. Inside, however, there's very little of the sterile/incomprehensible branch of modern art; most of the material on display is accessible, and some of it is very fine indeed. The displays are on three levels, and consist of a constant cycle of temporary exhibitions, either thematic or solo; downstairs there's an interesting bookstore.

You're hardly out of the New Museum before you come to the first of the entrances to the Guggenheim Museum SoHo, although in fact this leads into the very extensive museum store; access to the museum proper is via a somewhat unobtrusive little doorway a few paces further along. This is an annex of the main Solomon R. Guggenheim Museum uptown (see page 52), and it shows selections drawn from the main collection as well as temporary exhibitions.

Go to the traffic lights, cross, and come up the other side of Broadway. At number 594 is a building that (like several on this stretch of Broadway) contains a diversity of small art galleries and minor museums. The American Primitive Gallery on the second floor is a commercial gallery containing exactly what the name would suggest. On the building's first floor is the Alternative Museum—or is it? The museum was under reconstruction in early 2000 and proclaimed that henceforth it would be devoting most of its energies to developing a virtual version of itself on the internet. It'll be a pity if this means that the reality evaporates into cyberspace, for this museum has its part to play in the city's culture. Founded in 1975, it is a very political venue, its temporary exhibitions concentrating on divisive issues such as gender and race, and the artists whose shows it puts on are of the variety whose work is driven by personal politics. You may not *like* what you see here, but it cannot be denied that it stimulates.

Once you've finished with 594 Broadway (and you may want to explore some of its other galleries before leaving), go down Broadway to the corner with Prince Street to find the subway station.

A Chinatown Walk

Summary: One of the most fascinating and "special" areas of Manhattan, Chinatown has borders that are hard to define because they are constantly being pushed back as Chinatown grows. At the moment a sensible set of boundaries might be Spring and Delancey streets to the north, East and Worth streets to the south, Broadway to the west and Allen and Pike streets to the east, although this area also includes much that is Little Italy.

The story of Chinatown really begins with the repeal in 1943 of the fundamentally racist Chinese Exclusion Act of 1882, which had effectively kept the number of Chinese in the USA to an absolute minimum by making it difficult for them to settle here and impossible for them to obtain citizenship. Before 1943 the number of people in the Chinese ghetto around the foot of Mott Street had reached about 4,000, the vast majority of them young men—for the Act made it impossible for them to be joined by their families; their numbers had been swollen from a mere couple of hundred since the 1870s by the arrival of Chinese workers who, expelled from the West now that the Transcontinental Railroad was finished and there was no further demand for their near-slave labor, had little where else to go. Even with the repeal of the Act things didn't much improve for the growth of this immigrant community, for the number of Chinese immigrants permitted to the country as a whole was limited to only 105 annually. Even so, by the mid-1960s the population of Chinatown had reached some 20,000, and the abolition of immigration quotas based on national origin in 1968 allowed the numbers to soar. While Chinatown became the largest such community in the Western hemisphere, at the same time it became more culturally diverse, its population accepting increasing numbers of people from other countries, and not just Asian countries; at the same time other Chinese communities grew up elsewhere in New York.

This walk takes you on a looping route through the main areas of Chinatown.

Start and finish:	Canal Street and Centre Street.
Transportation:	Subway lines J, M, Z and 6 to Canal Street.
Length:	3 km (2 miles).
Time:	About 2 hours.
Refreshments:	In Chinatown there's no such thing as a bad restaurant.
Which day:	Not Sunday or Monday for the Museum of Chinese in the Americas.
Highlights:	Engine Company #31
	New York City Rescue Mission
	The Bridge of Sighs
	Columbus Park
	True Light Lutheran Church
	Church of the Transfiguration

Mariners' Temple Baptist Church
St. James' Church
Shearith Israel Graveyard
Museum of Chinese in the Americas

Come up out of the subway and stroll a block westward along Canal Street to reach Lafayette Street; the subway has several exits scattered around the junction of Canal and Centre, so you'll need to orient yourself, perhaps with the help of a passerby, to make sure you're going in the right direction.

On reaching Lafayette, turn left down it and cross Walker Street. Just beyond that you find the building of Engine Company #31. This was erected in 1895 by the architectural firm of Napoleon Le Brun & Sons, who were responsible for the design of many of Manhattan's firehouses in the late 19th century. This is probably their masterpiece, and is in imitation of early-16th-century châteaux of the Loire Valley. As the plaque says:

Today it seems surprising that such an elaborate design would be used for so utilitarian a structure. The entire spirit of the building—with its corner tower, steep roof, dormers, and stone and iron crestings—recalls a romantic fairy tale.

The New York City Rescue Mission
Across the street from it, at number 90, is the New York City Rescue Mission, founded by Jeremiah "Jerry" McAuley (1839–1884) in 1872. It is claimed to be the oldest rescue mission in the USA. McAuley's own circumstances were not ideal when he

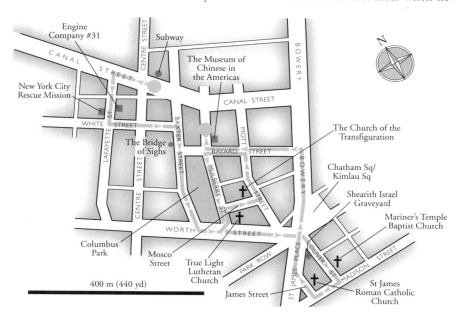

had the notion of founding the mission. He was born in Ireland, probably a bastard, and, brought up by his grandparents, spent a childhood in petty crime. When he was 13 his grandparents could take it no longer and packed him off to New York to live with his sister and her husband. Soon they kicked him out as well, and he made a living on Water Street as a thief and hooligan, and grew to know the inside of the jailhouse well. It was on what he claimed were trumped-up charges that he was eventually, at the age of 20, sent to Sing Sing for 15 years. There he taught himself to read and, after five years, on hearing the testimony of a fellow inmate became a reborn Christian.

In 1864 he was pardoned and released early from prison, but was dismayed to find the Christians he met outside did not share his strength of conviction. He became a Protestant, something that did not go down well with his fellows in the Irish community, and in 1872 he married his long-time girlfriend Maria. That same year he had a vision of himself saving, for Christ, the destitute and downtrodden from their sins. With the help of a wealthy patron, one Frederick Hatch, he purchased 316 Water Street (not far from the current headquarters here) and opened up his first mission, which he named Helping Hand for Men. For the remaining 12 years of his life he dedicated himself (as did Maria) to the destitute.

The Bridge of Sighs

Carry on down Lafayette to White Street and turn left. Cross Centre Street and pass between the main building of The Tombs (see page 144) and its northern tower, beneath a little closed bridge adorned with the rather splendid sculpture *Justice, or Solomon's Throne* (1992) by the Chinese-born New York artist Kit-Yin Snyder (*The Seven Columns of the Temple of Wisdom*, also by Snyder, are the seven tall columns sticking up out of the sidewalk nearby), and reach Baxter Street. Cross it and turn right. From the corner with Bayard Street, look up and to your right and you'll see the notorious Bridge of Sighs, across which the accused are led from their cells in The Tombs to the courts.

Around Columbus Park

Keep on down Baxter Street. On your left is an open space called Columbus Park, and typically it's filled with clusters of Chinese-American men engrossed in traditional card and board games, from chess to mah-jong to games you won't recognize. On your right are the rears of various of the official buildings and courts that huddle around Foley Square (see page 143).

Turn left along Worth Street. On your right as you walk along this block are the two Chatham Towers, erected in 1965 by architects Kelly & Gruzen. They are of architectural significance as very early examples of the exposed-concrete style of skyscraper, but that is all that can be said in their favor.

Cross Mulberry Street. A few paces beyond the intersection is the tiny True Light Lutheran Church. It is small, seemingly hurriedly put together and smeared with the grime of ages. It has, however, done eminent social work in a community that has much required it. The services here, as in most of the local churches, are divided between those held in English and those held in Chinese.

Go back a few paces along Worth Street to Mulberry Street, and turn up it to the right. When you get to Mosco Street, cut right to reach Mott Street, into which turn left.

Mott Street

Named for one Joseph Mott, who was during the late 18th century a successful butcher in the area, this is to Chinatown what Broadway is to New York City: the central spine to which all else is attached. If ever you had any doubts that Chinatown was *different* from the rest of the city, they will be dispelled the moment you turn the corner from Mosco Street. If you're a devotee of Chinese food you'll feel as if you've stepped into Paradise. Not every house-front is a restaurant, but it's a close-run thing, and the few that aren't are almost all food stores.

One place that isn't a restaurant is almost immediately on your left: the Church of the Transfiguration, since 1853 a Roman Catholic church but originally erected in 1801 as the Zion English Lutheran Church; the rubble used for the construction was the same as that employed in the building of St. Paul's Chapel (see page 147). Although now obviously most of its parishioners are of Chinese extraction (the signs outside the church are mainly trilingual in English, Mandarin, and Cantonese), this has not always been the case, as one can deduce from the World War I memorial plaque on the wall, most of the names on which are Italian. There's also a remarkably informative plaque about the architecture, which reads in part:

> It is Georgian in style with steeply pitched end gables, rich entablature and quoins and rectangular plan, with the tower set forward. The pitched window heads, however, are reminiscent of English Gothic parish churches. In 1853 the Roman Catholic Church of the Transfiguration bought the church, at which time it was remodeled and the bell tower replaced.

The architect for this remodeling was Henry Engelbert, who seems also to have done the heavy Gothic window frames at the same time. A Sisters of Charity girls' school opened here in 1856, one of the teachers during the 1880s being Mother Frances Xavier Cabrini (1850–1917), founder of the Missionary Sisters of the Sacred Heart. Other well-known names associated with the church have been Cardinal Patrick Hayes (1867–1938), of Hayes Code fame, who was educated here, and entertainer Jimmy Durante (1893–1980), who worshiped here, his father being a prominent Mott Steet barber.

Chinese War Memorial

Keep going up Mott Street to Bayard Street, named for Nicholas Bayard (1644–*c.* 1709), a nephew of Peter Stuyvesant (1610–1672) who served as New York's mayor and was later convicted of treason for his draconian measures while in office. Turn left to get to Mulberry Street, down which turn left again to walk down the eastern side of Columbus Park. Turn left on Worth Street (passing the True Light Church again) and reach a complicated intersection called Kimlau Square. Cross the bottom of Mott Street and then make a rightish turn to cross what is signed as

Chatham Square. (The two intersections called Kimlau Square and Chatham Square almost overlap, hence the confusion of signs.) In the traffic island is the Chinese War Memorial, erected in 1962, the architect being Poy G. Lee (1900–1968). On the other side of the square turn right to cross the foot of East Broadway, and go down Oliver Street.

Ancient Warships

On your left, just a short way down, is the brownstone-fronted Mariners' Temple Baptist Church. The frontage is in a very poor state of repair, but one can still appreciate the two slender Ionic columns. The building was erected as the Oliver Street Baptist Church in 1844–45 by Isaac Lucas, an architect of whom almost nothing is known beyond a brief mention in the church minutes. Indeed, it's possible that Lucas was the building superintendent and the architect someone else entirely.

Cross Henry Street and then go right when you get to Madison Street. Over to your left as you stroll down the block is the housing project known as Two Bridges, the name referring to the Manhattan and Williamsburg bridges. It was completed in 1967, and until quite recently was much troubled by drug-related crime. The section you're passing contains the Alfred E. Smith Residential Houses. Smith (1873–1944) was a major figure in city, state, and national politics. His honesty was exemplary in the city politics of the day, and, himself the son of poor immigrants and unable to finish his education through the need to help feed the family, he was a tireless supporter of the rights of ordinary working people. The houses named for him stretch all the way over to South Street, where he was born at number 174.

When you reach the bottom of James Street, turn right again. Just after you do so you find St. James' Church. Dedicated in 1837 and attributed to the architect Minard Lafever (1798–1854)—certainly the detailing of the brownstone facade is modeled on his published designs, but it may have been by someone else—this is the second oldest Roman Catholic place of worship in the city, the oldest being St. Patrick's Old Cathedral (see page 127). The pedimented Greek Revival frontage is adorned with a pair of Doric columns. Alfred E. Smith served here as an altar boy. In 1986 the church was scheduled for demolition, but after protests from citizens' groups it was reprieved and the street was renamed Ancient Order of Hibernians Place. This is a name you won't find in the street atlases but which you may have noticed as an ancillary name on the sign as you turned up here from Madison Street. One of the plaques on the church explains the name:

> *Near this Church of St. James in May 1836 the First Division of the Ancient Order of Hibernians in America was organized by Authority of a Charter sent from Ireland by the Venerable Board of Erin.*
>
> *This tablet is reverently dedicated in connection with the one hundredth anniversary of the organization of the Ancient Order of Hibernians in America as a tribute to those dauntless Catholic Irishmen who, penniless, alone in a strange land, founded the Ancient Order of Hibernians in America to be a bulwark to faith and fatherland, a protector of the weak and friendless and a defender of American democracy.*

Coming up to St. James Place, turn right to go back up toward Chatham/Kimlau Square. On your right as you approach the junction is the tiny Shearith Israel Graveyard, a remnant of the first burial ground used (from 1656) by the Congregation Shearith Israel, the first Jewish congregation in North America (formed 1654). The earliest parts of what you can see date from 1683—which makes the vaunted antiquity of the Mariners' Temple and St. James' Church seem like an adolescent brag—and the graveyard ceased to be used in 1828.

The Museum of Chinese in the Americas

The intersection around Chatham/Kimlau Square is complicated. You're aiming to get to the Bowery, so you have to cross the ends of (in fairly rapid succession) Oliver Street, Catherine Street, East Broadway and Division Street. Once you've crossed Division Street you can draw breath again and notice that, away ahead of you up the Bowery, there's a pretty view of the distant Chrysler Building.

Keep going up the Bowery until you reach Bayard Street, at which point cross both it and the Bowery and continue along the right-hand side of Bayard. Since you left Columbus Park you've been seeing only occasional signs of Chinatown, but now suddenly you're plunged right back into it. Cross Elizabeth and then Mott, but when you reach Mulberry turn right without crossing.

Almost at once you find the Museum of Chinese in the Americas, on the second floor of 70 Mulberry Street. The entranceway is not very prepossessing, as you go through a utilitarian hall and up the worn stairs, but you'll soon find that it's all worth it. (The building does have some interest for specialist architectural historians, being a late 19th-century schoolhouse.) This is a really intriguing little museum. Founded in 1980 as the New York Chinatown History Project, it was chartered as a museum in 1992 and changed its name to the current one in 1995. There are temporary exhibitions as well as two permanent ones, the first of which you encounter as soon as you are in the door: "Family Portraits," a photographic exhibition showing images drawn from the families of Chinatown. The main permanent exhibition is "Where is Home? Chinese in the Americas," an interpretive display of artifacts and personal testimony documenting what the curators describe as the Chinese Diaspora.

On leaving, turn right on Mulberry. Go up to Canal and turn left to reach the subway station.

Around City Hall

Summary: New York is a city of astonishing architecture, and nowhere is this more evident than on this walk in the environs of City Hall among the buildings occupied by some of the most influential decision-making bodies in the land and by various of the New York City, New York State, and federal courts. It might seem from this description that the walk is somehow not very *human*—concerned more with institutions and with stones and mortar than with life—but nothing could be further from the truth. At every level you will find this an enriching walk.

One hazard of this walk is that it's infernally easy to get lost if you don't follow the directions with hawklike zeal: The City of New York has chosen to omit street signs from many of the intersections.

Start and finish:	City Hall Park.
Transportation:	Subway lines 4, 5, 6, J, M, and Z to Brooklyn Bridge/City Hall.
Length:	About 2.5 km (1½ miles).
Time:	About 1 hour.
Refreshments:	There are plenty of cheap eateries and fast-food joints on lower Broadway.
Which day:	Avoid weekends if you want to enter the official buildings.
Highlights:	City Hall Park
	Tweed Courthouse
	Brooklyn Bridge
	City Hall
	Woolworth Building
	Sun Building/The Marble Palace
	Emigrant Savings Bank
	Federal Office Building
	African Burial Ground
	New York County Courthouse/State Supreme Court
	Criminal Court Building/The Tombs
	Civil and Municipal Courthouse
	Family Court
	Municipal Building
	Police Headquarters
	St. Andrew's Roman Catholic Church

There are various exits from the subway station, some quite widely apart. Follow the underground signs to the City Hall Park exit and you should emerge at the northeastern edge of the fenced park, on the northwestern side of Park Row.

City Hall Park

The tranquil appearance of this little park belies the events it has witnessed (and still continues to witness), for it is here that the famous tickertape parades conclude, with the feted heroes being formally greeted by the mayor as thousands cheer them on. Of course, the old telegraph machines are now a thing of the past and tickertape with them, so imitation tickertape has to be manufactured for public use. The sheer quantities of paper deposited on the streets of Manhattan during one of these parades are quite staggering, and clearing it all up afterwards is a hideously expensive job, so the city does not give its blessing to a parade lightly: The event concerned must be something really important, like V-J Day, the return of the *Apollo 11* crew, or a victory by the Yankees or Mets in the World Series. In the further past the parades have not been such joyous affairs, being political demonstrations or even riots, sometimes accompanied by extreme violence. It was here that the poor, mainly the Irish, made one of the foci of their wrath during the riots protesting the Draft Act of 1863, along the way murdering blacks and in particular seeking to lynch Horace Greeley (1811–1872), editor and proprietor of the *New York Tribune*, whose editorials supported the Act and whose offices were in Printing House Square, just a little way down Park Row and on the other side of it from where you now are. The Draft Act was indeed iniquitous—Lincoln had promised there would be no draft, and yet not only had necessity forced him into it but he had made the compromise that anyone who could afford to give the federal government $300 (a lot in those days) would be exempt—but the behavior of the mob, egged on by an inflammatory speech from Governor Horatio Seymour (1810–1886), was viler.

The Municipal Building

The impressive structure on the other side of Park Row is the Municipal Building, which you'll visit at the end of the walk; for the moment, pop in through the gate to look at the park. Just inside the railings is a statue (1890) of Horace Greeley by John Quincy Adams Ward (1830–1910). Just in front of it there's a plaque honoring newspaperman Joseph Pulitzer (1847–1911) and the fact that nearby stood the Pulitzer Building, home of his *New York World* and one of New York's earliest skyscrapers, causing marvel for its 16 storys when it was opened in 1890. The plaque, dated 1954, tells you that Pulitzer "upheld the highest traditions of American journalism." In fact, his circulation war with William Randolph Hearst (1863–1951), owner of the *Morning Journal*, did little for the reputation of tabloid publishing and brought the expression "yellow journalism" into the language. Also in the park is a celebrated statue (*c.* 1890) of the Revolutionary War martyr Nathan Hale (1755–1776), done by Frederick MacMonnies (1863–1937).

The Tweed Courthouse

Further into the park, facing onto Chambers Street, is the Tweed Courthouse, officially first the New York County Courthouse and then the New York City Building, but universally known by its familiar name, which refers to Boss William Tweed (1823–1878), whose corrupt regime it rapidly came to symbolize. The architects were John Kellum (1809–1871) and Leopold Eidlitz (1823–1908). It took 20 years to erect, from 1858 to 1878, because the vast bulk of the money the city legislature approved annually for its construction was embezzled by Tweed. When the scale of the crime was finally realized—it took New Yorkers an astonishingly long time—Tweed was hounded out of office and spent the rest of his life either on trial (several times), on the run (several times), or in jail (several times, eventually dying of pneumonia there).

Brooklyn Bridge: History

Exit the park by the gate where you came in and stroll southward down the park's edge. Within a few paces you are treated to an excellent view along part of the length of the Brooklyn Bridge, the same bridge whose purported sale by tricksters to the rich and gullible has become a comic cliché. Opened in 1883, it was the first bridge to span the East River between Manhattan and Long Island. The story of the bridge dates back to 1857 and has three main heroes, the first two being father and son John Augustus Roebling (1806–1869) and Washington Augustus Roebling (1837–1926): the bridge project quite literally killed the father but was conquered by the son, who could not have completed the conquest without the aid of the third hero, his wife, Emily Warren Roebling (1843–1903).

John, the father, was born in Germany, coming to the USA when he was 25. He was a genius and polymath, but his main passion was for engineering, and in particular bridge building. Peter Cooper (1791–1883), himself a great inventor, took the young man up, and introduced him to Abram S. Hewitt (1822–1903), Cooper's son-in-law and later a Mayor of New York. In 1857 Roebling wrote to Hewitt about the possibilities of building a bridge over the East River, and Hewitt had the letter widely bruited about. Others had proposed such a bridge before, but Roebling was the first whose proposals were practicable. The Civil War put a stop to any plans, but after it Roebling's notions were taken very seriously indeed by the Brooklyn business community. (New Yorkers themselves were unenthusiastic, realizing that the bridge would allow Brooklyn to seize some of the trade that currently was exclusively New York's.) At the end of 1866, during a bitter winter when crossing the East River was a frustratingly time-consuming venture by ferry, a group of prominent Brooklynites, notably William C. Kingsley (1833–1885) and Senator Henry C. Murphy (1810–1882), determined to let the young German-born engineer try to turn his dreams into reality.

Brooklyn Bridge: Construction

In May 1867 the New York Bridge Company was set up, with Murphy as Chairman and with the cities of Brooklyn and New York (the latter only after Boss Tweed and others had been sizably bribed) among the shareholders. In 1869 Congress passed a bill authorizing construction of the bridge, and on January 2, 1870 work was officially begun with the site for the bridge's Brooklyn end being cleared.

The Brooklyn Bridge was revolutionary in several ways. It was one of the first for whose construction pneumatic caissons were used underwater. It was probably the first to use steel cable for its suspension. For some while after its completion it had the longest span between towers in the world—486.3 m (1,595 ft 6 in). But John Roebling, the man whose vision had made it all possible and who was the project's chief engineer, never lived to see it finished, or even properly begun. In July 1869, while surveying the sites for the main piers, he managed to get his foot caught between an incoming ferry and the dock, and within a couple of weeks he was dead of tetanus.

A month later his son Washington, himself a fully qualified engineer, was appointed chief engineer in his place. All went well for two and a half years, but then in 1872 Washington was afflicted by the bends while working in one of the bridge's caissons, and for the rest of his life he was partially paralyzed and suffered from cramps and hyperacusis. He had to supervise the remainder of the construction from a wheelchair in his Brooklyn Heights home, using binoculars, while his wife, Emily (who took crash courses in engineering and mathematics in order to qualify herself), superintended the work on-site. This bizarre setup actually worked, and on May 24, 1883 the bridge was finally ready for dedication by US President Chester A. Arthur (1830–1886). New York Governor Grover Cleveland (1837–1908) was also in attendance. Washington Roebling could not be there, but watched the scene through his binoculars. That evening the dedication party came to his home to pay their profoundest respects to the man who had, in a very real sense, sacrificed his life to one of the world's greatest engineering feats.

But the drama was not over. The press had been stirring up scare stories, notably that the bridge was vulnerable to the rhythmic tread of soldiers marching in unison. As regiments of the National Guard trooped onto the bridge during the public Decoration Day, six days later, there was a panic in the crowd, and in the resulting stampede twelve people were trampled to death and some three dozen were injured.

The Brooklyn Bridge is regarded by many on both sides of the East River as a delight. From where you're standing on Park Row you can gain some appreciation of its beauty; from the deck of one of the around-Manhattan cruise boats you can appreciate it even better. If you have the time to spare, you can walk across it and back, returning to join our route at this point.

City Hall

Continue down Park Row. There's a sign for Spruce Street, despite the fact that it's nonexistent on this side of the road. However, on the far side of Park Row at this point is Printing House Square, whence the *New York Tribune* once published. The large white building in the park on your right is City Hall, which has been closed to visitors since August 1998; the cops on guard at the gate here are usually pretty friendly and will chat if there's anything you want to ask them.

City Hall was built in a mixture of mainly Louis XVI and partly Georgian style in 1803–1812 by architects Joseph-François Mangin (*fl*1794–1818) and John McComb Jr. (1763–1853), who had won an 1802 competition for the job. There was controversy once it was finished, for only McComb's name was inscribed on the foundation stone, yet it was stylistically obvious that the inspiration and almost certainly the bulk of the work had been that of Mangin. Mangin was a shadowy figure of whom little is known save that he arrived in New York from France in 1795, was a city surveyor

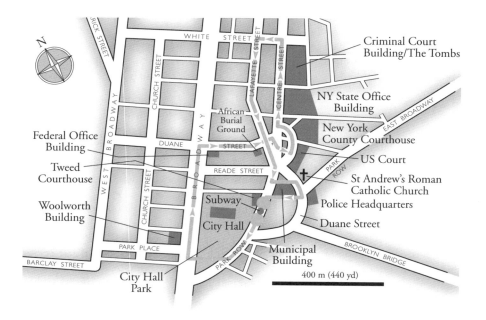

and the city's chief fortifications engineer, had an architect brother who worked with him in the firm Mangin Brothers, and was responsible for various pieces of institutional architecture including the New York State Prison and, probably, the initial designs for Castle Clinton. In 1858, fireworks launched from City Hall's roof to celebrate the laying of a transatlantic cable set the dome, cupola, and rotunda ablaze; they were reconstructed under the supervision of Leopold Eidlitz. The interiors, reputedly splendid, were restored in 1908–1917 by Grosvenor Atterbury (1869–1956).

The Woolworth Building
You can cut through the park here to an attractive fountain. From the fountain go briefly northward for a better view of City Hall (this is the best place for photographs of it) or go straight ahead to reach Broadway. Almost directly opposite you on Broadway is the Woolworth Building, which for a decade and a half after its completion in 1913—until the Bank of Manhattan Trust Building (see page 157) went up in 1929—was at 241 m (792 ft) the world's tallest building. The architect was Cass Gilbert (1859–1934), and he worked in the Gothic style that was just beginning to catch hold in New York. From City Hall Park you get a nice view of the building, which is a very lovely one, with its lavish neo-Gothic detailing; the crown at its top is in imitation of Rouen Cathedral's Butter Tower.

The building was the realization of a dream for the magnate Frank Winfield Woolworth (1852–1919), who, not content with enormous commercial success, sought also what he identified as respectable recognition. What better way than to have the tallest building in the world as one's headquarters and eponym? And Woolworth wanted his building not just to outstrip the record for height but to look as portentous as possible. He had seen the Houses of Parliament in London, and essentially told Cass Gilbert he wanted "something like that, only more so." This is exactly what Gilbert gave him. Some wag, observing the influence of cathedral architecture on the design, mockingly dubbed it the Cathedral of Commerce, an attempted insult which Woolworth turned around, adopting the expression as a boast. He paid the $13,500,000 costs of the building in cash, the same way that customers in his stores were required to pay for their purchases.

If the exterior is beautiful, the lobby is something beyond even that—an extravaganza of carving, gilt, stained glass, and mosaic. Among the carvings are witty figures of Woolworth (counting out his money) and Gilbert (holding a model of the building), as well as portrayals of some of the typical items one might buy in a Woolworth store. The mosaic ceilings and stained glass were the work of artisans following the designs of Otto Heinigke (1851–1915) and Owen Bowen (1873–1987).

The Green Clock

Exiting the Woolworth Building, turn left to go up Broadway. Cross Murray Street, Warren Street, and Chambers Street; just after you've crossed the last, look up to your right over Broadway and you'll see on the corner a green clock with "The Sun, it shines for all" engraved on it. This building was originally erected in 1846 as the flagship emporium of dry-goods retailer A. T. Stewart (*c.* 1802–1876), the architects being Trench & Snook. It soon became the place for fashion-conscious Manhattanites to be seen, but times changed, and in 1917 the "Marble Palace" was sold to Frank A. Munsey (1854–1925) to house the offices of his *New York Sun*. The *Sun* eventually set, in 1952, and the clock is really the only evidence left of the building's glory days. From this angle you get a good view, beyond the clock, of the Municipal Building. Nearer to you than that is the facade of the Emigrant Savings Bank Building, put up in 1908–1912 by architect Raymond F. Amirall. The bank was founded at the instigation of Archbishop John Hughes (1797–1864) in 1850 as a division of the Irish Emigrant Society, itself founded in 1817. This was the bank's second building on this site, and is today, as an architectural treasure, the property of the city; the bank's headquarters are now at 5 East 42nd.

Go on up Broadway to reach Reade and then Duane. If you have been in New York for more than five minutes you'll have seen that there are almost more branches of the drugstore Duane Reade than there are pedestrians. The chain takes its name not from a founder (as many people assume) but from the names of these two streets. The first of its 128 successful full-service drugstores in commercial and residential neighborhoods throughout the city opened in 1960 on Broadway between them, and is still here.

The Federal Office Building

Don't cross Duane Street but instead cross Broadway to number 290, the Federal Office Building. This was erected in 1994, with architects Hellmuth, Obata, Kassabaum, and is a prettier building than you can really appreciate from here. (You get better views of it from further up Broadway and in glimpses from Centre Street.)

The real focus of interest here is the art on display inside. The various works on show relate to the discovery during the building's construction that in the early 18th century there was a burial ground for African slaves nearby.

The first of the Federal Office Building's works of public art is visible above the Broadway entrance before you go in (use the door marked "Visitors' Entrance"). This is *America Song*, a relief done using concrete, granite, stainless steel, fiber-optics, and electrics by Clyde Lynds. The piece has a marvelous air of freedom about it, which is exactly Lynds' intention. The simple yet evocative verse (by an anonymous African poet) beneath it runs:

> *I want to be free*
> *Want to be free,*
> *Rainbow 'round my shoulder*
> *Wings on my feet.*

The Federal Office Building: Works of Art

Once inside the door you go through a security check to find yourself in a big, imposing, light-filled lobby. Straight ahead of you is the striking sculpture *Africa Rising* by Barbara Chase-Riboud (b. 1939), a significant sculptress and also a writer of note; in 1997–1998 she was involved in controversy over claims that the 1997 Dreamworks movie *Amistad* had been partly plagiarized from her 1988 novel *Echo of Lions*, a dispute settled out of court. *Africa Rising* is a lovely and moving piece.

Off on your right, in the central rotunda, is *The New Ring Shout* by sculptor Houston Conwill (b. 1947), architect/graphic artist Joseph De Pace (b. 1954), and poet Estella Conwill Majozo (b. 1949), a "dance floor" 12.2 m (40 ft) in diameter in illuminated terrazzo and polished brass. This is an extremely complex work, both technically and conceptually; highly recommended is the free leaflet available nearby that explains the fascinating symbolism in detail.

To discover one stunning artwork in the Federal Office Building is surprise enough; already you've met three, and there are two more to come. Keep going toward the Reade Street exit (not accessible to the public) and you find on the wall on your left a long silk-screened mural by Tomie Arai (b. 1949), *Renewal*. It's a narrative work, spanning roughly the period we know the African Burial Ground was in use, 1712–1792, as well as the Emancipation in New York in 1827. Arai has used also an overlapping presentation of the images in order to symbolize the process of archaeology. The strong reds of the mural warm the whole of the otherwise somewhat chilly-looking side-hall.

Finally, installed high on the wall by the Duane Street exit, there's a work known only as the Roger Brown Mosaic. At a very quick glance it might seem to be made up of hundreds of colored hexagonal tiles, but almost immediately you realize these are, toward the lower part of the work, in fact human skulls, while above those the "hexagons" are human faces in different colors. The closer you get to this work the more detailed you realize it is, and that the faces are not expressionless but gaunt and suffering. Roger Brown (b. 1944) intended this powerful piece to address not only the issues of slavery and oppression but also the more modern concern of the AIDS epidemic. He adds: "The city rises in the background as if growing out of the heap of human misery left behind."

The African Burial Ground

As you exit the Federal Office Building by the door through which you came in you'll notice on the other side of the street a further memorial to the Africans buried here. Cross the street if you want to and have a look at it: it's a very tranquil place.

Otherwise, go to your right down Duane Street. There's a nice view of the US Courthouse ahead of you. To your left, numbered 26 Federal Plaza, is a big black slab called the Jacob K. Javits Federal Building. In front of this is a sculpture called *Object in Five Planes* (1965) by Alexander Calder (1898–1976). On your right as you approach Elk Street is the African Burial Ground itself. This is in fact not the entire cemetery but simply a block left vacant on this site as a token of respect to the dead slaves. The full site once covered some 2 ha (over 5 acres), and some 20,000 slaves—either African or Black American—were buried here. This remnant is dedicated not just to the people buried here but to all the people who suffered under the tyranny of slavery in New York. Although a competition judged in Summer 2000 will decide a memorial to be erected here, as of early 2000 there's just a grass-covered lot one can look at through wire netting.

The US Courthouse and the New York Courthouse

Cross Elk Street and keep on down Duane Street. Directly opposite you as you reach the bottom end of Foley Square is the US Courthouse. Cross the complicated intersection to get to it. The US Courthouse was completed in 1936 by architect Cass Gilbert, still at work over two decades after completing the Woolworth Building. This is not one of his better designs, although the gold pyramid at its top is pleasing and the view of its lower parts you get from the sidewalk directly in front of it is enjoyable enough. To the left, behind it, you can see the top of the Federal Courthouse, erected by architect John Pederson Fox in 1994. You can go into the US Courthouse; the interior is overwhelmingly splendid (there was a fuss at the time over the cost of this) but not especially interesting otherwise. Do note that security guards will stop you from bringing cameras and tape recorders inside.

To your left as you stand facing the US Courthouse is a hexagonal building in very self-conscious imitation of the Greek Classical style. This is the New York County Courthouse/State Supreme Court, completed in 1927 by architect Guy Lowell (1870–1927), who had won a public competition in 1912–1913 based on his designs for a circular building, but then the committees took over and "improved" things, hence the hexagonal shape. The result is nevertheless rather fine, so perhaps for once the committees knew what they were doing. The building was put up where once the infamous Old Brewery had been; this was a slum building into which reputedly upwards of 1,000 people were packed. Foley Square itself was once known as the Five Points, and was one of those places into which you ventured only at risk of your life and/or virtue. Before that there was a pond called the Collect here, drained and covered over in 1811.

The Criminal Court Building and The Tombs

Keep going around Foley Square in this direction, crossing a small street which is Hamill Place. Pass by Louis J. Lefkowitz State Office Building, which is somewhat less interesting than its name suggests. Go rightish to head up Centre Street. Cross Hogan Place and you'll find yourself walking in front of an extremely attractive Art Deco building; it comes as something of a disillusion to discover that this is no elegant "Cathedral of Commerce" but the Criminal Court Building. It was done in 1939 by Harvey Wiley Corbett (1873–1954), one of the architects who contributed to the Rockefeller Center.

Just to the north of the Criminal Court Building, between it and White Street, is the Manhattan House of Detention for Men, internationally better known as The Tombs, which earned itself a reputation almost as bad as the Bastille or Lubianka. The trouble faced by the first two buildings set up here (one in the 1840s, the next in 1902) was that their foundations were laid in soggy landfill right next to the canal that crossed the lower tip of Manhattan between the East and Hudson rivers. The current building dates from 1983, and at least so far shows no signs of sinking like the other two.

More Temples of Law

Cross Centre Street and walk along a short block of White Street to Lafayette Street. Turn left here and walk a block to Franklin Street. The building you've been circumnavigating is the Civil and Municipal Courthouse, designed in 1960 by the firm of William Lescaze & Matthew Del Gaudio. The building itself is dreary, but it has some intriguing frescoes by William Zorach (1887–1966) and Joseph Kiselewski (1901–1986).

Cross Franklin and then cross Lafayette to your right. Walk past the Family Court. Erected in 1975 by architects Haines, Lundberg & Waehler, this is again not a very special building, but the sculpture in front of it, *Three Forms* (1975) by Roy Gussow, is worth a look. Inside the lobby, if you choose to make the foray, another interesting sculpture hangs from the ceiling: *Touchme* (1969) by Merle L. Steir.

Keep going down Lafayette and cross Leonard Street. Once you've done so, you're walking in front of the undistinguished City of New York Office of the Sheriff. Continue, crossing Catherine Lane and Worth Street to return to Foley Square, named for tavern-owner and Tammany Hall politician Thomas F. Foley (1852–1925). Walk down the edge of Thomas Paine Park, a testament to Paine (1737–1809), the great visionary patriot, and currently in the process of reconstruction. On the other side of the street you see another aspect of the Jacob K. Javits Federal Building, followed by a squat black box of a building which is the US Court of International Trade.

The Municipal Building

Negotiate the bottom of Foley Square as best you can. Directly ahead is an edge of the Municipal Building. Cross Duane Street and then Reade Street, then go left across Centre Street to find yourself at the northwestern corner of the Municipal Building. This was put up in 1914 by McKim, Mead & White, with William M.

Kendall (1856–1941) in charge, after a public competition in 1907–1908. Some critics complain that the Corinthian colonnade at the base is a mismatch with the Corinthian drum at the top with, atop that, the statue *Civic Fame* by Adolph Weinman (1870–1952), but in fact, as you'll have seen from the various vantages on the building you gained earlier during the walk, the whole is very consonant. The top is illuminated at night, so you may well have seen it from other parts of Manhattan (or even from Brooklyn) without knowing what it was. The building was extensively restored in 1992 by the firm Wank Adams Slavin. There's a fairly popular wedding chapel on the second floor, but in general admission is not encouraged. You can, however, go around the building and through its arches.

Behind the Municipal Building

Go through one of the arches to discover, in Police Plaza (designed by M. Paul Friedberg), an extraordinary bright orange piece of modern sculpture. It's called *5 in 1*, and is by Tony Rosenthal. It was completed in 1974 and restored in 1989. Beyond it is Police Headquarters, designed in 1973 by Gruzen & Partners. Small wonder the street on your right is named Avenue of the Finest!

On your left is St. Andrew's Roman Catholic Church, done in 1939 by Maginnis & Walsh and Robert J. Reiley. It comes as something of a surprise that such a small, modest building could have been erected so (comparatively) recently. There's no real interest to the church, either inside or out; its prettiness derives from its incongruous surroundings rather than from any architectural brilliance.

Retrace your steps through the Municipal Building and make your way back to the walk's starting point.

St. Paul's Chapel to Trinity Church ... the Long Way

FINANCIAL DISTRICT WALK 1

Summary: Even the thought of taking a walk through any area called "the Financial District" might be a bit offputting. You might envisage endless vistas of towering, featureless bank buildings. Nevertheless, this is for the most part an astonishingly pretty, highly engrossing walk through old New York, with superb historical churches at both beginning and end and an utterly delightful one in the middle.

Start:	St. Paul's Chapel.
Transportation:	Subway lines 2, 3, 4, 5, A, C, J, M, and Z to Fulton Street–Broadway Nassau.
Finish:	Trinity Church.
Transportation:	Subway lines 4 and 5 from Wall Street Station, or lines 2 and 3 from the other Wall Street Station.
Length:	About 3 km (2 miles).
Time:	About 2 hours, plus visiting time at the churches.
Refreshments:	There's not much on offer, alas, aside from hot-dog stalls and the occasional very expensive restaurant.
Which day:	Wednesday for the St. Nicholas Hellenic Orthodox Church, which is a strongly recommended part of the itinerary.
Highlights:	St. Paul's Chapel
	World Trade Center
	Austin J. Tobin Plaza
	St. Nicholas Hellenic Orthodox Church
	90 West Street/140 Cedar Street
	Trinity Twins
	Chamber of Commerce of the State of New York
	Liberty Tower
	Federal Reserve Bank of New York
	Legion Memorial Square/Louise Nevelson Plaza
	American International Group Building
	Chase Manhattan Plaza
	Trinity Church

There are several exits from the subway station, but try to engineer things so that you come out on Fulton Street, named for Robert Fulton (1765–1815), the inventor (and in earlier life, painter) whose *North River Steamboat*, later named the *Clermont*, launched in 1807 to operate on the Hudson, became the world's first commercially successful passenger steamboat. Once out of the subway station, turn left and then almost immediately left again to go up Nassau Street. At the end of a very short block, turn left into Ann Street. Ahead of you as you walk toward Broadway you can see the 12-story Underwood Building at 209 Greenwich Street.

St. Paul's Chapel

When you reach Broadway, cross over to find yourself standing in front of St. Paul's Chapel, the oldest public building still in use on Manhattan and the only surviving pre-Revolutionary church. It was built amid fields in 1766 by Trinity Church (see page 152) as a "chapel of ease"—that is, a chapel for people who might have difficulty making it to the main church. The architect was Thomas McBean, who based his design on London's St. Martin-in-the-Fields, built in Georgian Class-Revival style in 1726 by James Gibbs (1682–1754); it is possible that McBean, a somewhat shadowy figure, was a student of Gibbs. There have been many important ceremonies here, but by far the most significant was George Washington's act of worship here at a special service on the day of his inauguration, April 30, 1789. The pew where he sat is in the north aisle, with an oil painting above it of the Great Seal of the United States. At the time New York was the fledgling nation's capital, and Washington worshiped here over a period of some two years. On the other side of the chapel is the Governor's Pew, used by George Clinton (1739–1812), the first Governor of New York State; on the wall above it are the Arms of the State of New York. Among other events here was the funeral of President James Monroe (1758–1831). On the Broadway side there is an elaborate monument to Major-General Richard Montgomery (1736–1775), who died at the Battle of Quebec; his remains were brought here in 1818.

St. Paul's is historic rather than beautiful, but well worth a look anyway. The woodcarving is by Andrew Gautier and the ornamental *Glory* over the altar is by Pierre Charles L'Enfant (1754–1825), who also designed Washington DC. Usually you can't get into the chapel's pretty churchyard, in which there is an oak statue of St. Paul that bears examination.

After you've finished with St. Paul's, turn downtown on Broadway. Cross Fulton Street and look back; from here you get a good view of St. Paul's clocktower.

Occupying the entire block between Fulton Street and Dey Street, at number 195 Broadway, is the building of the H.J. Kalikow Company, formerly the AT&T Building. Opened in 1922, with William Welles Bosworth (1869–1966) as architect, this has a superb (if somewhat manic) lobby, full of fluted columns and, inset into the floor, plaques by Paul Manship (1885–1966).

The World Trade Center Plaza

Turn right into Dey Street (or exit onto Dey Street from the Kalikow lobby and turn right). From here it's hard to see anything else but the northern side of the infamous Twin Towers. Just before you reach Church Street, look to your left at the Century 21 department store's fantastic cast-iron door.

Cross Church Street to enter the Austin J. Tobin Plaza, originally called the Great Plaza of the World Trade Center but renamed in 1982—despite all this official naming, everyone calls it just the World Trade Center Plaza. There are various pieces of modern sculpture scattered around it, some of which merit a look but none of which is a knockout; and beneath it there's a very extensive shopping concourse.

The World Trade Center

The World Trade Center was a project initiated by the Port of New York Authority in the early 1960s as part of its program for the urban renewal of Lower Manhattan. Between 1970 and 1988, with Mimoru Yamasaki & Associates and later Emery Roth & Sons as architects, seven buildings were opened. Generally, however, when people talk of the Center—which they usually do with a shudder—it's the Twin Towers, opened in 1976, to which they're referring. At a height of 412 m (1,350 ft), these were the tallest buildings in the world at the time of their construction, although in fact they're not much taller than the Empire State Building, at 381 m (1,250 ft), erected nearly half a century earlier. It is often caustically remarked that the view from the observation platform here is infinitely better than that from the Empire State's, because from here you don't see the World Trade Center.

The architects are hardly to blame for the fact that the towers are so abhorrent. The Port Authority gave them the brief to create on a site of area under 6.5 ha (16 acres) a space of nearly 930 m^2 (10 million sq ft), so there was little they could do except build upward. What depresses and enrages about the Twin Towers is not their design—which is in fact not too grim—but the crassness of their scale in relation to the Lower Manhattan skyline. It was not an architectural but a political protest that led to the setting off of a bomb in one of the Center's underground parking lots in February 1993, causing the deaths of five people and a great deal of material damage.

About 50,000 people work here, a large enough number that the postal services have given the Center its own zip code. Daily another 70,000 or so visit. There are musical events most evenings in the Plaza. On the 107th floor of the northern tower is the feature called Windows on the World, in whose restaurant you can dine at great expense while looking out over the most splendid views of Manhattan and its surrounds. On the 110th floor of the southern tower there is a theme park called Top of the World, which includes the open-air observation deck. In short, quite a lot goes on here, and you may want to come back another day to explore the Center in full. For the moment, continue walking through the Plaza, bearing to your left until you encounter a flight of stairs that takes you down onto Liberty Street.

On occasion the Plaza is closed off. In this event, walk down Church Street (locally called Trinity Place) to reach Liberty Street; turn right and pick up the walk at the bottom of the stairs.

St. Nicholas Hellenic Orthodox Church

Emerging onto the sidewalk from the stairs, you can see over to your right a very massive-looking (though not particularly tall) skyscraper. This is the Dow Jones Building. There is very much prettier architecture on display from here, however. More or less opposite where you're standing there is, at the back of a parking lot, a very comely

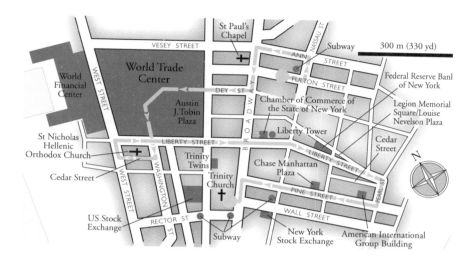

skyscraper, so cross Liberty Street carefully at the lights and head toward it down the small Washington Street. Stay on the northern side of Cedar and walk along a way to a small plain whitewashed building which you could easily mistake for a shelter used by the parking-lot attendants. This bleakish exterior masks one of the loveliest church interiors in all Manhattan, that of the tiny St. Nicholas Hellenic Orthodox Church.

Your best chance of finding this open (aside from on a Sunday) is on a Wednesday afternoon, although there's no guarantee – it seems to depend on the availability of volunteers. It is something akin to this approach that makes so utterly charming the interior—dark wood, backlit stained-glass windows, countless modern icons crowded on the walls, the lovingly tended altar, everything crammed together and glowing. Here there is no great art, no defiant statement, no *big* centerpiece designed to be gazed at in awe, but rather an accumulation made by countless anonymous lovers of their church that makes up a single, exquisite, and exquisitely *human* artwork.

The Little Twins and the Fake Empire State

Directly opposite is the building that brought you in this direction in the first place, 90 West Street (also numbered 140 Cedar Street). Twenty-three storys tall and built in 1907, this had the same architect as the Woolworth Building (see page 140), Cass Gilbert (1859–1934), for which it can be regarded as a practice run. At nights its richly ornamented top is floodlit.

Walk back up to Liberty Street and turn right to walk along its right-hand side. Cross Greenwich Street. When you come to Trinity Place (Church Street), look right at a splendid pair of buildings, the Trinity Twins or (since the erection of the World Trade Center) the Little Twins. If you look back and forth to make a visual comparison between the two sets of twins, old and new, your heart may sink at the sight of 70 years' worth of architectural retogression. The Little Twins are not in fact twins: The nearer one, the US Realty Building, opened in 1907 at 115 Broadway, is a story taller

(22 storys) than the further one, the Trinity Building, opened in 1905 at 111 Broadway. The architect was Francis H. Kimball (1845–1919), and he was concerned with these two buildings to set Trinity Church in a moodily neo-Gothic frame. The interiors are splendid as well. If you want, make a quick detour to check out one of the great, lavish lobbies, with their stained glass and their hammerbeam ceilings.

As you continue along this stretch of Liberty Street, look up and half-rightwards. What appears to be the Empire State Building peeking over the rooftops is actually the "Fake Empire State," the American International Group Building on Pine Street; the Empire State is a long way uptown from here. The little paved area to your right is Liberty Park.

Three Stunning Buildings in a Row

When you reach Broadway, cross over, sparing a shudder on your right at the piece of modern sculpture in front of 140 Broadway. Evocatively titled *Cube* (1973), this takes the form of a bright red-orange quasi-cube made out of stainless steel, perched seemingly on one apex and with a cylindrical hole punched through it. It is by Isamu Noguchi (1904–1988).

On your left, at 65 Liberty Street, is the Chamber of Commerce of the State of New York. This Beaux-Arts building was erected in 1901, with James B. Baker (1864–1918) as architect, but the organization is very considerably older than that. The city's first business association to have no government affiliations, it was founded in 1768 as the New York Chamber of Commerce at a meeting of 20 merchants in Fraunces Tavern (see page 158), and two years later was granted its Royal Charter. The Revolutionary War sundered the association, but in 1784 it was reorganized as the Chamber of Commerce of the State of New York. It was an early supporter of the Erie Canal proposal, and really came into its own in the decades following the Civil War, when it played an important role in the running of the city. It has remained a significant body ever since. The building you see here was its first permanent home.

There's another lovely building just next to it, at 55 Liberty Street: the former Chamber of Commerce Liberty Tower, originally opened in 1909 as the Sinclair Oil Company's headquarters and much more recently, in the early 1980s, converted into an apartment block. The architect was Henry Ives Cobb (1859–1931). Beyond that, to make it three stunning buildings in a row, there's the Federal Reserve Bank of New York at 33 Liberty Street, inspired by Florentine Renaissance palaces and completed in 1924 by York & Sawyer, the architects responsible for many other fine Manhattan buildings, such as that of the New-York Historical Society (see page 14). This one is a real dilly. You can guess even at a distance that it's a bank building, because it offers an affect of sturdy, massive impregnability, yet it is in no way offensively a fortress. Indeed, it's a very graceful building for all its gravitas, with a facade in different shades of Indiana limestone and Ohio sandstone and with wrought embellishments by the great metalworker Samuel Yellin (1885–1940). The building extends for five storys *below* ground level to provide the largest bank vault in the world, with room for more gold bullion then there is in Fort Knox—indeed, for about one-third of the world's known gold resources!

Modern Sculpture

Cross Nassau and then cross Liberty to the left to walk in front of the Federal Reserve Bank to Yellin's impressive doorway, noting particularly the ironwork quasi-frieze above the entry.

As you come down toward William Street you see on the side of a building a very battered, amateur mural version of the famous *Sunday Afternoon on the Island of La Grande Jatte* by Georges Seurat (1859–1891). Crude it may seem to you, but let your eyes drink it in—because they're just about to get a nasty aesthetic shock when you turn the corner. There you discover a tiny triangular park, with the alternative names of Legion Memorial Square and Louise Nevelson Plaza; and it was Louise Nevelson (1900–1988) herself who assembled the seven black metal pieces, collectively called *Shadows and Flags*, that adorn this space. There is worse to follow. If you go down to the bottom apex of the triangle and look back, you can see another modern sculpture, this time on the far side of the street next to the towering aluminum-and-glass slab that is Chase Manhattan Plaza: *Group of Four Trees* by Jean Dubuffet (1901–1985). This was presented to the bank by its former chairman, David Rockefeller (b. 1915), and one has seriously to question the man's motives. Constructed of fiberglass, aluminum, and steel, this black-and-white piece is a monstrous—five storys high!—version of the sort of pallid fungus you don't want to find in your cellar. There is some exquisite modern public sculpture in Manhattan, but for no inferrable reason the Financial District as a whole seems to have eschewed it in favor of such ultimately sterile exercises as the ones you can see from here.

Cross to continue down the left-hand side of Liberty Street. On your right is the very appealing facade of 80 Maiden Lane.

Along Pine Street

On reaching Pearl Street, turn right, then cross Cedar Street to turn right onto Pine Street. On your right, at 70 Pine Street, you find an entrance that has above it what appears to be a model of the Empire State Building. In fact, it's a model of 70 Pine Street itself, which is the "Fake Empire State" you saw earlier. Sixty-seven storys tall and done in Art Deco style, this is now the American International Group Building but was originally designed in 1932 by architects Clinton & Russell as the Cities Service Building. After American International moved here in 1978, the company conducted a major restoration, and the results of that effort can be well appreciated if you step into the lobby through the entrance further along (the main doors are now for emergency use only). The building is extremely graceful; from here on narrow Pine Street you can get only the vaguest impression of its tower, even by crossing the street and craning upwards. When it was built it was a dominant feature of the Lower Manhattan skyline, providing a lesser but nonetheless important visual counterpoint to its big sister further uptown.

A little further along on the left is the rear of 60 Wall Street, the J.P. Morgan Building (see page 157). Just as you get to the junction with William Street you find on the right the church called Our Lady of Victory, whose entrance is around the corner at 60 William Street. It's not a distinguished building, but its modesty brings

151

a refreshing touch to the street. Once you've crossed William Street you'll be pleased to notice as you glance to your right that we've considerably given you a second chance to admire Dubuffet's *Group of Four Trees*. It illuminates Chase Manhattan Plaza, a 60-story skyscraper erected in 1960 with Skidmore, Owings & Merrill as architects. For some while after World War II the importance of the Financial District seemed to be ebbing, and this declaration of confidence by the Chase Manhattan Bank (to the tune of $121 million) turned the tide.

Trinity Church Graveyard
Keep on, crossing Nassau Street and then Broadway. Directly ahead is the graveyard of Trinity Church. Here you can see (through railings) a dashing war memorial to those who died during the War of Independence. Among those buried here are the inventor Robert Fulton; Francis Lewis (1713–1802), one of the signatories of the Declaration of Independence; and Hugh Williamson (1735–1819), a signatory of the US Constitution. Beyond the cemetery you can see the Trinity Towers from a different angle. If you look behind you over Broadway you can see the former Equitable Building (opened in 1915), at 120 Broadway, which is another divinely attractive skyscraper; its architect was Ernest R. Graham (1866–1936), who, working for Daniel Hudson Burnham (1846–1912), also designed the Flatiron (see page 108). The building here, a sheer-rise giant of its day, aroused as much enthusiasm as the World Trade Center's towers in more recent times, and was directly responsible for the introduction in 1916 of the USA's first skyscraper zoning regulations.

Trinity Church
Go down Broadway a block to the immaculate Trinity Church itself. This neo-Gothic building was erected in 1846, with the architect being Richard M. Upjohn (1828–1903), and is the third on the site; the building is thus considerably younger than St. Paul's Chapel (see page 147), although the church itself is much older, being the oldest (and richest) Episcopal congregation in the city.

Trinity is one of the largest commercial landlords in Manhattan, currently owning no fewer than 27 commercial buildings in Lower Manhattan to a total of nearly 600,000 m² (6 million sq ft) of office, manufacturing, and retail space. Since 1969 it has mounted the Noonday Concerts in the church for the Wall Street community, and in 1983 it opened the Trinity Bookstore at 74 Trinity Place. Thanks to its continuing income it has been able to give grants to over 1,700 churches and religious organizations of different denominations all over the world.

The building, while splendid, nevertheless seems surprisingly modest to be the hub of all this city-wide, national, and even international activity, although its tower, at 85 m (280 ft), was the tallest structure in Manhattan at the time of building. The sandstone of which the church is made was quarried at Little Falls, New Jersey.

Immediately as you go through the outer door you find a plaque commemorating Queen Elizabeth II's 1976 visit. The doors are magnificent in themselves: Massively bronze and depicting biblical scenes, they were donated in 1896 by parishioner William Waldorf Astor (1848–1919) in memory of his father, John Jacob Astor Jr. (1822–1890), were designed by the Viennese artist Karl Bitter (1867–1895), and had their production

Plate 27: *As a city built on an island, Manhattan is entirely dependent on bridge and tunnel transportation links with the rest of the nation. The upper of these two is Manhattan Bridge, the other the famous Brooklyn Bridge (see page 138).*

Plate 28: *City Hall has had a rowdy history, because it is here that most of the city's political demonstrations make their destination—although in more peaceful times the same is true of the famous tickertape parades (see page 136).*

Plate 29: The World Trade Center's (in)famous Twin Towers. The joke goes that the view from the observation platform here is better than from that of the Empire State Building—because from here you can't see the Twin Towers! (see page 148).

Plate 30: The exotic palms and high glass atrium of the World Financial Center's Winter Garden create a delightful setting in which to take refreshment (see page 148).

Plate 31: *The urban canyons of the Financial District can, perhaps surprisingly, offer extremely interesting walks for the visitor (see page 146).*

Plate 32: The East Coast Memorial in Battery Park was dedicated in 1963 and commemorates members of the US armed forces who lost their lives during World War II in the US coastal waters of the Atlantic (see page 164).

Plate 33: From Battery Park you can enjoy beautifully evocative views of the Statue of Liberty far across the water (see page 162).

overseen (although he died before they were hung) by Richard Morris Hunt (1827–1895). The interior is not particularly special, although it has a pleasing ambience of matured antiquity. The high altar, designed by Frederick Clarke Withers (1828–1901) in 1877 and a gift from John Jacob Astor Jr. in memory of *his* father, William B. Astor (1792–1875), is divided into three panels of glass mosaics and semiprecious stones. The reredos, done in Carrara marble, red Lisbon marble, and Caen stone from Normandy, shows scenes from the life of Christ. The organ has nearly 9,000 pipes. It was originally built in 1924 by the Ernest Skinner Company of Boston and then rebuilt in 1958 and again in 1974 by Aeolian Skinner. There are separate keyboards at either end of the church. You might also want to have a look at the stained-glass windows, which are rare for their period. At that time US churches almost invariably had clear glass.

Once you've finished with Trinity Church you'll find the Wall Street 4 and 5 station almost directly outside, or you could walk a little way along Wall Street to the 2 and 3 line station.

The Wall Street Shuffle

FINANCIAL DISTRICT WALK 2

Summary: This second stroll through the Financial District starts where the previous one left off, and it would be possible to do both walks in a single (long) afternoon. The early part of the walk is characterized by more of the magnificent architecture you saw along the previous route; later the style moves from the splendid toward more human values, although this in no way diminishes the aesthetic quality. The walk ends at one of New York's most fascinating historic houses.

Start:	Trinity Church.
Transportation:	Subway lines 4 and 5 to Wall Street Station, or lines 2 and 3 to the other Wall Street Station, or lines 1, 9, N, and R to Rector Street.
Finish:	Fraunces Tavern.
Transportation:	Subway lines J, M, and Z from Broad Street.
Length:	About 2.5 km (1½ miles).
Time:	About 1 hour.
Refreshments:	As with the previous walk, there's not much on offer aside from hot-dog stalls and the occasional very expensive restaurant … and Delmonico's.
Which day:	Not Sunday for the Fraunces Tavern Museum.
Highlights:	New York Stock Exchange
	Federal Hall National Memorial
	Bank of Manhattan Trust Building (Trump Building)
	Merchants' Exchange (Regent Wall Street)
	J.P. Morgan Building
	Delmonico's
	India House
	Fraunces Tavern

If you've come by the 4 and 5 lines you'll emerge at street level more or less outside Trinity Church. From the other Wall Street Station, walk westward along Wall Street to Broadway (although in a moment you'll be walking eastward along the same stretch); from Rector Street Station come up Rector Street to Broadway. The itinerary assumes you start directly outside Trinity.

The New York Stock Exchange
Cross Broadway and enter Wall Street. Over to your right, just beyond the intersection with New Street, is the New York Stock Exchange. Walk a block further and

around into Broad Street to find the visitors' entrance at number 20. The New York Stock Exchange was founded in 1792 when 22 merchants (plus two more a few months later) signed an agreement for the trading of securities. It was called the Buttonwood Agreement because the merchants met daily under a buttonwood tree that grew near here, outside 68 Wall Street. However, even by the end of the year the market, such as it was, had become moribund and it remained that way for a quarter of a century. It is therefore more realistic to trace the history of the Exchange to March 1817, when 28 brokers agreed a constitution for the New York Stock and Exchange Board (the Stock Exchange is still often called the "Big Board"), and laid down membership rules. Bank and insurance stock predominated, although within a couple of decades railroad securities became paramount, remaining thus more or less until 1903, the year in which the current building was erected on the site of the building that had been the Exchange's headquarters since 1865. Before that the Exchange had been markedly peripatetic.

The architect here was George B. Post (1837–1913); an extension was added in 1923 by the architects Trowbridge & Livingston. You might want to retreat to the other side of Broad Street properly to appreciate the strength of the Classical facade, which has six fluted Corinthian columns, each nearly 16 m (52 ft) tall, and, above these, a triangular pediment containing bas relief figures collectively called *Integrity Protecting the Works of Man*. The originals of these were done by John Quincy Adams Ward (1830–1910) and Paul Wayland Bartlett (1865–1925) but, thanks to long-term urban erosion, what you see today are facsimiles.

Tickets to see the interior of the Stock Exchange are free, although you're advised to be here first thing in the morning to get them. There are self-guided tours, or you can sit in the Gallery for a while watching the frenzied activities of the traders on the floor below; the trading floor is 56 m (183 ft) long and 30 m (100 ft) wide and, were you to be able to see it empty, offers yet one more of Manhattan's magnificent interior spaces, with a height of 24 m (79 ft).

Federal Hall National Memorial

Go back up Broad Street to Wall Street. Diagonally opposite you is Federal Hall, the most striking feature of which is certainly the large statue (1883) of George Washington (1732–1799), by the same John Quincy Adams Ward who did the figures on the Stock Exchange's pediment and much else of the public sculpture of Manhattan during the latter part of the 19th century. The first Federal Hall built on this site (1699) was New York's second City Hall. One of the highlights of the old building's career is commemorated by a wall plaque:

Ohio Company of Associates

On this site the United States in Congress, assembled on the 13th day of July in the Year of Our Lord 1787 and of their sovereignty and independence the 12th, enacted an ordinance for the government of the territory northwest of the River Ohio, by which it was dedicated forever to freedom. Under another ordinance, passed here by the same body on the 27th day of the same month, Manasseh Cutler [1742–1823], acting for the "Ohio Company of Associates," an organization of soldiers of the Revolutionary Army, purchased from the Board of Treasury for settlement a portion of the waste and vacant land of the territory on April 7th 1788. Rufus Putnam [1738–1824], heading a party of 48, began the first settlement at Marietta, and on July 15th Arthur St. Clair [1734–1818] as first Governor established civil government in the territory. From these beginnings sprang the states of Ohio, Indiana, Illinois, Michigan and Wisconsin.

This was a significant event indeed: It was the genesis of the Northwest Territory. Cutler was an interesting character. He was a schoolteacher, whaling merchant, lawyer, and congregational minister by turn, and was cited for heroism as a War of Independence chaplain. When he said that the territory was "dedicated forever to freedom" he actually meant it. In those times the victorious rebels often spoke of freedom without any conception that this might extend to slaves (Washington himself was one of the largest slaveowners in the land), but Cutler had profound anti-slavery views and was probably responsible for those sections of the Northwest Ordinance prohibiting the owning of or trade in slaves.

The building was remodeled in 1788 by Pierre L'Enfant (1754–1825), and the following year served as the venue for Washington's inauguration. The new building was designed in 1834 by Ithiel Town (1784–1844) and Alexander Jackson Davis (1803–1892), and actually built in 1842. It served as the US Custom House until 1863, when that moved to 55 Wall Street (see page 157). Thereafter it was put to miscellaneous use until, in 1955, the National Park Service took it over and designated it a memorial to Washington. It is widely regarded as New York's most distinguished example of Greek Revival architecture. The entrance is up a steepish flight of stairs and between the central pair of eight 10 m (33 ft) Doric columns. The domed rotunda inside bears examination, and there are also temporary art exhibitions.

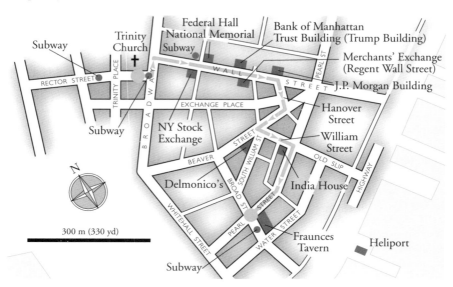

The "Crown Jewel of Wall Street"

Further along on the left is the "Crown Jewel of Wall Street," the former Bank of Manhattan Trust Building, at number 40; today it is one of the several Trump Buildings scattered around the city. When it was being put up, in 1929—with architects H. Craig Severance (1879–1941) and Yasuo Matsui—it was thought that, at 72 storys, it would be the tallest building in the world. And so it was, but only briefly, for in a genuine case of architectural rivalry the Chrysler Building (see page 96), completed the following year, had a spire secretly added to its plans to bring it the laurels, and the "Crown Jewel" had to make do with claiming the world's highest usable floor and observation deck. Although you can't see it from street level, the top of the skyscraper is distinguished by a superbly ornate pyramidal crown and a Gothic spire. Donald Trump (b. 1946) gave the building a welcome complete refurbishment in 1996.

The Regent Wall Street

On the opposite side of the street, 37 Wall Street offers another very pretty frontage. Number 55, also on the right-hand side of the street, was built in 1836–1842 by architect Isaiah Rogers (1800–1869) and heightened by McKim, Mead & White in 1907. Before that, since 1823, there had been on this site the old Merchants' Exchange, which was destroyed in the fire that swept Lower Manhattan in 1835. The basement of this new Merchants' Exchange was initially used as a prison! In 1863 the US Custom House moved in, and remained until 1907, when it moved to Bowling Green (see page 167). The building then became the headquarters of the National City Bank, which in 1955 merged with the City Bank–Farmers Trust Company to whose building at 20 Exchange Place (see below) an enclosed foot-bridge used to lead. This formed what is the USA's biggest bank, Citibank. During bank hours you could go in and have a look around at the excellent ceiling and at the tall arched windows with their Corinthian columns. At the start of 2000 the building changed functions again, and it is now the Regent Wall Street, a swank hotel. The old banking hall has become a banqueting hall.

A little along on the left, at number 60, is the J.P. Morgan Building, erected in 1988 with architects Kevin Roche, John Dinkeloo & Associates. This is topped by a stepped pyramid, and the center of the ground floor is a public atrium that goes through to Pine Street. The building as a whole has not received very good press, but in fact it's handsome enough, and the atrium, while hardly great art, is rather jolly in a kitsch fashion. There are various stores and you can get light refreshments.

Hanover Street

Just before 59 Wall Street (another fine-looking building), Hanover Street goes off to the right. It's a tiny, cramped, and somehow exceptionally pretty little street, one of the fabled Manhattan canyons but appealing because it's in miniature. Down on the right, Exchange Place leads off. At number 20, though better viewed from the intersection than close up, is a graceful 57-story Art Deco skyscraper built in 1931 as the headquarters for the City Bank–Farmers Trust Company by Cross & Cross. If you stroll down to it you can see the carved granite coins around its entrance. An entrance on its Hanover Street side, just past the intersection, leads into the Exchange Club.

Delmonico's

Go on a few paces and turn right to walk down Beaver Street. Directly ahead of you you can see the apex of the reddish and very handsome triangular Delmonico's Building, housing the famous restaurant. The original Delmonico's was opened a little way away, at 21–25 William Street, in 1827 by two Swiss brothers, Giovanni (d. 1842) and Pietro Delmonico; it was after their nephew, Lorenzo Delmonico (1813–1881), took over in 1831 that the restaurant rose to the heights of fame. By the end of the century it was the best-known restaurant in the land. In 1838 it relocated here, although it has since occupied various other sites in the city. Prohibition closed it down during much of the 1920s, but it was reopened by Oscar Tucci, who ran it until 1977. Since then it has had a troubled time (unlike its namesake hotel on Park Avenue at 59th). In 1982 it was reopened again at this site, and in 1998 there was yet a further reopening. Perhaps this time it'll have more success.

The present building was erected in 1891, the architect being James Brown Lord (1859–1902). The columns to either side of the doorway were, it is said, brought here from the Pompeii excavations.

Old Slip

Turn left down William Street, glancing to your right at the beautifully quaint old houses (many with ground floors now converted into restaurants) on South William Street. Cross William Street and keep on down it. Just after the intersection with Stone Street is a squat, deep-red Italianate building, India House. Since 1921 this has been the home of a businessmen's lunch club formed in 1918 by Willard Dickerman Straight (1880–1918). It was originally built in 1854 as the headquarters of the Hanover Bank.

To your left is Hanover Square Park, with a statue of Abraham De Peyster (1657–1728), who was Mayor of New York 1691–1693 and for a few months in 1700 was Governor. By the time he died he was one of the wealthiest merchants in the colony. The park was restored in 1978.

Pass along the front of India House to turn right onto Pearl Street. Just as you do so, look down Old Slip toward the river. This short street gets its name because it is built upon the filled-in old slipway. Its most obvious building, on the left-hand side as you look from here, is number 100, done in Renaissance Revival style in 1909 by Hunt & Hunt as the original 1st Precinct House for the NYPD. Since 1992 it has been the home of the New York City Landmarks Preservation Commission, a body founded in 1965 to identify and preserve historic districts, buildings, and other landmarks; their plaques are on many of the buildings described in this book.

Fraunces Tavern

Go along Pearl Street to reach Broad Street. On the corner to your left is Fraunces Tavern, one of New York's most historic buildings and a fascinating place to visit. It was built in 1719 at the behest of the French-born merchant Stephen (Étienne) de Lancey (1663–1741) at the corner of what were then called Queen and Canal streets. After his death it became a tavern, the Queen Charlotte. In 1762 it was bought by Samuel Fraunces (1722–1795) as part of his string of taverns in New York and Philadelphia; the tavern's name changed, for obvious reasons, at the Revolution.

It earned a widespread reputation for its fine English-style food and its desserts. Among its habitual patrons was George Washington, and in 1783 he chose the Long Room here as the venue for his victory farewell to the officers of the Continental Army. After the War of Independence, while New York was the nation's capital, the building was rented to the fledgling government and housed the departments of War, the Treasury, and Foreign Affairs before reverting to use as a tavern. In 1904 it was bought by the Sons of the Revolution in the State of New York as its head-quarters—justifiably, since it was here in 1876 that the first Sons of the Revolution association was organized. Preservation architect William H. Mesereau (1862–1933) was hired to restore/reconstruct the building, and in 1907 it was reopened as a museum and restaurant.

The restaurant has gone but the museum, spread over five buildings, is still going strong. Its focus is early American history, and to this end it has, in addition to the exhibits (both temporary and permanent), programs of lectures, commemorative concerts, family Saturday workshops, tours, and the like. The museum is worth its modest admission charge for the permanent exhibitions alone. In the Long Room, where Washington gave his celebrated address, there is a complete re-creation of an 18th-century public dining room; the Clinton Room, named for Governor George Clinton (1739–1812), who celebrated the British departure from New York in 1783 at the tavern, evokes an early 19th-century dining room; the Orientation Gallery and the section called "More than a Place to Drink" inform about the history of the tavern and of early New York; and "A Flash of Color" displays historic flags and standards, notably the various historical banners that have served as US national symbols.

Once you've finished at Fraunces Tavern, go a little way up Broad Street to the subway station.

A Stroll Through Battery Park

Summary: This walk begins where the previous walk left off, and doesn't take long if you're interested only in the pleasant stroll. On the other hand, Castle Clinton and the two museums will absorb quite a lot of time if you want to go through them properly, so don't underestimate the route. The biggest highlight of all is the excellent view you get of the Statue of Liberty—you'll be passing the slip for ferry departures should you decide to take an excursion there.

The area of Battery Park was called Capske Hook by the early colonists in imitation of a Native American word meaning "rocky ledge." From earliest times its position was recognized as of navigational importance, in that it offers access to both the Hudson and the harbor, and later, for the same reason, it was reckoned to be of military significance also. Its name change came because of the gun batteries once stationed here. Nearby, approximately where the Museum of the American Indian now stands, the Dutch built Fort Amsterdam over a period of years leading up to 1635; it was renamed Fort George after the British took it in 1664, and demolished in 1788. Much of the present area of the park was constructed on landfill during the 18th and 19th centuries (the stones from Fort Amsterdam/George were used as part of that landfill) and this process continues: During the building of the Brooklyn–Battery Tunnel in 1940–1952, for example, some 0.8 ha (2 acres) was added. To the north and west of the park is Battery Park City, 37 ha (92 acres) built from 1968 entirely on landfill, rather more than a quarter of it derived from the debris created during the construction of the World Trade Center (see page 148); the very end of the walk strays into the southern part of this area.

Start:	Fraunces Tavern.
Transportation:	Subway lines J, M, and Z to Broad Street.
Finish:	Bowling Green.
Transportation:	Subway lines 4 and 5 from Bowling Green.
Length:	About 2.5 km (1½ miles).
Time:	About 1 hour, plus visits.
Refreshments:	There are snack bars in Battery Park and more elevated eateries on the Battery Park City side of Pier A.
Which day:	Not Saturday for the Museum of Jewish Heritage.
Highlights:	Staten Island Ferry
	Shrine of St. Elizabeth Ann Seton
	New York Unearthed
	Statue of Liberty National Monument
	East Coast Memorial
	Castle Clinton

The Immigrants
Korean War Memorial
American Merchant Mariners' Memorial
Robert F. Wagner Jr. Park
Museum of Jewish Heritage
Museum of the American Indian/US Custom House

Emerging from the subway station, go to Fraunces Tavern (see page 158 for more information on this) at the corner of Pearl Street and Broad Street. Continue down Broad Street and cross Water Street. A very pretty clock sticks out from the otherwise anonymous building at 4 New York Plaza. At the bottom of Broad Street you reach South Street, the two halves of which are separated by the speeding traffic of Franklin Delano Roosevelt Drive. Turn right.

Staten Island Ferry

All along the East River side of South Street, on your left, are various termini for ferries to Governors Island, Weehawken, Port Liberté, and Jersey City. Last along this row is the terminus for the Staten Island Ferry; the boats go frequently (see page 177) and there is no charge for the half-hour trip, which offers excellent views of the Statue of Liberty. If you take the trip you'll find on Staten Island plenty of quiet and some fine historic buildings. Recommended visits are to the following:

- Conference (or Billopp) House, built before 1688, where an unsuccessful Revolutionary War peace conference was held in 1776;
- the Historic Richmond Town feature in La Tourette Park, which reconstructs 18th- and 19th-century life on the island and includes Voorlezer's House, built *c.* 1695;
- the Alice Austen House Museum, a farmhouse restored to look as it did in the 1890s and commemorating the work of the Victorian photographer Alice Austen (1866–1952);
- the Seguine Mansion, a stately Greek Revival grand home built in 1838 on the island's southern shore, facing Prince's Bay;
- the Memorial to Giuseppe Garibaldi (1807–1882) and the Garibaldi–Meucci Memorial Museum, housed in the home of the Italian inventor Antonio Meucci (1808–1889), where Garibaldi once sheltered; and
- Staten Island Zoo.

Shrine of St. Elizabeth Ann Seton

Turn briefly right up Whitehall Street, then cross to the left to go around Peter Minuit Plaza. Minuit (1580–1638) was the Dutch Director General of the colony of New Netherland who signed a treaty with the local native Americans and purportedly bought (in fact, as far as the aborigines were concerned, part-leased) the island of Manhattan for goods worth $24. As you swing around to the right into State Street you see, dwarfed by the surrounding skyscrapers, a tiny church built of red brick and with two tiers of pillars. Cross Water Street to reach it.

The church is the Church of Our Lady of the Rosary with, next door to it, the Shrine of St. Elizabeth Ann Seton (1774–1821). Born Elizabeth Ann Bayley into an upper-class New York Episcopalian family, she married William Magee Seton, scion of a wealthy trading family, at the age of 19. In 1797 she founded the Society for the Relief of Poor Widows with Small Children, but only six years later, in 1803, found herself a widow with five children. In 1805 she converted to Catholicism, to the wrath of her family; shunned, she moved with the children to Baltimore in 1808, where she founded a Catholic elementary school for girls. In 1809 she founded the USA's first Catholic religious order, the American Sisters of Charity. She was beatified in 1963 and canonized in 1975—the first US-born saint.

The Rectory
The Rectory, at number 7, was originally the John Watson House, and was erected in Federal style by the architect John McComb Jr. (1763–1853) in *c.* 1800. It's an interesting house in itself for, while the Ionic columns of the facade are in a curve to match that of the street, the house is actually L-shaped—hence the unusual balcony over the double entrance. Seton lived here for a couple of years from 1801, and her daughter Rebecca was born here. Of course, at that time the house was not isolated as it now is but was one of a community of similarly grand Federal mansions.

A little further up State Street, at number 17, is a program (annex) of the South Street Seaport Museum called New York Unearthed, dedicated to New York's archaeological history. The building was put up in the 1980s as yet another of the identikit skyscrapers of the period. When the landlords failed to be able to rent sufficient offices the museum was opened instead.

The Statue of Liberty
You're now going to head for Battery Park, on the other side of State Street. Go back to Water Street and cross it, then cross rightwards over State Street.

Enter Battery Park and veer leftwards to go around the Promenade, roughly parallel with the Hudson River. Down by the river you'll see a line of pay binoculars, and possibly a little cluster of people feeding quarters into them. When you follow with your eyes their line of attention it'll probably be the first time that you notice the Statue of Liberty out in the distance over the water. On a good day you can see "The Lady" surprisingly clearly. In fact, in such conditions you're better off eschewing the optically shoddy binoculars and relying on the naked eye.

Originally called *Liberty Enlightening the World*, the statue stands on Liberty Island, known until 1956 as Bedloe's Island, and was a gift made in 1885 to the people of the newborn United States of America from the French people, who had had their own revolution just a few years after the American one. The idea for it came from the French historian Edouard de Laboulaye (1811–1883), who did not live to see his notion reified. Work started in 1875 under the sculptor Frédéric-Auguste Bartholdi (1834–1904). His smaller-scale model for the statue can be seen near the Pont de Grenelle in Paris. For the real thing, copper sheets were hammered into shape and

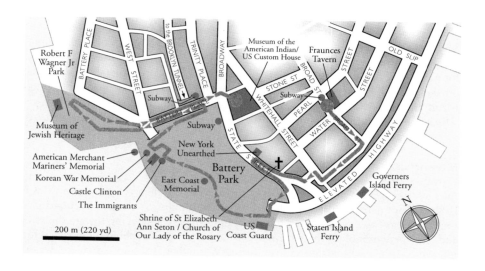

mounted on a steel framework constructed under the supervision of first Eugène-Emmanuel Viollet-le-Duc (1814–1879) and then Alexandre-Gustave Eiffel (1832–1923), of Eiffel Tower fame. When the statue was completed in 1885—it weighed well over 200 tonnes and stood 46 m (151 ft) tall—it was taken to pieces again and shipped across the Atlantic for reassembly *in situ*. Its pedestal was done by Richard Morris Hunt (1827–1895) and the mounted statue was dedicated by President Grover Cleveland (1837–1908) on October 28, 1886. Declared a National Monument in 1924, it was restored in the mid-1980s by a joint French and US workforce for centennial celebrations in 1986. The famous sonnet "The New Colossus," written by Emma Lazarus (1849–1887) in 1883, and its plaque were added to the pedestal in 1903. The sonnet reads:

> *Not like the brazen giant of Greek fame,*
> *With conquering limbs astride from land to land;*
> *Here at our sea-washed, sunset gates shall stand*
> *A mighty woman with a torch, whose flame*
> *Is the imprisoned lightning, and her name*
> *Mother of Exiles. From her beacon-hand*
> *Glows world-wide welcome; her mild eyes command*
> *The air-bridged harbor that twin cities frame.*
> *"Keep, ancient lands, your storied pomp!" cries she*
> *With silent lips. "Give me your tired, your poor,*
> *Your huddled masses yearning to breathe free,*
> *The wretched refuse of your teeming shore.*
> *Send these, the homeless, tempest-tost to me,*
> *I lift my lamp beside the golden door!"*

163

Ellis Island

A short way upriver from where you're now standing you can catch a ferry to the Statue of Liberty National Monument (tickets on sale in Castle Clinton), which since 1965 has included also Ellis Island. From 1892 to 1924 Ellis Island was the gateway for more than half of the immigrants entering the USA. After a massive restoration during 1984–1990, it was reopened to the public with two new features: the Ellis Island Immigration Museum and the American Immigrant Wall of Honor, on which the descendants of immigrants have inscribed the names of their venturesome ancestors.

Memorials

Retreat a little from the river, past a snack bar, and you find a statuary memorial to the men and women of the US Coast Guard who served their country in World War II. Walk from here parallel with the river until you come to a massive sculpture of the American Eagle portrayed in full predatory savagery and facing toward the river and eight gray monoliths that are inscribed with the names of those members of the US armed forces who lost their lives during World War II in the US coastal waters of the Atlantic. This monument, the East Coast Memorial, was dedicated in 1963 by President John F. Kennedy (1917–1963), who lost his own life later that year.

Continuing, you come to a little fenced plaza within the park. On your left is where you can catch the ferry to Liberty and Ellis islands; on your right is another memorial, this time dedicated to wireless operators who for whatever reason have been lost at sea in course of their duties.

Most of the way across the plaza stands a statue, with a sword-bearing angel in front of it, of the Florentine navigator Giovanni da Verrazano or Verrazzano (*c.* 1485–1528), leader of the first European expedition credited with discovering Manhattan Island, which it did in April 1524 aboard the French caravel *La Dauphine*. The natives seemed friendly but the weather turned foul, and Verrazano decided to go back to sea and continue his quest for the Northwest Passage without he or any of his men having set foot on the island. The statue, cast in the Roman bronzeworks, *New York State*, was erected in 1909.

Castle Clinton

Come out of the plaza by the exit nearest you. The gray stack on your right is a memorial to General William Booth (1829–1912), founder of the Salvation Army. On your left you'll see a low, circular walled structure made of red sandstone. This is Castle Clinton, built in 1808–1811 as West Battery or Southwest Battery and renamed soon after, in 1815, in honor of De Witt Clinton (1769–1828). At the same time it became the HQ of the US Third Military District, which it remained only until 1820, when the HQ moved to Governors Island. Built on the site of various previous strongholds, it was one of a series of seven forts proposed for the city's defense by Colonel Jonathan Williams; the architecture is normally credited to John McComb Jr. but it seems that Williams did most of it himself with McComb being responsible only for the entrance. When originally constructed it stood some 60 m (200 ft) offshore, with a drawbridged wooden causeway connecting it to the mainland; as a result of landfill efforts from the 1850s onward, it is now set comfortably back from the water's edge. The defenses were impressive—those walls are nearly 2.5 m (8 ft) thick, and the fort held 28 cannon—but Castle Clinton never saw any military action, and in 1823 was decommissioned as redundant.

Taken over and converted by private enterprise, in 1824 it became Castle Garden, a hall for popular entertainment that, after renovation in 1848, was in its day the largest such hall in the USA, seating over 6,000; singer Jenny Lind (1820–1887), the "Swedish Nightingale," made her US debut here in 1850.

The city took the fort back in 1853, and between 1855 and 1892 it served as the Emigrant Landing Depot; before it was replaced by Ellis Island, seven or eight million hopeful immigrants (estimates vary) were processed through here. McKim, Mead & White were commissioned in 1896 to convert it yet again (adding two storys), this time as the New York Aquarium, a highly popular attraction that was a particular favorite of President Franklin Delano Roosevelt (1882–1945). Rumor has it that it was in order to spite Roosevelt that city planner Robert Moses (1888–1981) determined to demolish it so that the site could be used for one end of his proposed Battery–Brooklyn suspension bridge, and then, when that plan failed, for a ventilation unit for the Brooklyn–Battery Tunnel. The Aquarium moved in 1941 to the Bronx Zoo and Moses succeeded in demolishing part of the building (essentially, the McKim, Mead & White additions) before the public furore could no longer be ignored, and then America's entry into World War II put a hold on all his schemes.

In 1950 the US Department of the Interior took the fort over and declared it a National Monument. It was restored during the 1970s and again during the 1990s; it now serves as a National Parks Visitor Center, and it is here that you can buy tickets for the Statue of Liberty/Ellis Island ferries. In the summer there are concerts in the fort.

A Stirring Statue

As you come out of the fort you see directly ahead the rear of a genuinely stirring statue, *The Immigrants*, "dedicated to the people of all nations who entered America through Castle Garden." It was done by Luis Sanguino (b. 1934) in 1973; this Spanish artist also did the statue of Ernest Hemingway (1899–1961) in Pamplona in 1968. Although not photorealistic, the faces and postures of the group of figures speak eloquently of the mixed emotions of the immigrating millions—their desperation to leave misery, poverty, and perhaps persecution behind; their eagerness to find paradise of a sort in the New World. It is one of New York's finest and most memorable public statues. Just behind it is the Hope Garden, which in summer is full of roses.

More Memorials

Walk around past Castle Clinton and diagonally toward the river to reach the Korean War Memorial, whose main figure depicts in cookie-cutter fashion an armed US soldier in an obelisk of black marble. The piece was done by Mac Adams (b. 1943); the memorial was dedicated in 1991 to all the US servicemen who lost their lives during the 1950–1953 conflict. It's best seen in evening light.

Continue in the same line right down to the river, toward the almost churchlike clocktower of Pier A, added in 1919 to a structure built in 1886 by architect George Sears Greene Jr. (1837–1922). It is the city's last surviving historic pier, and in the late 1990s underwent very substantial renovation (on the far side from where you're walking) to become a visitors' complex. Nearer to you is an astonishing piece of sculpture that is the American Merchant Mariners' Memorial, done in 1991 by the Venezuelan-born sculptress Escobar Marisol (b. 1930) and

> *dedicated to all merchant mariners who have served America from the Revolutionary War through the present day in the prosecution of war and in the pursuit of peaceful commerce [...] The sculpture was inspired by a photograph of the victims of a submarine attack on an American merchant ship during World War II. Left to the perils of the sea, the survivors later perished.*

It's an extremely dramatic piece: One of a group of obviously desperate men is reaching down to aid a colleague in the water of whom only the upwardly stretching arm and shoulder are visible. The focus of the sculpture changes depending on the state of the tide in the Hudson.

Robert F. Wagner Jr. Park and the Museum of Jewish Heritage
Follow the path around toward the exit from Battery Park, walking roughly parallel to Pier A. If you like, make a detour over to your right to have a look at the flagpole, presented to the city by the Dutch government in 1926 as a memorial to Peter Minuit; on the other side of the base is a relief map of the old Fort Amsterdam.

Exiting Battery Park, walk back along parallel with the other side of Pier A and into the Robert F. Wagner Memorial Park. You're now in Battery Park City, although you may not immediately be struck by any obvious difference, and are heading for the rather curiously shaped building a couple of hundred metres away—the Museum of Jewish Heritage, opened in September 1997 and with architecture by Kevin Roche (b. 1922). Before you reach it, however, you might want to browse around the park; although as a park it's rather dull, there are some interesting pieces of modern sculpture on view, notably *Ape & Cat (at the Dance)* (1993) by Jim Dine (b. 1935), *Resonating Bodies* (1996) by Tony Cragg (b. 1949), *Eyes* (1995) by Louise Bourgeois (b. 1911), and *Raven Puts the Light in the Sky* (1980) by Ken Mowatt (b. 1944).

The museum's core exhibition comprises some 15,000 objects—documents, photographs, artifacts, home movies, and documentary film footage along with audio and video testimony—amassed since 1986, and the collection is still expanding as Holocaust survivors and their descendants donate new material. Of the core collection, some 2,000 photographs, 800 historical and cultural artifacts, and 24 original documentary films are on rotating display.

The US Custom House
Coming out of the Museum of Jewish Heritage, retrace your steps through the Wagner Park and then keep going past the outside of Battery Park along Battery Place. In due course you reach a very complicated intersection, where Broadway

ends and Battery Place and State Street diverge. On the other side of this intersection, with its entrance facing at right-angles to where you stand, is a very grand-looking Beaux-Arts building, the US Custom House (more fully the Alexander Hamilton US Custom House). To reach it, carry on a little along the sidewalk toward the very pretty entrance (dating from 1905) to the Bowling Green Subway Station, then cross at the WALK/DON'T WALK sign.

Opened in 1907 and with architect Cass Gilbert (1859–1934), this was New York's third Custom House, following those at what are now Federal Hall National Memorial (see page 156) and the Regent Wall Street (see page 157). The sculptor Daniel Chester French (1850–1931) was responsible for the four seated figures that flank the entrance: from left to right they are *Asia, America, Europe,* and *Africa.* Above, along the cornice, there are twelve smaller figures representing the great trading powers of both the ancient and modern world.

The Museum of the American Indian

The Custom House is today the home of the George Gustav Heye Center, opened in 1994 as part of the Smithsonian Institution's National Museum of the American Indian; Heye (1874–1957) was a wealthy New Yorker who amassed the core collection of Native American artifacts. The Center is one of three divisions of the museum, the other two being the Museum on the Mall in Washington DC and the Cultural Resources Center in Suitland, Maryland. W. Richard West, himself a Southern Cheyenne and the museum's director, has explained the moral importance of the New York site:

Indians migrate to New York, now as in the past, for the same reason other do: to seek their fortunes. But beyond that, an ancient place of exchange among Indians, has become a center of new thinking about Native cultures. The Hopi of Arizona have a prophecy of a time when they would travel to the east to meet with the nations of the world in a "house of mica." Through the exhibitions and programs of the National Museum of the American Indian's Heye Center, the Custom House, too, is becoming a place for the exchange of ideas among peoples.

There are some one million items in the museum as a whole, of which about 70 percent are devoted to the indigenous peoples of North America and the remainder to those of South America. The geographical scope runs from the Arctic to Tierra del Fuego, and includes the Caribbean. And there is for an ethnographic museum a refreshing approach to the question of who many of these items actually belong to: "Human remains and funerary objects, religious and ceremonial artifacts, communally owned tribal property, or any holdings acquired illegally are returned upon request to individual descendants or tribal groups who can demonstrate a cultural affiliation and factual claim to the property in question." You'll almost certainly want to spend the rest of the day here, even if you got here in the morning! Astonishingly, admission is free. Once you feel able finally to drag yourself away, you can either cross the intersection to the subway entrance you saw earlier or, more safely, go across the bottom of Broadway and a few tens of paces back along the other side of Battery Place.

Further Information

All times are given based on the the 24-hour clock.

AN UPPER WEST SIDE MUSEUM WALK (UPPER WEST SIDE WALK 1)
(pages 10–15)

Refreshments
CAFÉ LALO
201 West 83rd Street; tel 212 496-6031.
Mon–Thur 08.00–02.00, Fri 08.00–04.00,
Sat 09.00–04.00, Sun 09.00–02.00.

Attractions
THE CHILDREN'S MUSEUM OF MANHATTAN
Tisch Building, 212 West 83rd Street; tel
212 721-1223. Wed–Sun 10.00–17.00.

HAYDEN PLANETARIUM/FREDERICK
PHINEAS AND SANDRA PRIEST ROSE
CENTER FOR EARTH AND SPACE
As per American Museum of Natural
History.

AMERICAN MUSEUM OF NATURAL HISTORY
Central Park West at 79th Street; tel 212
769-5100. Sun–Thur 10.00–17.45, Fri–Sat
10.00–20.45. Guided tours of the museum's
highlights (no extra charge) go at 10.15,
11.15, 12.15, 13.15, 14.15 and 15.15. The
various eateries within the museum have
their own hours and these—as well as the
range of eateries available—change
periodically; best to check at the desk on
arrival or to phone beforehand.

NEW-YORK HISTORICAL SOCIETY
2 West 77th Street; tel 212 873-3400.
Tue–Sun 11.00–17.00. Library Tue–Sat
11.00–17.00.

FROM THE DAKOTA TO THE LINCOLN CENTER (UPPER WEST SIDE WALK 2) (pages 16–23)

Refreshments
PANEVINO RISTORANTE
Avery Fisher Hall, Lincoln Center Plaza; tel
212 874-7000. Sat and matinee days
11.30–14.00, performance evenings
17.00–20.00.

CAFÉ VIENNA
Avery Fisher Hall, Lincoln Center Plaza.
Nightly 17.00 to end of intermission; open
from 12.00 on matinee days.

Attractions
CONGREGATION SHEARITH ISRAEL
99 Central Park West at 70th Street; tel 212
873-0300.

CHRIST AND ST. STEPHEN'S CHURCH
120 West 69th Street; tel 212 787-2755.
Open to the public Mon–Fri 08.30–17.30.

DOROTHY AND LEWIS B. CULLMAN CENTER
(NEW YORK PUBLIC LIBRARY FOR THE
PERFORMING ARTS)
Lincoln Center Plaza; tel 212 642-0142.

MUSEUM OF AMERICAN FOLK ART
2 Lincoln Square; tel 212 977-7170.
Tue–Sun 11.30–19.30.

LINCOLN CENTER GUIDED TOURS
These go from the foyer of the
Metropolitan Opera House daily at 10.30,
12.30, 14.30 and 16.30, and last about an
hour; get there 15 min before tour starts.
Advance reservations are strongly advised
(tel 212 875-5350 between 10.00 and
16.30), as is checking with tour desk (same

number) the day before your planned tour in case of last-minute schedule changes.

NEW YORK STATE THEATER
Lincoln Center Plaza; tel 212 870-5570.

METROPOLITAN OPERA HOUSE
Lincoln Center Plaza; tel 212 362-6000. Backstage tours Mon–Fri 15.45, Sat 10.00, but check first because times alter periodically.

AVERY FISHER HALL
Lincoln Center Plaza; tel 212 875-5030. Mon–Sat 10.00–18.00, Sun 12.00–18.00; also open 30 min after start of any performance.

CORK GALLERY
Avery Fisher Hall, Lincoln Center Plaza; tel and hours as per Avery Fisher Hall.

VIVIAN BEAUMONT THEATER
Lincoln Center Plaza; tel 212 239-6200.

JUILLIARD SCHOOL
Lincoln Center Plaza; tel 212 769-7406.

ALICE TULLY HALL
Lincoln Center Plaza; tel 212 875-5050. Office hours (and hence doors open) Mon–Sat 11.00–18.00, Sun 12.00–18.00. Hours extended on performance nights to 30 min after start of performance.

WALTER READE THEATER
Lincoln Center Plaza; tel 212 875-5600. Daily 13.30 until 15 min after end of last performance.

STANLEY H. KAPLAN PENTHOUSE AND DANIEL AND JOANNA S. ROSE REHEARSAL STUDIO
Lincoln Center Plaza; tel 212 875-5050.

FROM COLUMBUS CIRCLE TO THE SWEDISH COTTAGE (CENTRAL PARK WALK 1) (pages 24–35)

Refreshments
THE TAVERN ON THE GREEN
Central Park West between 66th and 67th

streets; tel 212 873-3200. Mon–Thur 12.00–15.30 and 17.00–23.00ish, Fri 12.00–15.30 and 17.00–23.30ish, Sat–Sun 10.00–15.30 and 17.00–23.30ish.

LOEB BOATHOUSE CAFÉ
East Side between 74th and 75th streets; tel 212 517-2233. Mon–Fri 12.00–16.30 and 17.30–22.00, Sat–Sun 11.00–16.30 and 17.30–22.00.

TRUMP INTERNATIONAL HOTEL AND TOWER
1 Central Park West; tel 212 299-1000.

THE CAROUSEL
Mid-Park at 64th Street; tel 212 879-0244. Hours vary according to the weather, but all being well are daily Apr–Nov 10.00–18.00, Nov–Apr 10.00–16.30.

CHESS & CHECKERS HOUSE
East Side at 65th Street; tel 212 794-6564. Hours as for the Dairy. Indoor tables available weekends only.

THE DAIRY
East Side at 65th Street; tel 212 794-6564. Tue–Sun Apr–Oct 10.00–17.00, Nov–Mar 10.00–16.00.

SHEEP MEADOW
Apr–Nov 11.00–dusk except when wet.

LOEB BOATHOUSE
East Side between 74th and 75th streets. *Rowing-boat rental:* Mid-Apr–mid-Oct 10.00 to 1 hr before dusk. Tel 212 517-2233. *Chauffeured gondola rental:* Mar–mid-Oct 17.30–22.00. Tel 212 517-2233. *Bike rental:* Mar–Oct 09.00–17.00. Tel 212 861-4137.

HENRY LUCE NATURE OBSERVATORY
Belvedere Castle, Central Park; tel 212 722-0210. Tue–Sun 10.00–16.00.

SWEDISH COTTAGE MARIONETTE THEATRE
West Side at 79th Street; tel 212 988-9093. Phone this number or check http://www.centralpark.org/old/map/marionette.html for performance details.

FROM FREDERICK DOUGLASS CIRCLE TO GRAND ARMY PLAZA (CENTRAL PARK WALK 2)
(pages 36–45)

CONSERVATORY GARDEN
Fifth Avenue between 104th and 106th Streets; tel 212 860-1382. Daily 08.00–dusk.

NEW YORK ROAD RUNNERS CLUB
9 East 89th Street; tel 212 860-4455 and 212 996-6577.

KERBS MEMORIAL BOATHOUSE
East Side at 72nd Street; tel 212 360-8133 and 212 673-1102. Model boat rentals Sun–Fri 10.00–19.00, Sat 14.00–19.00.

TISCH CHILDREN'S ZOO/CENTRAL PARK WILDLIFE CENTER
East Side between 63rd and 66th Streets; tel 212 861-6030. Mon–Fri 10.00–16.30, Sat–Sun 10.00–16.30. Last tickets sold 30 min before closing.

THE ARSENAL
Fifth Avenue at 64th Street; tel 212 360-8111.

PLAZA HOTEL
Fifth Avenue at 59th Street; tel 212 759-3000.

SHERRY–NETHERLAND HOTEL
781 Fifth Avenue; tel 212 355-2800.

MUSEUM MILE (EAST SIDE MUSEUM WALK 1) (pages 46–54)

Refreshments
CAFÉ WEISSMAN
The Jewish Museum; tel 212 423-3230. Sun–Mon and Wed–Thur 11.00–17.45, Tue 11.00–20.00.

SOLOMON R. GUGGENHEIM MUSEUM CAFÉ
Solomon R. Guggenheim Museum; tel 212 423-3657. Mon–Wed 08.30–18.00, Thur 08.30–15.00, Fri–Sat 08.30–20.00.

Attractions
CHARLES A. DANA DISCOVERY CENTER
Central Park at Harlem Meer; tel 212 860-1370. Tue–Sun 10.00–16.00.

EL MUSEO DEL BARRIO
Heckscher Building, 1230 Fifth Avenue at 104th Street; tel 212 831-7272; fax 212 831-7927. Wed–Sun 11.00–17.00.

MUSEUM OF THE CITY OF NEW YORK
Fifth Avenue at 103rd Street; tel 212 534-1672. Wed–Sat 10.00–17.00, Sun 12.00–17.00. Tue preregistered groups only 10.00–14.00.

INTERNATIONAL CENTER OF PHOTOGRAPHY
1130 Fifth Avenue at 94th Street; tel 212 860-1777; fax 212 360-6490. Tue–Thur 10.00–17.00, Fri 10.00–20.00, Sat–Sun 10.00–18.00.
There is also a midtown branch: 1133 Avenue of the Americas at 43rd Street; tel 212 768-4682; fax 212 768-4688.

THE JEWISH MUSEUM
1109 Fifth Avenue at 92nd Street; tel 212 423-3230. Sun–Mon and Wed–Thur 11.00–17.45, Tue 11.00–20.00.

COOPER–HEWITT NATIONAL DESIGN MUSEUM
Fifth Avenue at 91st Street; tel 212 849-8400. Tue 10.00–21.00, Wed–Sat 10.00–17.00, Sun 12.00–17.00.

CHURCH OF THE HEAVENLY REST
Fifth Avenue at 90th Street; tel 212 369-8040. Mon–Fri 10.00–17.00, and at virtually any time Sun. Open for evening prayer 18.00 Tue and for Holy Eucharist 18.30 Wed.

NATIONAL ACADEMY OF DESIGN
1083 Fifth Avenue at 89th Street; tel 212 369-4880. Wed–Sun 12.00–17.00, Fri 10.00–18.00, Mon–Tue closed.

SOLOMON R. GUGGENHEIM MUSEUM
1071 Fifth Avenue at 89th Street; tel 212 423-3500. Sun–Wed 09.00–18.00, Fri–Sat 09.00–20.00.

GOETHE-INSTITUT NEW YORK/GERMAN
CULTURAL CENTER
1014 Fifth Avenue at 83rd Street; tel 212
439–8700; fax 212 439-8705. Information
Center/Library Tue, Thur 12.00–19.00,
Wed, Fri, Sat 12.00–17.00.

THE METROPOLITAN MUSEUM OF ART
1000 Fifth Avenue at 82nd Street; tel 212
535-7710. Tue–Thur and Sun 09.30–17.15,
Fri–Sat 09.30–20.45. Some galleries open
only from at 11.00 on Sun. Tickets include
(on same day) THE CLOISTERS, the
museum's branch for medieval art, which is
in Fort Tryon Park at the northern tip of
Manhattan: Tue–Sun 09.30–16.45 Nov–Feb
and 09.30–17.15 Mar–Oct.

FROM THE METROPOLITAN MUSEUM OF ART TO ST. VINCENT FERRER CHURCH (EAST SIDE MUSEUM WALK 2) (pages 55–59)

Refreshments
THE ORIGINAL SOUP BURG COFFEE HOUSE
& RESTAURANT
922 Madison Avenue; tel 212 737-0095.
Every day 05.00–20.00.

TORAYA
17 East 71st Street; tel 212 861-1700.
Mon–Sat 11.00–17.30.

PASTAFINA PASTA & PIZZA RESTAURANT
876 Lexington Avenue; tel 212 535-6240.
Daily 11.00–22.30.

Attractions
OWEN GALLERY
19 East 75th Street; tel 212 879-2415.
Tue–Sat 10.00–17.30.

THE WHITNEY MUSEUM OF AMERICAN ART
945 Madison Avenue at 75th Street; tel 212
570-3676 and 212 570-3652. Tue–Wed and
Fri–Sun 11.00–18.00, Thur 13.00–20.00.
There is a branch (Whitney Museum of
American Art at Philip Morris) at 120 Park
Avenue at 42nd Street. Mon–Fri
11.00–18.00, Thur 11.00–19.30. Gallery
Talks and Sculpture Court Mon–Sat
07.30–21.30, Sun 11.00–19.00.

ST. JAMES' CHURCH
865 Madison Avenue; tel 212 288-4100 and
212 774-4200. Open 08.00–19.00 for
prayer and contemplation.

THE FRICK COLLECTION
1 East 70th Street; tel 212 288-0700.
Tue–Sat 10.00–18.00, Sun 13.00–18.00.

THE AMERICAS SOCIETY
680 Park Avenue; tel 212 249-8950.
Tue–Sun 10.00–18.00.

7TH REGIMENT ARMORY
643 Park Avenue; tel 212 744-2968. Open
by appointment only.

CHINA INSTITUTE
125 East 65th Street; tel 212 744-8181.
Open only during exhibitions. Mon and
Wed–Sat 10.00–17.00, Tue 10.00–20.00,
Sun 13.00–17.00.

ST. VINCENT FERRER CHURCH
Lexington Avenue at 66th Street; tel 212
744-2080. Open various hours—best to
phone ahead.

FROM THE MUSEUM OF AMERICAN ILLUSTRATION TO THE MUSEUM OF TELEVISION AND RADIO (EAST SIDE MUSEUM WALK 3) (pages 60–65)

Attractions
MUSEUM OF AMERICAN ILLUSTRATION
128 East 63rd Street; tel 212 838-2560. Tue
10.00–20.00, Wed–Fri 10.00–17.00, Sat
12.00–16.00.

THIRD CHURCH OF CHRIST, SCIENTIST
583 Park Avenue; tel 212 838-2855.
Reading Room at 147 East 62nd Street (off
Lex) open Mon–Tue and Thur–Fri
12.00–19.30, Wed 12.00–19.00, Sat
10.00–16.00, Sun 13.00–16.00.

CENTRAL PRESBYTERIAN CHURCH
593 Park Avenue; tel 212 838-0808.

CHRIST CHURCH UNITED METHODIST
CHURCH
520 Park Avenue; tel 212 838-3036. Open
07.00–09.00 for prayer and meditation.

ASIA SOCIETY AT MIDTOWN
502 Park Avenue; tel (main headquarters)
212 288-6400. Open only during events.

SPANIERMAN GALLERY
45 East 58th Street; tel 212 832-0208.
Mon–Sat 09.30–17.30.

F.A.O. SCHWARZ
767 5th Avenue; tel 212 644-9400.

IBM BUILDING
590 Madison Avenue.

AT&T BUILDING
550 Madison Avenue.

TRUMP TOWER
725 Fifth Avenue.

MUSEUM OF MODERN ART
11 West 53rd Street; tel 212 708-9480.
Sat–Tue and Thur 10.30–17.45, Fri
10.30–20.15.

AMERICAN CRAFT MUSEUM
40 West 53rd Street; tel 212 956-3535.
Tue–Sun 10.00–18.00, Thur 10.00–20.00.

MUSEUM OF TELEVISION AND RADIO
25 West 52nd Street; tel 212 621-6600.
Tue–Wed and Sat–Sun 12.00–18.00, Thur
12.00–20.00, Fri 12.00–21.00.

ST. PATRICK'S CATHEDRAL AND
THE ROCKEFELLER CENTER
(pages 66–73)

Refreshments
RAINBOW ROOM
GE Building, 30 Rockefeller Plaza, 65th
floor; tel 212 632-5000.
This was closed for renovation during
Spring 2000, so phone first to make sure it's
reopened.

Attractions
ST. THOMAS' EPISCOPAL CHURCH
1 West 53rd Street at Fifth Avenue; tel 212
757-7013.

ST. PATRICK'S CATHEDRAL
Fifth Avenue from 50th Street to 51st Street;
tel 212 753-2261; fax 212 755-4128; Parish
House (for all correspondence) 460
Madison Avenue, New York, NY 10022.
Every day 07.00–20.45.

SAKS FIFTH AVENUE
611–21 Fifth Avenue; tel 1-800 347-9177.
Mon–Fri 09.00–21.00; Sat 09.00–17.00;
Sun 12.00–18.00.

DAHESH MUSEUM
601 Fifth Avenue at 48th Street; tel 212
759-0606. Tue–Sat 11.00–18.00.

RADIO CITY MUSIC HALL
1260 Sixth Avenue at 49th Street; tel 212
632-3975. Tours hourly, last 1hr Mon–Sat
10.00–17.00, Sun 11.00–17.00.

GE BUILDING
30 Rockefeller Plaza; tel 212 632-3975.
Always open.

NBC EXPERIENCE
30 Rockefeller Plaza; tel 212 664-3700.
Mon–Sat 08.30–17.30, Sun 09.30–16.30,
extended Nov 26–Jan 2 to Mon–Sat
07.00–22.00, Sun 09.00–21.00. Tours every
15–30 min, last about 70 min. Children
under 6 not admitted.

CHRISTIE'S NEW YORK
20 Rockefeller Plaza; tel 212 636-2000.
Every day 10.00–17.00.

GOTHAM BOOK MART & GALLERY
41 West 47th Street; tel 212 719-4448.
Mon–Fri 09.30–18.30, Sat 09.30–18.00.

THEATERLAND (pages 74–85)

Refreshments
GAIETY BAR (MCHALE'S)
Eighth Avenue at 46th Street; tel 212 997-
8885.

OLLIE'S
200B West 44th Street; tel 212 921-5988.

SARDI'S
234 West 45th Street; tel 212 221-8440.

BARRYMORES RESTAURANT
267 West 45th Street; tel 212 391-8400.

MOTO
328 West 45th Street; tel 212 459-9393.

KODAMA
301 West 45th Street; tel 212 582-8065.

CHEZ SUZETTE
675 Ninth Avenue; tel 212 581-9717.

LAKRUWANA
358 West 44th Street; tel 212 957-4480.

Theaters
NB: The phone numbers given are for the box offices. The repeated phone numbers represent centralized reservations.

WINTER GARDEN THEATER
304 West 47th Street; tel 212 439-6200.

BROADWAY THEATRE
1681 Broadway; tel 212 239-6200.

VIRGINIA THEATRE
245 West 52nd Street; tel 212 239-6200.

NEIL SIMON THEATRE
250 West 52nd Street; tel 212 307-4100.

TIMES SQUARE CHURCH
217–39 West 51st Street.

GERSHWIN THEATRE
222 West 51st Street; tel 212 307-4100.

CIRCLE IN THE SQUARE THEATRE
1633 Broadway; tel 212 307-2700.

AMBASSADOR THEATRE
215 West 49th Street; tel 212 239-6200.

EUGENE O'NEILL THEATRE
230 West 49th Street; tel 212 239-6200.

WALTER KERR THEATRE
219 West 48th Street; tel 212 239-6200.

LONGACRE THEATRE
220 West 48th Street; tel 212 239-6200.

CORT THEATRE
138 West 48th Street; tel 212 239-6200.

PALACE THEATRE
1564 Broadway; tel 212 307-4100.

BROOKS ATKINSON THEATRE
256 West 47th Street; tel 212 307-4100.

ETHEL BARRYMORE THEATRE
243 West 47th Street; tel 212 239-6200.

BILTMORE THEATRE
261 West 47th Street.

RICHARD RODGERS THEATRE
226 West 46th Street; tel 212 307-4100.

LUNT–FONTANNE THEATRE
205 West 46th Street; tel 212 307-4100.

MARRIOTT MARQUIS THEATRE
1535 Broadway; tel 212 307-4100.

LYCEUM THEATRE
149 West 45th Street; tel 212 239-6200.

ROUNDABOUT THEATRE
227 West 42nd Street; tel 212 719-1300.

BELASCO THEATRE
111 West 44th Street; tel 212 239-6200.

LAMBS THEATRE
130 West 44th Street; tel 212 239-6200.

SARDI'S
See details under Refreshments.

HELEN HAYES THEATRE
240 West 44th Street; tel 212 307-4100.

ST. JAMES THEATRE
246 West 44th Street; tel 212 239-6200.

MAJESTIC THEATRE
245 West 44th Street; tel 212 239-6200.

BROADHURST THEATRE
235 West 44th Street; tel 212 239-6200.

SHUBERT THEATRE
225 West 44th Street; tel 212 239-6200.

BOOTH THEATRE
222 West 45th Street; tel 212 239-6200.

MINSKOFF THEATRE
200 West 45th Street; tel 212 307-4100.

DUFFY THEATRE
1553 Broadway; tel 212 307-4100.

PLYMOUTH THEATRE
236 West 45th Street; tel 212 239-6200.

MUSIC BOX
239 West 45th Street; tel 212 239-6200.

ROYALE THEATRE
242 West 45th Street; tel 212 239-6200.

IMPERIAL THEATRE
249 West 45th Street; tel 212 239-6200.

JOHN GOLDEN THEATRE
252 West 45th Street; tel 212 239-6200.

MARTIN BECK THEATRE
302 West 45th Street; tel 212 239-6200.

PRIMARY STAGES
354 West 45th Street; tel 212 333-4052.

42ND STREET—THE SOUL OF MANHATTAN (pages 86–98)

Refreshments
CHEZ JOSEPHINE
414 West 42nd Street; tel 212 594-1925.
Mon–Sat 17.00–01.00.

BRYANT PARK GRILL
25 West 40th Street; tel 212 840-6500.
Mon–Sun 11.30–15.30 and 17.00–20.00.

GRAND CENTRAL OYSTER
BAR•RESTAURANT
Grand Central Terminal; tel 212 490-6650.
Mon–Fri 11.30–21.30; Sat 17.30–21.30.

Attractions
NEW YORK PUBLIC LIBRARY
Fifth Avenue & 42nd Street; tel 212 661-7220. Main research facilities Mon, Thur–Sat 10.00–18.00; Tue–Wed 11.00–19.30. Other departments are closed also Mon, and on the other days generally have more restricted hours of access.

CHRYSLER BUILDING
405 Lexington Avenue.

UNITED NATIONS HEADQUARTERS
First Avenue and 42nd–48th Streets.
Mon–Fri 09.00–16.45, Sat (and holidays) 09.15–16.45. Children under 12 must have adult accompaniment. Guided tours (about 1 hr) go every 10–15 min from visitors' entrance and are expensive.

FROM PENN STATION TO THE EMPIRE STATE BUILDING
(pages 99–106)

Refreshments
TICK TOCK DINER
481 Eighth Avenue at 34th Street; tel 212 268-8444; fax 212 268-8443. Never closes.

Attractions
GENERAL POST OFFICE BUILDING
421 Eighth Avenue; tel 212 967-8585. Open 24 hours a day, every day.

MADISON SQUARE GARDEN
Seventh Avenue between 31st and 33rd; tel 212 465-6776. Tours every hour on the hour Mon–Sat 10.00–15.00, Sun 11.00–15.00.

MACY'S
Herald Square, 151 West 34th Street; tel 212 695-4400. Mon–Sat 10.00–20.30, Sun 11.00–21.00.

EMPIRE STATE BUILDING
350 Fifth Avenue; tel (Helmsley–Spear Inc., managing agent) 212 736-3100.
Observatories: Every day 09.30–24.00; last tickets sold at 23.30. *New York Skyride:* tel 212 279-9777. Every day 10.00–22.00.

FROM THE FLATIRON TO THE STRAND BOOKSTORE (pages 107–112)

Refreshments
OLD TOWN BAR & RESTAURANT
45 East 18th Street; tel 212 529-6732.
Mon–Fri 11.30–00.30, Sat 12.00–01.00, Sun 12.00–22.00. Food stops serving at 23.30 Mon–Sat and 21.30 Sun.

PETE'S TAVERN
129 East 18th Street; tel 212 473-7676.
Similar hours and prices to those of the Old Town Bar.

Attractions
THE FLATIRON BUILDING
175 Fifth Avenue.

THEODORE ROOSEVELT BIRTHPLACE
28 East 20th Street; tel 212 260-1616.
Wed–Sun 09.00–17.00. Tours every hour on the hour 09.00–16.00.

STRAND BOOKSTORE
828 Broadway; tel 212 473-1489. Mon–Sat 9.30–22.30, Sun 11.00–22.30.

TWELFTH STREET BOOKS
11 East 12th Street; tel 212 645-4340.
Mon–Tue 10.00–20.00, Wed–Thur 10.00–19.00, Fri–Sat 10.00–21.00, Sun 11.00–18.00.

FROM UNION SQUARE TO THE FLATIRON (pages 113–118)

Refreshments
MAYROSE DINER
920 Broadway (at 21st); tel 212 533-3663.
Mon–Sat 07.00–00.00, Sun 07.00–21.00

Attractions
UNION SQUARE GREENMARKET
Early morning until twilight, depending on weather and traders' whim. Best on Wed, Fri, and Sat morning through to mid-afternoon. At other times there can be little or no evidence of the market's existence, although usually you'll find at least a stall or two.

GREEN ARC
Every day 12.00 until twilight, except in inclement weather.

A RAMBLE IN GREENWICH VILLAGE (pages 119–123)

Refreshments
PÓ
31 Cornelia Street; tel 212 645-2189. Tue 17.30–23.00, Wed–Sat 11.45–14.15 and 17.30–23.00, Sun 11.45–14.15 and 17.00–22.00.

LITTLE HAVANA
30 Cornelia Street; tel 212 255-2212.
Tue–Sun 17.00–23.00.

MARIE'S CRISIS CAFÉ & PIANO BAR
59 Grove Street; tel 212 243-9323. Daily 16.00–04.00. Music nightly from 21.30; singalongs on Fri.

Attractions
THE BITTER END
147 Bleecker Street; tel 212 673-7030.
Mon–Thur 20.00–02.00, Fri–Sat 20.00–04.00, Sun 19.30–02.00.

THE BOTTOM LINE
15 West 4th Street; tel 212 228-6300.
Typically doors open at 18.00 for the first show, which is at 19.30, and at 22.00 for the 22.30 show.

SOHO (pages 124–129)

Attractions
DEITCH PROJECTS
76 Grand Street; tel 212 343-7300. Tue–Sat 12.00–18.00.

THE DRAWING ROOM
40 Wooster Street; tel 212 219-2166. Tue and Thur–Fri 10.00–18.00, Wed 10.00–20.00, Sat 11.00–18.00.

ANIMAZING GALLERY
474 Broome Street; tel 212 226-7374.
Mon–Sat 10.00–19.00, Sun 11.00–18.00.

THE ARTIST'S SPACE
38 Greene Street, 3rd Floor; tel 212 226-3970. Tue–Sat 10.00–18.00.

GOURMET GARAGE
453 Broome Street; tel 212 941-5850. Daily
07.00–22.00.

ST. PATRICK'S OLD CATHEDRAL
263 Mulberry Street; tel 212 226-8075.

PUCK BUILDING
295–309 Lafayette Street.

MUSEUM FOR AFRICAN ART
593 Broadway; tel 212 966-1313. Tue–Fri
10.30–17.30, Sat–Sun 12.00–18.00.

NEW MUSEUM OF CONTEMPORARY ART
583 Broadway; tel 212 219-1222. Wed
12.00–18.00, Thur–Sun 12.00–20.00.

GUGGENHEIM MUSEUM SOHO
575 Broadway at Prince Street; tel 212 423-3500. Thurs–Mon 11.00–18.00.

AMERICAN PRIMITIVE GALLERY
594 Broadway, Suite 205; tel 212 966-1530.
Mon–Fri 10.00–18.00, Sat 11.00–18.00.

THE ALTERNATIVE MUSEUM
594 Broadway, Suite 102; tel 212 966-4444.
Tue–Sat 11.00–18.00.

A CHINATOWN WALK (pages
130–135)

ENGINE COMPANY #31
87 Lafayette Street.

NEW YORK CITY RESCUE MISSION
90 Lafayette Street; tel 212 226-6241.

TRUE LIGHT LUTHERAN CHURCH
195 Worth Street; tel 212 962-1482.

THE CHURCH OF THE TRANSFIGURATION
25–9 Mott Street; tel 212 962-5157.

MARINERS' TEMPLE BAPTIST CHURCH
12 Oliver Street; tel 212 233-0423.

ST. JAMES' ROMAN CATHOLIC CHURCH
32 James Street; tel 212 233-0161.

SHEARITH ISRAEL GRAVEYARD
55–7 St. James Place.

THE MUSEUM OF CHINESE IN THE AMERICAS
70 Mulberry Street, #209; tel 212 619-4785. Tue–Sat 12.00–17.00.

AROUND CITY HALL (pages 136–145)

WOOLWORTH BUILDING
233 Broadway. Lobby open Mon–Fri
07.00–18.00.

THE *SUN* BUILDING
280 Broadway.

EMIGRANT SAVINGS BANK BUILDING
51 Chambers Street.

FEDERAL OFFICE BUILDING
290 Broadway.

AFRICAN BURIAL SITE
Duane Street at Elk Street. African Burial
Ground Memorialization info line tel 212
264-6949; fax 212 264-4082.

US COURTHOUSE
40 Centre Street.

NEW YORK COUNTY COURTHOUSE
60 Centre Street.

CENTRAL CRIMINAL COURT
100 Centre Street.

CIVIL AND MUNICIPAL COURTHOUSE
111 Centre Street.

FAMILY COURT
60 Lafayette Street.

MUNICIPAL BUILDING
1 Centre Street North.

St. Andrew's Roman Catholic Church
20 Cardinal Hayes Place; tel 212 962-3972.
St. Andrew's boasts that there are "Daily
Mass and Confessions at almost every time
of the day!," so if you go into the church for
reasons unconnected with worship do
respect the rights of others.

ST. PAUL'S CHAPEL TO TRINITY CHURCH ... THE LONG WAY (FINANCIAL DISTRICT WALK 1)
(pages 146–153)

There are weekly guided walking tours of
this area; tel 212 908-4110 and 212 606-4064
for more details of the several walks. Big
Onion Tours (tel 212 439-1090) offers a
full range.

Refreshments
Windows on the World Restaurant
World Trade Center, Church Street between
Liberty and Vesey; tel 212 938-1111.

Attractions
St. Paul's Chapel
Broadway and Fulton Street; tel 212 602-
0800. Daily 08.00–16.00.

World Trade Center
Church Street between Liberty and Vesey;
tel 212 323-2340. General information
daily 09.30–21.30; tel 212 435-7377 or
212435-4170. Concourse shopping hours
Mon–Fri 07.30–18.30, Sat 10.00–17.00;
closed Sun. Events tel 212 435-4170.
Tourist attractions tel 212 435-7397.

St. Nicholas Hellenic Orthodox
Church
155 Cedar Street; tel 212 227-0773. Open
Wed afternoons and all day Sunday (no
fixed hours).

Federal Reserve Bank of
New York
33 Liberty Street; tel 212 720-7839.
Reservations required for guided tours,
which include the multimedia Visitor
Center.

Trinity Church
Broadway at Wall Street; tel 212 602-0800.
Daily 08.00–16.00. *Welcome Center* Sun–Fri
10.00–12.00 and 13.00–14.30. *Guided tours*
daily 14.00 plus after 11.15 Holy Eucharist
on Sun; tel 212 602-0872 for groups over
five. *Museum* Mon–Fri 09.00–11.45 and
13.00–15.45, Sat 10.00–15.45, Sun
13.00–15.45.

THE WALL STREET SHUFFLE (FINANCIAL DISTRICT WALK 2)
(pages 154–159)

Refreshments
Delmonico's
56 Beaver Street; tel 212 509-1144.

Attractions
New York Stock Exchange
8 Broad Street; tel 212 656-5168. Mon–Fri
09.00–16.30.

Federal Hall National Memorial
28 Wall Street; tel 212 825-6888. Mon–Fri
09.00–17.00. Free tours and programs start
at 12.30, 14.00 and 15.30.

Fraunces Tavern
54 Pearl Street; tel 212 425-1778. Mon–Fri
10.00–16.45, Sat 12.00–16.00, open all days
until 19.00 during evening programs.
Guided group tours lasting 45 min–1 hr
(10 adults or more; advance reservation
required—tel 212 425-1778). Occasional
walking tours from Fraunces Tavern last 2
hr and are led by guides from Big Onion;
tel 212 425-1778 and, if you get answer-
phone, press 10.

A STROLL THROUGH BATTERY PARK (pages 160–167)

Staten Island Ferry
Battery Park at South Street; tel 718 815-
2628. The one-way trip takes 30 min. Ferry
schedule available from www.ferrytime.com
or at above phone number, but basically ferries
leave Manhattan Mon–Fri hourly
00.30–06.30, half-hourly or more frequently
06.30–23.30, Sat–Sun hourly 00.30–12.00,
half-hourly 12.30–19.30, hourly 20.30–23.30.

CONFERENCE HOUSE
Conference House Park, 7455 Hylan
Boulevard, Staten Island; tel 718 984-6046.
Apr 15–Nov 15, Fri–Sun 13.00–16.00.

HISTORIC RICHMOND TOWN
La Tourette Park, 441 Clarke Avenue, Staten
Island; tel 718 351-1611. Jul–Aug Wed–Fri
10.00–17.00, Sat–Sun 13.00–17.00;
Sep–June Wed–Sun 13.00–17.00.

ALICE AUSTEN HOUSE MUSEUM
Alice Austen Park, 2 Hylan Boulevard,
Staten Island; tel 718 816-4506. Mar–Dec
Thur–Sun 12.00–17.00.

SEGUINE MANSION
Lemon Creek Park, 440 Seguine Avenue,
Staten Island; tel 718 667-6042. Periodic
tours of the Mansion offered spring through
fall by New York City Urban Park Rangers.
Call number above for tour dates, details; call
718 984-0503 for group reservations.

GARIBALDI-MEUCCI MEMORIAL MUSEUM
420 Tompkins Avenue, Staten Island; tel 718
442-1608. Tue–Sun 13.00–17.00.

STATEN ISLAND ZOO
614 Broadway, Staten Island; tel 718 442-
3100. Daily 10.00–16.45.

SHRINE OF ST. ELIZABETH ANN SETON/
CHURCH OF OUR LADY OF THE ROSARY

8 State Street (Rectory at number 7); tel
212 269-1557. Mon–Fri 06.30–17.00.
Other times by appointment.

NEW YORK UNEARTHED
17 State Street; tel 212 748-8628. Mon–Fri
12.00–18.00.

STATUE OF LIBERTY AND ELLIS ISLAND
National Park Service, Liberty Island; tel
212 363-7620. Circle Line ferry tel 212
269-5755. American Immigrant Wall of
Honor tel 212 883-1896. Ferry runs every
30 min 09.30–17.30 from Gangway 5,
Battery Park.

CASTLE CLINTON NATIONAL MONUMENT
Battery Park; tel 212 344-7220. Daily
08.30–17.00.

MUSEUM OF JEWISH HERITAGE—A LIVING
MEMORIAL TO THE HOLOCAUST
18 First Place, Battery Park City; tel 212
509-6130. Sun–Wed 09.00–17.00, Thur
09.00–20.00, Fri 09.00–15.00 (17.00 in
summer).

MUSEUM OF THE AMERICAN INDIAN
(GEORGE GUSTAV HEYE CENTER)
US Custom House, 1 Bowling Green; tel
212 668-6624 (recorded information) and
212 514-3705. Fri–Wed 10.00–17.00, Thur
10.00–20.00.

Bibliography

Burrows, Edwin G., and Wallace, Mike. *Gotham: A History of New York City to 1898.* Oxford University Press, New York, 1999.

Burton, Dennis. *Nature Walks of Central Park.* John Macrae/Henry Holt, New York, 1997.

Carroll, Raymond, and Berenson, Richard J. *Barnes & Noble Complete Illustrated Map and Guidebook to Central Park.* Silver Lining/Barnes & Noble, New York, 1999.

Dolkart, Andrew S., with the New York City Landmarks Commission. *Guide to New York City Landmarks.* Wiley, New York, 1998 edition.

Ellis, Edward Robb. *The Epic of New York City: A Narrative History.* Old Town Books, New York, 1990 (reissue of a 1966 original).

Howard, Kathleen (ed.). *The Metropolitan Museum of Art Guide.* Metropolitan Museum of Art, New York, 1983.

Jackson, Kenneth T. (ed.). *The Encyclopedia of New York City.* Yale University Press, New Haven & London, in conjunction with the New York Historical Society, New York, 1991.

Laermer, Richard. *Native's Guide to New York.* Norton, New York, 1998 edition.

Leapman, Michael. *The Companion Guide to New York.* Companion Guides/Boydell & Brewer, Woodbridge, 1991 edition (reissued 1996).

Morrone, Francis. *The Architectural Guidebook to New York City.* Gibbs Smith, Layton, 1998.

Taylor, B. Kim. *The Great New York City Trivia & Fact Book.* Cumberland House, Nashville, 1998.

Time Out. Time Out New York. Penguin, London, New York, Victoria, Toronto, Auckland, 1998 edition.

One particular website/webzine merits special attention: *The City Review* at http://www.thecityreview.com/home.html.

Index